Billarooby

Billarooby

JIM ANDERSON

GRAFTON BOOKS
A Division of the Collins Publishing Group

LONDON GLASGOW
TORONTO SYDNEY AUCKLAND

Grafton Books
A Division of the Collins Publishing Group
8 Grafton Street, London W1X 3LA

Published by Grafton Books 1989

A CIP catalogue record for this book is available
from the British Library

ISBN 0 246 13431 3

Printed and bound in Great Britain by
Mackays of Chatham PLC, Chatham, Kent

To the memory of
my mother

Acknowledgements

I would like to thank my sisters Janet Grace and Joyce Roy, my brother Lindsay Anderson, Felix Dennis, Steve Rosenberg, Luther Nicholls, Orville Schell, the Marin Arts Council (for their timely grant), and in particular Charles Fox, without whose initial encouragement this book would never have been written. One night many years ago by his fire I was rambling on about my father, the drought, and the prisoner of war camp, and he said, 'There's a good story there somewhere.' We hammered out an early form of the plot together and he did a ruthless editing job on the first draft. I hope that the good story has finally been found.

Contents

ONE

Camp

1

BILLAROOBY was a small community on the Lachlan River, a few miles northwest of Wudgewunda in New South Wales, Australia. There was a one-teacher school but no shop, no post office, no electricity or telephone, and no church, although there was a service every Sunday morning up in the MacAdamses' woolshed, which had been specially consecrated for that purpose. Ironically, if it hadn't been for the guarantee of that regular service, it is very possible that Dad would not have bought his sixty-five acres in Billarooby, and we Armstrongs would have gone elsewhere and remained the nice, ordinary, country family that Mum always insisted we were.

When we settled down there in the spring of 1942, my sister, Heather, was twelve, and I had just turned eleven. Heather was named that because they could tell right from the start that she was tough, like the plant, but my name, Lindsay, was my grandmother's maiden name, and Dad called me that in one of his many attempts, mostly futile, to appease Granddad.

Our house was on the edge of a plateau above the river flats on which Dad grew his vegetables. It had verandahs on three sides and a faded red roof of galvanized iron. The house was very old and dilapidated but made out of wattle and daub, which, next to the rare magnificence of a stone house like the MacAdamses', was the strongest and coolest form of construction around. There was a washroom, and a kitchen tank from which water ran right into the house. The main drawback was the floor. It wasn't concrete, or boards like other houses we had lived in, just beaten red earth. Mum had put down layers of newspaper and spread her beautiful carpets, but one night I had overheard a bitter argument.

'You seem pleased that we have gone down in the world,' Mum had shouted.

'It's the price we have to pay,' Dad replied.

'The price for what?' Mum's voice had risen to a scream.

In the yard, which Mum had planted with all the flowers she liked best back at River Hall, our rather more grand home in Suffolk, England, there was a Lombardy poplar, a ragged privet hedge, and a huge, shady pepper tree.

I remember only too well the day it all started. I was in the hammock, daydreaming away, and Mum approached from the house, talking to herself.

'My God, my God, this heat, I can't stand it. I won't put up with it, I won't. We're all going to die. I know we're going to die.'

She sloshed a bowl of dishwater over the petunias right by me and, for the thousandth time, sighed for the misty green of England. Mum was always going on about the heat, and Australia, and worse. She took a look down to the flats, let the bowl fall to the gravel, and then slowly pulled her dress off over her head. I stared at the dimpled whiteness of her shoulders and then guiltily looked elsewhere.

'Jack, Jack, Jack, Jack, *Jack!*' she cried out in exasperation.

I shrank back into the hammock, and the movement caught her eye. Startled, she clutched the dress to the front of her petticoat.

'You were supposed to be down helping your father. What a boy you are! He'll have a piece of you.' Her voice was sharp.

I said nothing, and Mum tipped me out of the hammock.

'Get a move on. And don't let the flies sit on you like that.'

I waved at the flies and headed for the house. Mum gave me a push as I went by. Mum hardly ever cuffed me, but she had a push like a shove.

'You can come down with me, but I'm sick of you hiding behind my skirts. Do your hair,' she called after me.

I stuck my head into the basin in the washroom and then pushed my wet hair back with my hands. Mum was always critical of my hair, which was badly cut (she cut it) and ash blond, a colour that no one else in our family had ever had. Sometimes grown-ups called me Snowy, which I hated but mostly let pass. As the water dripped down over my face, I inspected my eyes in the mirror. There was no doubt where their colour came from. Down from the sky, and blue as a blind man's.

'No, I'm reading,' I heard Heather say petulantly from her room. 'Dad won't mind.' Dad was always letting Heather off work in the fields. He would have minded about the book she was reading, however. It was *Gone with the Wind*. I don't know where she had got it. Certainly not from our shelf of wholesome Everyman's Classics.

'You'll miss Auntie Annabel's tea.'

'Mum, it's only the Douglasses.'

'But it's so we can all meet Brown.'

'Mum, will you stop that.'

I heard Heather slap the page to indicate she thought the conversation had gone on long enough. Mum's eyes caught mine. Brown had been badly wounded in the war, and every Sunday up in the woolshed, since we had come to Billarooby, there were prayers for his full recovery. He had been in the Repatriation Hospital in Sydney but had arrived home unexpectedly two days before. The doctors had been giving him the tomtits, said Auntie Annabel, and he had done a flit. He was now fixed up in his room down on the flats at the dairy, where he lived with his father, Slow George Douglass, and Auntie Annabel, his father's unmarried sister. Heather was always very blasé – it wasn't even an act – but I was looking forward to meeting Brown almost as much as Mum.

Mum gave up on Heather. 'Get some exercise. Those eggs had better be collected before I come back.'

Heather stuck her tongue out at me as I went by her door, so I slammed it in her face. Heather and I put up with each other, but I cannot say we had managed friendship. Friendship was not Heather's style. She was big for her age, and took physical advantage of it. 'You little squit' was her favourite epithet for me, and it was often accompanied by a slap. It was said that we had the same face, but I couldn't see it, of course. For one thing, she wore round glasses with black wire frames, and she had ten times as much hair, which she did in plaits and ribbons. Her voice had a horrible sibilance from her growing up too fast.

*

The mantelpiece clock, and then the grandfather clock, chimed four. 'Late,' said Mum from in front of the full-length mirror. She finished buttoning up her grey cotton work smock and began stroking her hair with the silver brush. Her hair was long and lustrous and a beautiful auburn colour.

Mum's name was Lillian. Mr MacAdams had described her as 'an English rose trapped in the southern sun.' Since arriving in Australia she had developed tiny freckles on her face. Every time we had moved further west and the sun grew hotter and the air drier and dustier, Mum cried a little about the loss of her peaches-and-cream complexion. Her freckles eventually grew so large they became a tan, and the darker colour actually went very well with her hair and her large hazel eyes. I knew she had secretly come to like the change, but it was not something that she would ever allow to Dad.

She dropped the photograph of Brown into her handbag and again caught my eye. Auntie Annabel had been up for tea the previous week and had accidentally left the photograph behind. Now Mum was regretfully returning it. 'Real striker in his uniform, ain't he?' Auntie Annabel had said when she saw the effect it had on Mum.

'I'll be a few more minutes.' Mum pushed her handbag to one side and began fiddling with her hat. 'Why don't you wait for me down in the orchard.'

I ran down past the lavatory (or dunney, as they called it in those parts), which was thirty yards below the house, to the bottom of the hill and climbed the mulberry tree. From the top there was a fine view in every direction. Dad's vegetable crops – peas, beans, beets, carrots, tomatoes, corn and pumpkins, even cucumbers and lettuces – stretched in lush, glistening rows from the Douglasses' dairy fence all the way to the Lachlan, which flowed by to the west beneath lines of gum and willow. Across the river rose rocky hills. Their outlines were softened by a covering of beautiful blue haze, and I always yearned to walk in them. 'What is beyond those hills?' I asked one day when Mr Buchanan, our schoolteacher, came round to see Dad, and he replied, 'The great emptiness – and that includes Dubbo.' He laughed, and it was good for Mum to hear him laugh about it because she was frightened by Billarooby. To her it was like the end of the line, the edge of nowhere. Dad had created an oasis down there by the river, but what if . . .

'Jack, they have droughts all the time.'

'Not for years. There's a different pattern now.'

'There was that big one in 1927–28. Slow George's wife just up and left him.'

'The Lachlan never goes dry.'

We had all spent long hours in the fields. There was a fire in Dad's head that kept him going from before dawn until after dusk, every day except Sunday. Mum had tried to keep up, but she had become exhausted with the effort. Dad had refused to get help, but then Mum had noticed an advertisement in the *Wudge-wunda Star* for Landgirls – respectable, educated young ladies who were available for farm work as part of the war effort. It was a scheme being promoted by the Women's Land Army and Auxiliary to make up for all the young men who had gone off to fight. Mum had persuaded Dad to apply for two of them, and since their arrival a week before, she had been very happy. At last she had time for the housework, her sewing, and a little neighbourhood visiting.

I could see the Landgirls now, their backs bent to their hoeing, way down by the river, and closer, at the pump, I could see Dad. I wasn't looking forward to the encounter with him in the least, and was glad Mum would be there to protect me. I suppose that made him right about me being a 'mother's boy' and justified his scorn. But I didn't know what to do about it.

Mum was coming at last and going for the flies with a fury. Over one arm she carried her tea dress, to change into after 'a little light weeding,' which was all she ever intended to do now that the Landgirls had arrived. It was made of olive green Swiss voile with small white dots.

I suddenly was impatient to meet Brown, and gave a sigh as I saw that Mum was going to go into the lavatory before she joined me in the orchard.

It was at that instant that life in Billarooby took a momentous turn. As I watched her hurry down the path to the burst of rocks and the acacia tree where the dunney was, I had a feeling that someone else was watching her too. And checking quickly, I found that somebody was. Not fifty yards away, in the eroded gully that ran from the orchard all the way to the river, a man was standing. He had on a red shirt, red trousers, and a white cap. I couldn't be sure, but it seemed that there was a long scar running down one side of his face. And he was grinning. His eyes left Mum and settled on me, up there in the tree. Then he beckoned with a wave of his arm.

'Mum, there's a Chink,' I yelled. My first thought was that it was one of the Chinese gardeners who irrigated their plots along the river on the other side of Wudgewunda. But what was he doing so far from home?

Mum heard my voice, and her eyes searched for me in the orchard. I waved and pointed down the gully, but she didn't see me.

'Chinaman,' I yelled. 'Chink' was rude.

'Wait,' she called. She shooed the flies out of the dunney with her whisk and then closed the door. I looked back to the gully, but he was gone. Could I have imagined it? I let out a cry of disappointment. But our eyes had met. He had beckoned me. Then I saw a flash of red farther down towards the river. There he was, moving fast, clambering over the Pirates' Log. He dropped down the other side, once more out of sight.

'Mum,' I yelled again. My heart was pounding and I almost ran after him then and there.

'I'm sure you imagined the whole thing,' she said as we hurried along the path between the irrigation channels. Everywhere crickets were chirping. Two Wanderer butterflies flew by, stuck together. Myriads of insects swarmed in the humid air. A frog plopped into the water. 'Oh, these flies.'

I hated it when I was told that I imagined things, and in my anger, made a great leap across the channel. 'Mum, I'll prove it to you.'

'Your father's waiting.'

'I'll just go by the river and look,' I shouted, running off between the beans. 'I'll be at the pump at the same time as you.'

'Lindsay!' Mum made one last desperate attempt to call me back. But I was well off. 'Don't you try to cross that river.'

Her voice was almost lost on the hot breeze.

2

MUM WAS RIGHT ENOUGH to warn me. The Lachlan, early that summer, was a broad, muddy expanse that she knew I had not fully accepted was impossible for me to cross. It flowed deep and swift between its steep banks and was full of snags that created dangerous eddies and whirlpools. There were often places where fallen trees had stilled the river into large pools, and some of these could be swum in, but even these were perilous. They were bottomless and dark and concealed the fearsome Bunyip, a monster of ancient Australian legend, which loved to lurk in such opaque places, always ready to pounce on unwary passers-by and careless swimmers, particularly young tenderfeet like me. Well, that was the scare story. At school, Mr Buchanan, who couldn't swim a stroke, was always lecturing us on the dangers.

As I leapt along the cow trails threading their way up and down the bank and saw no sign of the man in red, I began to suspect that somehow he had managed to do what I could not – cross the river – and when I reached the ford, which was just beyond Dad's pump, at the southwest corner of our farm, I was sure of it. I waded in. The current was swirling around my knees before I stopped and moved back a little. It would be Christmas before it was low enough to cross there. 'Dry up, dry up,' I cried, and then immediately felt guilty, for it was one of Mum's greatest worries that the river would go on us.

I stood still, enjoying the cool of the water on my bare legs and the shade of the red river gums. The steady chug of the pump came from across the flats, and I sighed. Mum would be just about there by now.

The second I started for the pump, the scarred face of the man in the gully loomed large in my head. Maybe he hadn't crossed at all. He might have gone along the bank above the ford. It was wilder territory up there, territory I had yet to explore. I sniffed the air. Fox. It would just take a minute and then I would weed the beets. If I could confirm that a Chinaman had been nosing around our property, Dad might not mind that I was late.

I hadn't gone twenty yards before I knew that I was right. There were brambles beaten down, and a patch of nettles that he had walked straight through. I reached a stand of silky oaks, thickly infested with yellow-belly spiders, and found even better evidence, for someone had cleared a path through the oaks by rolling up the webs with a stick and scraping the spiders off on to the tree trunks. I could see, discarded on the other side of the trees, the stick that it had been done with. Dislodged spiders still struggled to free themselves from the trap of their own silvery webbing.

When I picked up the stick, it cast a spell on me.

I found myself on a bend in the river where the bank flattened out and the sun shone brightly. After the gloom of the infested silky oaks, it seemed like open parkland. I was in the midst of a spacious grove of river gums of enormous girth and height. The trees stood grandly and at ease, elderly survivors that had long since carved out generous areas for themselves. The outer bark hung in long, tattered strips, and beneath, their trunks were fresh and smooth, except for some bulbous growths. The limbs were full of ample forks like armchairs waiting to be sat in.

There was something peculiar about the joy in those beautiful, pale trees, a strangeness in the whisper of the leaves. Then I thought about how free they were and how wonderful it would be to be a tree, with 360-degree vision and, unlike our family, a permanent place in the world. I put down the Chinaman's stick, placed my arms around the nearest one, and closed my eyes.

Even as I sank into the cool caress of the trunk on my cheek, my head filled with the horrible memory of a cyst that had once been removed from the crook of my left arm. The cyst had grown and grown until it was as big as a hot water bottle and spread almost from shoulder to wrist. Mum treated it like a boil (our family was subject to boils when we first came to Australia), with poultices, but it went from red to purple, from hard to soft. It wasn't until it turned yellow that I was taken many miles away, to a doctor in Cowra, which was the nearest town. He was angry that I hadn't been brought in sooner. 'Might have to lose that arm.' He called a fellow doctor and they removed the cyst that same morning.

I opened my eyes in fright and looked up. Right above me was one of the large pitted growths. In my imagination I saw the doctor cutting it open. There was a tray of knives, pus and blood were flowing down, the smell of chloroform filled the air. I backed away from the tree, shaking my head to get rid of everything, particularly the chloroform. I saw that I had dug my nails deeply into the soft, new bark.

I circled warily. There was freedom in that grove, but the freedom included some kind of dying. I decided to release the spiders from the stick.

As I watched the spiders crawl unsteadily away into the grass, I had the strange feeling once more that someone was watching. I looked around, and there, not twenty yards away, squatting on the broad trunk of a tree newly fallen into the river, was the man in red.

'Hey, who are you?'

I approached him slowly. He was smiling at me but did not move from his position. His elbows rested on his knees, and his hands were clasped under his chin. As I came to the edge of the water and looked up at him, he continued to smile in the friendliest way. It seemed the most natural thing in the world to take the next step and climb out along the trunk over the water to him. He reached out a hand, but I was perfectly capable of doing it myself.

A few seconds and I was standing in front of him. He looked up at me. He did indeed have a scar. A really bad one. It had only recently healed, and I could see where it had been stitched. His cheekbone was very red and there was a spot of dried blood. His skin was a light brown with a yellowy tinge, and he had an owl's beak of a nose. He was much too young to be one of the Chinamen.

'How do you do?' I said, suddenly remembering my manners.

I stuck out my hand and he shook it.

Still he said nothing. There was silence but for the chuggle of the river going by.

I thought he might be deaf and dumb, and then something in his eyes brought a realization upon me with a rush: he couldn't speak English. I was overwhelmed with sympathy.

'Lindsay,' I said loudly, jabbing myself a few times in the chest with my forefinger. 'Lindsay.'

'Ah!' He pointed to himself and said, 'Tadao.'

He began speaking rapidly in a high-pitched voice and pointed across the river.

'You come from over there?'

He stood up and moved farther out along the trunk. He climbed through the tangle of branches and leaves until he was up to his knees in the swirling water.

'You can't cross here,' I called. The river still rushed by, in a deep, dark channel at least twelve feet wide.

He began talking again, pointing to the water.

'Oh, I really wouldn't. The current is very strong. Can't you see?'

But suddenly, just as I was thinking I could start teaching him English, in he plunged. His cap came off and got caught on a branch. The current swept him several yards downstream, but he was a strong swimmer and very soon reached the far bank. He slipped in the mud, grabbed some of the thick bracken fern, and hauled himself to safety. Easier than it looked, he gestured. I suppressed a wild thought. I could swim, but I couldn't possibly take the risk. In any case, my clothes would be soaked and Mum would be furious. He called out something to me and then clambered up the steep bank. At the top he gave a wave, and was then lost from sight.

'You lost your cap,' I shouted. It was still there, in an eddy, swirling slowly round and round. I fished it out with a stick, rinsed it, and gave it an inspection. It was neatly embroidered with chrysanthemums, which I found very strange – a man having flowers on his cap. I sniffed it, and the sweet smell of greasy hair produced a strong feeling of connection with him. The man who had visited our farm was no longer a stranger to me.

'Come back,' I cried into the empty air. 'Oh, please come back.'

Perhaps the loss of his cap was a punishment for having watched Mum go to the lavatory. Anyway, I had a trophy. I could prove to Dad that there had been an intruder on the flats and I had almost caught him.

I should have gone back to the farm right then, of course, but I didn't. Anything to delay that confrontation with Dad. I don't know quite at what point I decided to follow the man in red, Tadao, but I found myself running farther and farther along my side of the bank, convinced that somehow, I, too, would find a way to cross. And, as if in answer to a prayer, around the very next bend, find a way I did.

It came in the form of a cable dipping low across the water. It was suspended from steel tripods, and from the end of the cable, on my side of the bank, hung a small cradle. I approached cautiously. Even as I considered the mechanism (it was simple enough), a voice came from above me. 'Aha, a victim for my trap!'

It was Mr Kelly. As he descended the bank he buttoned up his low-hanging, baggy shorts, which didn't begin to cover his pendulous gut. He had a house on stilts, somewhere farther up the Lachlan, and was the owner of Kelly's dump. He dealt in scrap. He was about fifty years old and very large. A curly underbrush of greying hair covered his entire torso, the thickest of all where it grew down into his shorts. It spread across his shoulders and thinned out only when it reached his biceps.

I had seen Mr Kelly several times, but only as he drove furiously by in his old truck. Many years before, I had heard, he had killed another man in a drunken fight.

'Here, take a pew,' he said in the most generous way, and before I could say anything, I had been swallowed up by his arms, his huge lap, and the rails of the cradle. His hairy body was wet with sweat and he had an overpowering, unwashed beery smell. He released the catch and we were off, swooping low over the water like kingfishers. The swirling surface rushed up towards us and I panicked for a moment, but as the forbidden far bank came gliding to our feet, the panic was replaced by a wicked thrill.

'You like my dandy contraption, my little matee?' He might have killed a man, but he always used jokey, elaborate language.

'Yes. Thank you.' I eased myself quickly out of his lap, but not quickly enough. He reached out and grabbed my arm.

'And which way would you be going, my young gallant?'

I pointed to the blue hills, now much closer and nowhere near as blue.

'I wouldn't if I were you.'

'I'm older than I look.'

'You're the Armstrong bleeder, aren't you? What are you doing so far from home?'

I was silent.

'Razor cut your tongue? Well, you tell your dad that this afternoon that friendly gentleman Pict named Bruce Kelly got you safe and sound across the Lachlan, warned you about the hills, and showed you, as a very special privilege, his pretty crop of domestic mustard.' Mr Kelly gestured, and I saw through the trees a field of spindly plants with pale yellow flowers.

Mr Kelly's grip tightened on my arm and I grew more and more uncomfortable. It was partly my impatience to be off – the chance of catching up with the man in red was slipping further and further away – but more Mr Kelly himself. All that hair. And his face. It was a big, round baby face, with grey stubble and little squinty eyes. I began to wonder if I had fallen into the clutches of the Bunyip himself.

'Mr Kelly, that's me, of the Billarooby Kellys, who have lived here longer than the MacAdamses and even longer than the fucking Douglasses. Two lovely wives left me, through no fault of mine. Sluts, the both of them.'

He took a long swallow from the bottle of beer he was carrying, and then offered it to me. I shook my head.

'Mr Kelly, that's me. The man who killed a man.'

'That's not something to boast about,' I found myself saying.

'Friendly little bugger, aren't you.' He dug his fingers in a little more, bent down, and said, 'Kill once, you can kill twice. What's that in your hand?'

'My cap, sir.'

Mr Kelly let go of my arm, shoving me at the same time.

'Well, I'll be fucked. *Your* cap!'

Somehow he knew it wasn't mine.

'How'd you get hold of it?' he demanded, suddenly threatening.

I put the cap behind my back and had the sense to say nothing.

'You'll find what they've got in those hills soon enough. See if I give a shit. My little sonny sir.'

I could have quoted Mr Buchanan and told him that people who don't give a shit quickly become boring old farts, but I just stood there mesmerized.

Mr Kelly took a Chesty Bond singlet hanging out of the back pocket of his shorts, wiped his red, sweaty forehead with it, then pulled it on. It was so filthy Mum would have been disgusted. I was disgusted.

'A boot in the arse is what you need.'

His good mood returned and he twinkled down at me in a way that I would come to know well. He lunged forward, spun me round, and delivered the needed boot. Then he moved off towards his field of mustard without another glance at me.

I followed a tussocky track up a slope covered in thick brown grass. There were several yellow box trees and clusters of huge boulders with patches of pink lichen. Suddenly I gave a leap into the air as I realized that at last I was in the yearned-for rocky hills. My eyes drank in this new world, so different from the river flats and the soft soils of Dad's irrigated fields. There came a brief pang of guilt and I looked back. In the distance was our farmhouse on the edge of the plateau, and closer by was Mr Kelly's head and shoulders as he made his way through his yellow mustard field. He was heading for a tin-roofed shack.

A flock of chattering lorikeets skittered overhead. Their flash of red and purple in the sunlight was a good omen. It was a day for adventure, whether I caught up with the man in red or not. I turned away from the sight of Mr Kelly and began to run.

The track wound upward. I flushed a hare out of a clump of grass and it bounded splendidly off. There was no mistaking it for a lowly rabbit. Overhead soared a broad-tailed hawk. The boulders gave way to open grassland, and sheep grazing peacefully on the slopes gave puzzled looks as I loped by. I found myself drawn to the horizon, where an outcrop of rocks, crowned by graceful kurrajong trees, thrust into the sky like the ruins of a medieval keep. That's what I would do, I decided: climb that outcrop, have a last look for the man in red, and then head back for the farm and the weeding.

But it wasn't easy. Long before I reached the outcrop, the track went into a dip and merged with a freshly graded road coming from the other direction. Almost immediately there was a cattle grid and a fence to which a metal sign was wired. On it was stencilled:

GOVERNMENT PROPERTY
KEEP OUT
GUARDS HAVE ORDERS TO SHOOT
ANYONE PROCEEDING WITHOUT
AUTHORITY BEYOND THIS POINT.
Australian Military Forces.

If I had obeyed that sign, everything might have turned out very differently for our family in Billarooby. As it was, one of Mr Buchanan's sayings came to my mind: 'Take no chances, you miss a lot of choices.' I looked in every direction, found the road deserted, and took a chance.

I crossed the cattle grid, veered off to the right, and was soon high in a jumble of rocks. There were flannel flowers and dog rose growing amongst them. My run became a scramble, and I fleetingly worried about pythons and bandy bandys, spitting cats and rat wallabies. I slipped and scraped my knee, but nothing stopped my blind rush upward.

'Ah!' Below me was an open plain. The afternoon sun bathed it in a brazen light and I shaded my eyes to get a better view.

I knew at once what it was.

There were neat rows of brand-new bungalows, dark green, with galvanized iron roofs, glittering like salt in the sunlight. A large Fibro building, with a huge red cross painted on its roof, glowed white. Other buildings were scattered about. Ploughed and harrowed ground was all ready for planting. An area closed off with wire netting had several chooks pecking in it. An Australian flag hung limply in the windless air, and enclosing everything in the shape of an immense circle were three concentric fences of tangled barbed wire, with tall towers at intervals around the perimeter. Men with rifles stood in little cabins at the top. The circle was divided into four sections by barbed wire – lined roads, which formed a cross. One road was covered in thick grass, the other with tar, which was blistered and bubbling, black in the heat.

It was a prisoner of war camp. Somewhere in the back of my head I remembered Mr Buchanan passing a remark about one being built, but it had been of no interest to me and I had forgotten. Now, as I heard a whistle blow and saw a line of men appear from behind one of the huts, I realized who it was that I had been following. These men were dressed in red clothes and they were behind heavy barbed wire because they were Japanese, the scourge of the Pacific. The man I had followed was no Chinese gardener but a Japanese prisoner who had escaped.

I shrank back into the rocks. For the first time I felt that I had come too far from home, and I looked around in dread, almost expecting the escaped man to be behind me.

'Japs,' I whispered. 'Japs are worse than Hitler.' I rose to flee. I would never come here again.

I took one last look at the camp, so close below. The Japanese were now running round and round their exercise yard at a fast pace. Two more of them had appeared, one swinging a bat, the other tossing a ball up into the air. I saw that the yard had been marked out for softball. They shouldn't let Japs play games, I thought.

I began to wonder. Why were there not soldiers out looking for the man in red, and why had he been moving back towards the camp?

I was not prepared for what happened next. A black horse came into view from the north, galloping fast. As it came closer, I could see thick white foam oozing from its mouth. The rider was an old man in uniform, his cap braided with red and gold. He held himself very stiffly, and his long nose was stuck up haughtily above a grey handlebar moustache. An officer. Maybe even a general or something equally important.

In the rocks thirty feet below me there was a sudden movement. A flash of red. It was the escaped prisoner. His face was turned to the right, towards the approaching horse and rider. He stood, and then ran out into the open, waving a stick.

'Don't be crazy!' I cried out involuntarily.

The rider did not seem to see him coming until the last moment. The prisoner screamed something and threw a stone, which missed. He swung his stick, but the horse sheered away and quickly outdistanced him. The prisoner ran in pursuit. A great shout arose from the camp as the other Japanese saw what was happening and rushed to get a better view. They clung to the barbed wire and began a strange chip-choppy chant. From one of the towers came the sound of a rifle shot, and then another. A group of soldiers appeared from behind a long white building just outside the main gate of the camp and took a look. Some of them began running towards the rider, who shouted a command and then, wrenching his horse around, galloped back. As he did, he drew a whip and raised it high. The prisoner swung at the horse again, and missed. The rider lashed him hard across the shoulders, causing him to stagger forward. The stick went flying, but the prisoner, instead of trying to retrieve it, threw his head back and gave a strange cackle. Then he stood to attention and stretched his arms out like Jesus Christ on the cross, as though daring the very worst. The rider charged, forcing his horse straight into him. There was another cut with the whip; the prisoner fell to the ground and lay motionless. Dust from the horse's hooves rose in the air. The rider steadied his horse, and then, leaning over in the saddle, gave the man two terrible cracks with the whip, back and forth, right across the face. He paused, and then gave a third one for good measure. I saw blood explode on the prisoner's cheek, as clearly as if he were next to me, although he was a good forty yards away.

I had seen such a thing before. The exploding blood. 'Grand-dad!' I gasped, and closed my eyes.

When I dared look again, the rider was cantering in the direction of the main gate, and the soldiers had reached the fallen man. They began hauling him roughly towards the camp. A whistle was blown, orders given; guards forced the other prisoners, silent now, back from the barbed wire.

I watched until the injured man was dragged through the gate and out of sight. Then I ran from the camp without another glance. The sun scorched my back, but still I felt covered in a clammy sweat and I stumbled twice, my legs almost jelly. Mr Buchanan was always telling us to watch out for the terrible things man does to his fellow man. I had just seen one of those things. The man with the whip had committed a most cruel act, and I felt sorry for the Japanese. I did not even want to think of him as a Japanese, and found myself wishing that I had climbed down from the outcrop and somehow given him his cap back.

3

As I left the rush and gurgle of the river behind me and ran towards the pump, the sound of Dad singing came across the flats. He had a fine baritone voice, and it was one of his favourite hymns. Anything but hymns was profanity to Dad. Or so he said.

> 'He is the Good Shepherd,
> He is the Lord and Master.
> He is the shepherd of Albion,
> He is all in all,
> In Eden in the Garden of God,
> And in heavenly Jerusalem.
> If we have offended, forgive us:
> Take not vengeance against us . . .'

As I crept up behind the stringy bark, no more than ten yards away from the pump, Dad went into the second verse and I knew that meant he was in a good mood. The hymn was a serenade for Mum, who had already changed into her pretty tea dress. She gave Dad a big kiss on the cheek, and I saw how happy they were together right then. I took a wild bet that they hadn't even missed me.

'Oh, Jack, it's paradise down here.'

'It's the water.' Dad patted the pump, which was built out of a converted Model T truck. It was propped up on blocks and the rear tyres had been removed. Dad was always patting the pump. The Lachlan was our lifeblood, he said, and the pump was the farm's heart.

Dad was six feet tall and known for his silences as well as his singing. His skin was rough and ruddy from the sun. Mum said his high blood pressure added to the redness, but one of Dad's vanities was that he was somehow descended from a noble American Indian chief, and before he married he had even gone to Quebec, looking for the remnants of the Iroquois nation. He had a very upright stance and an aquiline nose. His hair, almost black, was always well greased and slicked back. He allowed Mum no cosmetics of any kind, but he did not regard his own brilliantine as a cosmetic. Mum always made sure he wore clean and well-starched clothes, even in the muddy fields. I have to admit that he was good looking, although there was a slight weakness to his chin that he had covered up with a beard when he first arrived in New South Wales. Even though all the other men around shaved, he would have kept it if Mum had not found it too prickly.

There was a permanent hard welt near where his left nostril joined his cheek. It was something that Granddad had done to him.

'Be nice to your father,' Mum would often say to me when he and I were not seeing eye to eye. 'You know he did not get off to a good start in life.'

Granddad himself told Heather and me the story. My grand-mother, whom Granddad loved very much, had died giving birth to Dad. Granddad said he would have preferred to have kept her and lost the baby for he already had three other sons. One morning he had taken Dad away from the nurse, gone to the registrar, and put his name down simply as Jack, almost as though he had not wanted him to have a name at all. The name chosen by my grandmother, if it was another boy, had been James Gunning William.

When Dad was two years old, Granddad had suddenly uprooted his family from his farm near Prestwick, in Ayrshire, Scotland, and gone south to Suffolk. He said it was to get away from the 'Valley of the Catholics,' but really it was because of Grandma. Every year thereafter, until his death twenty-five years later, Granddad had travelled north on the train by himself to put flowers on her grave.

Mum massaged Dad's back for him and then, glancing towards the dairy, ran a hand quickly inside his overalls. I had seen Mum do things like that before, and mostly Dad stopped her. That day he didn't, but after a few moments he drew out his watch and said, 'Where is that young blighter?'

It was my cue.

'I'm here,' I said, stepping out from behind the tree. 'Dad, I'm sorry I haven't done the beets yet, but I had to chase an intruder off the farm. I'll do them right now. I won't even come to afternoon tea, if that is what is correct.' It all came out in a rush, so determined was I to make amends.

'Get those flowers out of your hair!' shouted Dad.

'Oh, Lindsay, look at you,' cried Mum. 'Where have you been? You don't run away for over an hour without telling us.'

'Where's the scraper?' I asked. Then I saw it leaning up against the pump and ran to get it, but it was no good. Dad was already unbuckling his belt and looking as though he was going to beat me black and blue.

'No, Jack, look at the state he's in. Lindsay, dear, what happened to your legs?'

I looked down. They were bleeding from dozens of scratches. And swollen and stinging like mad. I had accidentally blundered through the nettles on the way back.

'Your shoes are caked. Did you go in the river?'

The more Mum fussed about with her handkerchief, the closer I got to crying, and when I thought about the horrifying incident I had seen and what Dad might do to me, I couldn't help it any longer. I began bawling my eyes out.

'There was a Chinaman in the gully watching Mum and I chased him off the farm for you. All the way up past the ford. He lost his cap in the river and I had to go into the water to get it to prove there was a Chinaman. Because you never believe me.'

I pulled the cap out of my pocket and showed it to them.

'It's the truth. And when I was coming back to do the beets, I ran into Mr Kelly and he wouldn't let me go.'

'You've been gone almost two hours,' said Dad slowly. His welt had gone white. The vein in his temple throbbed.

'I got lost. I was on the trail of that fox that got into the chooks.'

Mum kept wiping at my face with her handkerchief and I continued to cry. Dad hated to see me cry. It was all part of my weakness.

'Leave his face alone. Chinaman my eye. He's been up to something. You crossed the river on that cable.'

I shook my head.

'What are you so upset about, Lindsay? Did Mr Kelly do something to you?'

'Dad's going to beat me because I didn't do the weeding yet.'

'You know he's going to do no such thing. We're going to afternoon tea with the Douglasses this very second, and Miss Douglass is going to put something on your legs for you. Now stop your tears. What will Brown think?' She removed some dirt from my suspenders, gave them a snap, and then took Dad by the arm. He still had his hands on his belt buckle. 'Jack, calm down. There *was* someone in the gully. Lindsay saw him from the tree.'

Dad pushed Mum's hand away roughly. 'If you had been here when you were supposed to be, you wouldn't have been running off after some nonexistent Chinaman.' Dad picked up a clod of earth and threw it. I could have ducked, but I let it hit me. 'Did he smile at you?'

'Jack!'

'I'd have been better off with another girl.'

'That's enough,' said Mum, putting her arm about Dad's waist and turning him gently towards the gate to the Douglasses' dairy. 'Quite enough.'

There was a long silence from Dad. 'All right. You do them after tea, and you'll finish if it takes all night.' He rammed his Stetson down on his head, cleared his throat, and spat some phlegm on the ground. Then he had another thought. 'You didn't go near that camp over there, did you?'

'No,' I said. I dropped my eyes in the face of his stare and in that instant decided I was not going to go to afternoon tea after all. I didn't want to be anywhere near Dad for a while.

'If my ears stuck out like that,' I said to myself as they moved off, 'I'd get a doctor to tie them back.'

'Come along, Lindsay,' Mum called back with a smile. 'Sponge cake.'

'I hate sponge cake.'

'But what about Brown? Your hero.'

'I'm going to do the weeding.'

I had flashes of Auntie Annabel's tea service with its orange scalloped rims, of her blue budgerigars nuzzling in their cage, of the black upright piano along the back wall of her parlour, and of the sponge cake with its raspberry jam and whipped cream filling two inches thick; I had a picture of Brown being wheeled in, all bandaged up, ready for me to help him, but I swung the scraper determinedly up in the air and brought it down with a whack.

The sun dipped down behind the line of trees along the Lachlan, and at exactly the same time, or so it seemed, I smelled the Landgirls. I turned round. They were almost on top of me, going by on their way home from work.

The Landgirls had been with us quite a few days but I still hadn't really got used to them. Their names were Joan Cash and Betty Dresser. I was impressed when they said they had been friends ever since they went to kindergarten together. They came from the Sydney suburb of Marrickville and had been shorthand typists before volunteering for work with the Women's Auxiliary and the farming life. They were doing it for their boyfriends, they said, who were both in Libya with the 9th Battalion.

Joan was short and plump and shapely – so shapely that she always seemed to be bursting at the chest. Betty was tall and lank, with round shoulders, and always stood a step behind Joan, like her shadow. Joan's hair was fancily curled and a very bright blonde, while Betty's was long, dark brown, and straight as a poker, but with a fringe that was permanently frizzed.

'Take your pick,' said Joan, holding out a bag. The chocolates inside were all melted together. I pulled off a piece and stuck it in my mouth. The Landgirls had access to army rations unavailable to the rest of us, and offered everything they had. They had almost got Mum into rouge.

Joan took a little compact out from somewhere in her overalls and began to freshen up her lipstick. Her mouth was very large and soon was glistening red. She ran her tongue around her lips and gave me a crooked smile. Joan was always very much at home wherever she was. I looked away quickly.

'Water?' Betty handed me her canvas bag.

I drank as much as I could, poured a little over my head, and then handed it back to her. 'Thank you. It's so hot.'

'Ciggy?' asked Joan. She lit one and blew smoke down at me.

I shook my head shyly.

She stood very close, her hips thrust forward, emanating strong odours of perfume, sweat, cigarette smoke, and Dad's phosphate-rich dirt. I had a sudden wish to push my face into her shorts.

'Haven't you done your dash for today, kiddo?' asked Joan, picking a little piece of tobacco off the tip of her tongue.

'I have to finish if it takes all night.'

'Oh, sweetie, don't take him so seriously,' said Joan.

'He's been an old grouch all day long,' said Betty.

'Needs a few beers down his muzzle.'

'Joan!'

There had been a crisis when the Landgirls first arrived at our farmhouse. While they were unpacking in the room at the back Mum had prepared for them, Dad had started an argument in the kitchen. 'We asked for two quiet Protestant ladies, Lillian. There's been a mistake.'

'Jack, they're city girls. You have to give them a chance.'

'They're whores, both of them. Her hair's dyed. I won't have them living under the same roof. They'll have to live out in the shed.'

'Jack, there's no way we can block it off from the hens.'

'I'll cut a window.'

'You'll put me in a new floor first. They're still going to eat with us.'

'Damnation!'

'The fat one does look a little cheap, but you've planted so much, Jack. Be more tolerant, dear.'

It was almost two days before Dad even spoke to them, and Joan complained noisily about the fact that we did not have a wireless, but they took to farm work with a will, and that, along with their seemingly endless supply of army luxuries, soon softened Dad up. He barked away at them, but in no time at all they were part of the family.

It was dark by the time I finished the weeding. Mum and Dad had come back and gone up the hill, the kookaburras had long finished their sunset chorus along the river, the wallabies were grazing on the other side of the fence, and the moon was high and pale in the sky. I walked home along the path through the irrigation channels, slapping at the mosquitoes. When I reached the gully by the orchard where I had first seen the Japanese, I stood and stopped for a moment, shuddering in the warm night air at the thought of him.

The mopoke flew by on soundless wings. Something had disturbed him from his hunting perch on the old lightning-struck tree halfway up the hill. Then I heard a snort. It was Dipper, our blue cattle dog. She appeared, wagging and grinning.

'Oh, Dipper,' I cried, crouching down to hug her. 'You're about to have pups and you came all the way down the hill. The weeding's done and Dad's going to be pleased with me.'

I lifted her floppy spaniel ear – she wasn't a purebred heeler by any means – and whispered into it, 'I saw the war in action this afternoon, and I'm not going to tell a soul about it except you.' I paused and then added, 'And Mr Buchanan, because I have to clear up a few points.'

4

MR FRED BUCHANAN, our teacher, sat with his feet up on the desk, smoking a cigarette and listening to us sing.

> 'From a draw to a death,
> From a death to a view,
> From a view to a death in the morning.
>
> 'Do you ken John Peel with his coat so gay,
> Do you ken John Peel at the break of day . . .'

It was Thursday afternoon and 'Singing for Schools' was on the wireless. I loved to sing. I had a voice and I could hit the notes. Even Dad had to admit that. It was Heather with the tin ear. Mr Buchanan let the broadcaster have it all his own way, and apart from encouraging us with occasional shouts, he divided his attention between the school clock and the two stockmen rounding up sheep in Mr MacAdams' bottom paddock. He was impatient for Dad to arrive.

Mr Buchanan was a very good teacher. Everyone agreed on that. I have forever been grateful to him not only for the intense drilling he gave in essential English grammar, arithmetic, geography, and history, but for getting me to read such things as *Candide* and *Of Mice and Men* at an early age. He kept up a breakneck pace, and that was with him drinking all day long and giving over both Thursday and Friday afternoons to recreational purposes. Thursday afternoons that summer was swimming, thanks to Dad. 'I'll teach the whole school,' Dad had said when he found out that no one there – out of all fourteen of us – could swim except Heather and me, of course, and the Cutler twins, who were the other English kids living in the district. Mr Buchanan loved the lessons as much as anybody and got pretty silly every time Dad got hold of him in the water for his turn.

The broadcast finished and Mr Buchanan came to life. He swung his legs off the table, stubbed out his cigarette, turned off the wireless, and scurried across to the piano. He took us through 'Do You Ken John Peel' again and again until we got it right, went straight into my favourite song, 'There Is a Tavern in the Town,' as an encore, and then banged down the piano lid.

He lit another cigarette and then looked round at us ferociously. The ferocity was fake. It was the uncertainty about what he was going to do next that kept us on our mettle.

He had straggly brown hair with some sparse sunbleached strands that he wore scraped over his bald pate. Hats hurt his head, he said, and his skin up there was crinkly and rough from the sun. Mr Buchanan lived right by the school in a small white house with a verandah out front and a lawn of buffalo grass full of cigarette butts. After school and on weekends he would sit in a rocking chair on his porch, watching the road and reading. Some men in the district called him Legs because of his habit of wearing shorts to show off his heavily muscled calves. He had once been a competition long-distance walker.

Mr Buchanan was friends with all the local farmers and their wives but did not have a sex life. We all knew that Auntie Annabel had a crush on him, but he said that she was not for him. Her nose was too long and her petticoat always showing. He sympathized with her problems, however, for his were the same. He too had failed in love, and celibacy and cynicism were his lot.

The worst anyone said of Mr Buchanan was that he was a sticky beak. 'He has no family of his own,' I heard Mrs Mac-Adams say to Mum one day, 'that's why he likes to pry. All the more reason never to tell him anything.' Some people who are the first to want to know are the last you want to tell, but Mr Buchanan was not one of those. Everyone in Billarooby, just about, told him everything.

'We have fifteen minutes before Mr Armstrong arrives. Any questions, any last requests?'

I put up my hand. 'When do the Japanese get here, sir?'

'Good God.' Mr Buchanan threw his cigarette out into the

playground and lit another. 'What on earth makes you think they would ever come to a dump like this?'

'If they come, sir, we hide in the trench behind the dunney,' said Jimmy Cutler beside me on the bench. The very thought of the dunney made him sputter into laughter.

'The Japs won't even reach Australia, let alone here. You can take my word for it.'

'They killed two hundred and fifty people in Darwin, sir.'

'Bombing. Not the same. Takes six Japs to down one Aussie. You all know that.'

'I read that we have a population problem, sir,' I said. 'There's more than six Japs – '

Mr Buchanan interrupted. 'The Americans are giving them a licking. General MacArthur's eating lunch up in Port Moresby these days.'

He put his fingers to his eyes, stretched the skin, turned them into slits, put out his tongue between bared teeth, and gave a cackle – his imitation of a Jap. The little kids up on the front bench tittered.

'See, your average Jap.' Mr Buchanan seized his pointer and moved to the full-colour picture on the wall, taken from a prewar *Life* magazine, of a Japanese samurai in chignon and ceremonial robes and regalia, standing with his curved sword behind his head, like the King of Hearts. It was the only thing in the whole schoolroom I coveted.

'The face may be fearsome, but look at that ridiculous outfit. Don't tell me you're going to be frightened of someone who dresses like that.'

He suddenly grabbed the leather strap he kept hanging by the window and brought it down with a stinging whap on the front desk. Nettie Bridges gave a little shriek of terror, then covered her mouth up.

'That's enough of Japs. Let's get back to more important matters. It's Thursday today and Mr Armstrong will be here any minute. OK. So how do we get the name of Thursday? Who remembers besides Lindsay?'

Heather glinted at me through her glasses. She knew, but annoyance at Mr Buchanan's presumption kept her aloof. No hands went up and Mr Buchanan sighed. 'All right, Lindsay, go ahead.'

'From Thor, sir, the Viking god of war and thunder. He was also the protector of the other gods from their enemies.'

'Very good.' He grinned at me. 'And did you know that Frederick the Great had his coffee made with champagne?'

'Yes, sir.'

'And where did you read that?'

'*Arthur Mee's Children's Encyclopaedia,* sir.'

'Which is over there!' shouted Mr Buchanan, flinging his hands dramatically in the direction of the bookshelves. 'For all of you young bastards to read.'

Eric Kiddy let out a loud fart, and everyone suppressed giggles. We were restless, ready for swimming.

'Oh, sir, make him go outside. He's going to do another one,' said Heather, waving her hand about. Gordon Morrison, on the other side of her, pretended to, and she backhanded him. Gordon had to feed five hundred chooks before coming to school each morning, and was the toughest kid in the district. His father had knocked out one of his front teeth in a fight.

Mr Buchanan advanced. He had once lifted Eric bodily and dumped him in the horse trough. At that moment, however, a commotion from the front paddock had us all on our feet. The horses were whinnying, dogs were barking.

'It's the black dog, sir,' said Jennifer Cutler, 'after Bones.'

'OK, we'll break for the day. Jenny, Jimmy, go rescue him. The rest of you can watch, but don't go through the fence.' Mr Buchanan grabbed Eric Kiddy's ear and led the rush outside.

I stayed behind to covet the samurai and look at the wall map of the world, which was covered in shiny brown varnish and had a million cracks.

Mr Buchanan came strolling back in, a cigarette in one hand, a flask of brandy to his lips.

'Why aren't you out there with the rest of them?' He hurriedly got rid of the flask in his table drawer and wiped his mouth with the back of his hand. 'They're getting ready to go.'

'I was wondering if the Owen Stanleys were on this map, sir. I found out Brown Douglass was wounded in those mountains.'

'New Guinea's a long way from here, Lindsay.' Mr Buchanan vaguely made a measurement on the map with his hand.

'I think the Japanese problem is more serious than you let on, sir.'

'You reading the papers again?'

'I heard they were coming here to rescue the Japanese prisoners, sir.'

Mr Buchanan looked surprised. 'Well, there's an idea,' he said sarcastically.

'I went to the camp, sir.'

'With your dad?'

'No, sir. I walked. Across the river.'

'Good Lord. It must be miles.'

'A prisoner had escaped. I saw them catch him.'

Mr Buchanan got slightly shifty. He checked through the window to see if anyone was coming, then sat down on his table. He gave his crotch a long scratch.

'What did you see?'

'A man on a horse whipped him, sir, while he was down, and made him bleed.'

Mr Buchanan twirled an imaginary moustache and raised his eyebrows in a query.

'Yes, sir. Who is that?'

'That is Monsieur le Commandant.' Mr Buchanan went to his drawer and took another swallow of brandy. He was nervous about Dad's arrival. 'The Colonel.'

'I read nothing about it in the *Star*, sir.'

'You won't.'

'It looked bad, very bad.'

'Things are not always what they seem Lindsay. Remember we are at war. You can get away with murder.'

Mr Buchanan smiled, and then put both hands on my shoulders.

'Take no notice of me. You're right. The Colonel did a terrible thing. Bit of a Tartar, that Colonel. It was outside the rules. That prisoner has been transferred to another camp.'

'Perhaps they should have transferred the Colonel, sir, and set the prisoner free.'

'Hmm.' Mr Buchanan stroked his chin for a moment. He seemed to think that wasn't such a bad idea. 'They're treated well enough, on the whole. Good food, games, and they're going to give them English lessons.'

He checked through the window yet again, and then went to his personal cupboard. I knew I was going to be shown a Secret File. He took out a rolled-up piece of paper.

'I bought this in Sydney during the winter holidays.'

It was a coloured poster showing a Japanese soldier running down a burning street with a naked white woman slung over his shoulder. There was a pistol in his hand, a rising sun insignia on his shoulder, an evil grin on his face. In the flames it read 'THIS IS THE ENEMY.'

Mr Buchanan waited for my reaction. I stared at the picture for some time. There was another Japanese in the blue of the background, wielding a bayonet.

'Doesn't it put the wind up you?' he asked, putting it away quickly. 'Terrible thing to do to a lady.'

'Pretty scary, sir, I suppose.'

'Still want to set the Japs free?'

'They're not all like that, sir.'

'Very true. But you go wandering around that camp you might run into a stray bullet. Don't want to lose you. Composition class would never be the same.' Mr Buchanan grinned.

'I was wondering, sir, would it be a dreadful thing to have a prisoner as a friend? The war and all that.'

'Bit useless, I'd say. Bad as unrequited love.' Mr Buchanan sighed. 'If you'd like to see the camp in a safe and proper fashion, I will take you one day. I have a mate in the Twenty-fourth Garrison Battalion. They're the soldiers who guard it.'

Mr Buchanan kept surprising me about the camp. Somehow I had assumed that no one in Billarooby except myself had ever visited it or knew anything about it.

'Does your mum know you went?'

'No, sir. She wouldn't like me to have anything to do with the war. She doesn't like it.'

'Well, I don't either. If it wasn't for the war, I'd be living it up in Sydney.' Mr Buchanan looked out the window again. 'And what about your dad? You tell him?'

'You must never tell Dad, sir. Never.'

'OK. Then, mum's the word.' Mr Buchanan laughed at his joke

and then said, 'But only if you promise not to go there alone again.'

I had no trouble with that. 'I promise.'

'Good. The closest I want you to get to the war is that trench out in the back on a false alarm.'

Into the silence that fell, I said, in a way that I hoped was portentous, 'Dad didn't go to war.'

'Smart man. Not everyone went to war. Brown Douglass rushed off. Look what happened to him.'

'Dad had a severe medical problem, sir.'

'Really?' Mr Buchanan sat down on the front desk and began swinging his bare legs. 'And what was that?'

'His lungs, sir. But my granddad was angry. It was the day of the terrible fight. He said his lungs were perfectly all right.'

'Well, your dad's the one who would know.'

'I'm not sure, sir. You see, Granddad died suddenly.'

'We all have to go sometime, Lindsay. You can make book on it.'

I stared at him uncertainly. Mr Buchanan gave his encouraging smile. 'And was that your mother's dad?'

'Oh no, sir. Mum is an orphan. Her parents both died.'

'Well, dearie me. What did they die of?'

'I think they just got sick and died, sir.' I paused and then added, 'Of cancer,' although that was something I really wasn't supposed to mention to anyone.

'So your dad snapped her right up out of the orphanage, eh?'

'From the haberdashery in Haverhill, sir. He was her very first boyfriend, and he took her to live with Granddad.'

'And your granddad died unexpectedly, you said?'

'Yes, sir. I was there when it happened.'

'Well I never. This might be a good little story for composition, Lindsay.'

Mr Buchanan's eyes gleamed at me rapaciously and I began to think twice. I had already said far more than I intended. I had wanted to unburden myself but had not really anticipated such intense interest. He was just about to drag more out of me when the screen door creaked open. It was Dad. He had been listening out on the verandah, getting up steam, and he had a scowl on his face enough to curdle blood.

'Get over here,' Dad shouted, looking around for something to chase me with.

Mr Buchanan jumped up, very flustered. He repaired his hair rapidly with his fingers. 'I'm sorry, Jack. We were discussing the war, and one thing led to another . . .'

Dad was so angry he wasn't listening. Before Mr Buchanan realized the sort of thing Dad could get up to when he was mad, his best cane had been seized from the hook behind his table and Dad was storming over to get me. I retreated behind the back desk, and then Mr Buchanan got over his amazement and into action. He was between me and Dad in a trice.

'Jack, forgive me, but this is my schoolhouse, and that is my best cane.' Mr Buchanan held out his hand. 'If you must cane somebody, cane me. I was asking the questions.' For a moment Dad could have gone either way, but suddenly his face cleared and he subsided like a spent balloon.

A couple of seconds went by while they stared at each other, and then Dad handed over the cane, all civility once more.

'My son should not be talking to you about family affairs, Fred. He's a regular little gossip. I'd be grateful if you would curb his tongue rather than encourage it.'

'I'm sorry, Jack. I admit at once to curiosity. If not inquisitiveness.'

Mr Buchanan grinned and even touched Dad lightly with his fist in the middle of his chest. On the heart. There was silence while Dad got his words together. Mr Buchanan waited expectantly.

'There's no secret about my father. I have no idea why I should have been so upset. He shot himself in a hunting accident. Years ago now.'

'Ah.'

'The old fellow slipped getting over a stile, and his gun went off.' Dad twisted his Stetson slowly around in his hands and stared at me. 'Lindsay knows all about it. Tell him, Lindsay.'

I felt a slow flush mounting in my face. 'I was only six, sir.'

'Tell him,' said Dad fiercely.

'I was down by the riverbank, sir, picking up the pheasant when I heard the gun go off. I thought Granddad had bagged another one. Then I heard Dad yelling for me, sir. I went running up to the top of the bank and saw Granddad fallen by the stile. Dad was in the middle of the field running towards Granddad too. We reached him at the same time. And then Dad sent me off for help, but I saw all the blood. Granddad had blown his head off. He was drunk, sir.'

'Anything more, son?' Dad spat out the 'son' at me. Mr Buchanan was looking disappointed.

I stared at Dad, and the way he looked made me burst into tears. Dad turned away from the sight.

'I can't remember anything more, sir. I can't.'

Mr Buchanan gave me a little hug. 'Your poor old granddad. Don't think about it. One day when you're older, you can write it down for me. He's a whiz at composition, Jack. In fact, he's the best pupil in the school at just about everything. Next to Heather.' Mr Buchanan grinned, and once more he reached out, as if his compliment had earned him the right to touch Dad yet again.

'Never get his shoulder to it.'

'Ah well, he's like me, Jack. I'm not cut out for the land either.'

There was a silence and Dad's mood seemed to shift once more. Mr Buchanan walked us towards the door an arm to each of us, and I dried my eyes.

Dad stopped and told me to go outside, but I could tell that he was going to talk to Mr Buchanan about Granddad, all the things I couldn't remember, the things he refused to tell me 'for my own protection,' so I hesitated.

Dad motioned to me impatiently.

'Tell the others we're coming,' said Mr Buchanan.

I went out, but I couldn't resist hanging around.

'My father was very difficult in his later years,' Dad began, then broke off and shouted, 'Get away from that door.' I heard his footsteps and ran.

I was not to find out what Dad said to Mr Buchanan about Granddad for almost a year. And when I did, it was to provide me with the most traumatic day I ever had at the Billarooby school.

As I went by the golden wattle tree, I looked back. Dad and Mr Buchanan had come outside and were taking a leak together up against the box-thorn hedge. I knew from previous observation that Mr Buchanan would be sneaking glances at Dad's dick while they did so.

All through the swimming lesson and into the evening I worried about what Dad might have said to Mr Buchanan. It set me off, and in the early hours of the morning I had my nightmare for the first time since our arrival in Billarooby. I knew that Mum and Dad had been hoping that the change in climate might have caused it to go for good. But I screamed and screamed and Mum came running into my bedroom and held me tight. Dad stood scowling in his pyjamas by the open door.

'He'll have to sleep with us,' said Mum as she led me along the corridor.

'Help me,' I sobbed. The nightmare was always the same.

'We can't help you if you don't ever tell us what it is,' said Mum.

'It's too terrible.'

'You baby,' called Heather from her room. 'You little sniveller.'

'I don't want him to start coming in to us again,' said Dad. 'He's fourteen years old.'

'Eleven, Jack.'

I heard Dad's teeth snap, top against bottom. I had never told Dad what my nightmare was, and I hoped to God he would never guess, but he didn't like it. To him, it was all part of my weakness. Sometimes he yelled at me, sometimes he was just coldly angry. I knew that whenever I woke him up, he could never get back to sleep afterwards.

Mum motioned me into the middle of their big bed, between them. There was a time when I loved the chance to snuggle up against Dad's pyjamas, but I shook my head and lay down on Mum's side, as far away from Dad as I could get and still be in the bed.

I drank in the warm, wonderful smells coming from Mum's nightgown and felt her arms around me, and gradually my shudders stopped. It's only a nightmare, I kept insisting as I drifted into sleep.

5

IT WAS A SQUEEZE getting to church that week. Dad never drove the truck on Sundays, only the sulky. It was one of the inflexible rules that he had developed. But with me sitting on the boards and Heather on Mum's knee, we managed to all fit. The Landgirls loved it. They had never been in a sulky before. Dad was in a sour mood because the 'Godless whores' had both decided to become churchgoers.

Mum had herself shaded with the pink and green parasol that Dad objected to from time to time as a vanity. 'Let the sun touch you like the good Lord intended.' Dutiful as she was, Mum knew that this was cant. 'Tell me the difference between my parasol and your hat, just tell me,' she would say.

The Douglasses' lorry passed us as we clip-clopped by the Morrisons' poultry farm. A hand waved from the window.

'Brown,' said Mum.

I sat bolt upright. Mr Buchanan had said that wild horses would not drag Brown to church.

'I thought he was in bed,' said Heather.

'Crutches,' said Mum. 'He's getting stronger every day.'

'You girls could have gone with the Douglasses,' said Dad, 'if you had just walked down to the road, as I suggested.'

'Lay off,' said Joan. 'It's ninety-five in the shade.'

'We're sorry, Mr Armstrong,' said Betty.

We turned into the long gravel driveway of Moorellen, the MacAdamses' property. I clung to the brass rail of the front guard and watched our mare Belinda's sweating flanks and her tail as it expertly swished away the flies. The Douglasses' lorry was way ahead of us, and I wanted to whack Belinda with the whip, have her sprout wings and catch Brown up. The leather creaked and squeaked; the metal-rimmed wheels ground ever so slowly on the gravel.

When we entered the woolshed, Brown was already seated, three rows from the front, beside his father, Slow George. On his other side sat Mr and Mrs MacAdams. Auntie Annabel was at the organ playing the congregation in. Her eyes were closed, her glasses far away, beyond her wart, on the end of her nose, her face held up to the dusty iron beams. She was giving it her all. Usually it was for Mr Buchanan, her secret boyfriend, but on this day it was for Brown, her favourite nephew, as well. As we took our seats a couple of rows behind, Mrs MacAdams' voice rose above the noise of the organ. She was asking Brown about his condition.

'Must she talk so loud?' Mum asked.

'It's her woolshed,' said Heather, and then to me (I was craning my neck around Mrs Bridges, Billarooby's biggest lady, to get a look at Brown) she said, 'Get her to remove her shoulder pads.'

'Stop fidgeting,' said Mum, and it was then that I noticed who was sitting on the other side of the MacAdamses. I was shocked, for it was none other than the Colonel.

The Reverend Pitts dedicated the opening hymn to Brown.

> 'Halleluja, Halleluja,
> Hearts to Heaven and voices raise;
> Sing to God a hymn of praise,
> He who on the cross a victim
> For the world's salvation bled.
> Jesus Christ the King of Glory
> Now is risen from the dead . . .

Dad's voice rose strongly above everyone else's. He was singing his way out of his discomfiture over the Landgirls, whose cheap perfume was wafting over the worshippers. He had told them before they got into the sulky that they stank to high heaven, and had tried to make them take a last-minute scrub.

Dad and the Reverend Pitts were a match, and one of the few good things about church every Sunday, besides Auntie Annabel's flirty faces at Mr Buchanan from behind the organ, was the way that Dad and the Reverend Pitts tried to outsing each other. It was friendly competition. The Reverend had already asked Dad if he was interested in being a church warden in place of Dad Packman, who had dropped the collection plate three weeks in a row. Dad certainly looked as if he could do the job. On Sundays he wore his three-piece lightweight tweed suit with a herringbone pattern. He sweltered away, but it did not bother him. Comfort was a glad sacrifice, he maintained, to the proprieties of the Sabbath.

The Reverend Pitts had a cold, wet hand, winter or summer. I knew because it was impossible to get out of the woolshed without shaking it. He had a roving eye (unbecoming in a man of his years, said Auntie Annabel) and smelled strongly of Lifebuoy. His nose was red and porous, and a problem to him.

The Reverend Pitts always went on about the war, and if it hadn't been for Mr Buchanan, he would have had me convinced that Billarooby would be bombed like Darwin and Broome. According to him, only the good Lord and our brave fighting men were between us and the earthly doom forecast in Revelation. As we went down on our knees for the prayers, he reminded us of all the men from the district in the front lines – John Corish, Andy Gordon, Tom McCaddie, John Gunn, Roy Douglass . . . The names rolled off his tongue, and then he gave thanks for the safe return of Brown.

'. . . who for so long lay critically injured, in danger of losing those pinions without which we could not walk God's good earth. The noblest of the noble, the bravest of the brave, who was happily not called upon to make the supreme sacrifice, now safely returned to the bosom of his family and to all of us here in this little community. We are pleased that he has chosen to honour us with his presence today. While he is not one of our most regular churchgoers, sooner or later the good Lord gathers in His flock, and willingly it is that they come when the time is ripe. An innocent lamb has been restored to us from the slaughter and it is with open arms that we welcome him back. May his heart be filled with love of the Lord forevermore . . .'

I found all this a lot of nonsense, religion being my first rebellion, but I didn't mind the fuss being made. It was a very special occasion, Brown coming home from the war.

'My boy, my boy, my boy,' Slow George was saying in a choked voice. Mrs Bridges was sagging leftward, and I could see that Slow George had his arm clasped around Brown's back. Brown's arm reached out in return and went around his father's shoulder. Slow George gave a loud sniff, and I saw tears rolling down his cheek. Something stirred deep within me at this show of tears and male emotion. Beside me Dad stiffened, for it was considered unseemly in our family to show anything more than a stiff upper lip, particularly in a public situation, definitely in church.

Reverend Pitts moved on to the announcements, and he finished them with a welcome to the church, for the first time, of his good friend, and Mr and Mrs MacAdams' good friend, 'Lieutenant Colonel Allan Smith, commandant of Prisoner of War Camp Number Twenty-four, Wudgewunda.'

I took a furtive look around, but no one was taking exception. He seemed to be in good standing with everyone. The Colonel stroked his eyebrows calmly.

The announcements gave way to the sermon, and half an hour into it Mum began to fan herself rapidly. Joan caused a disturbance by lighting a cigarette, and Betty had to tell her to go outside. The woolshed was made of corrugated iron and was a sweltering place, full of the heavy smells of tallow, tar, disinfectant, lanolin, and the stale linger of shearers' sweat. Brown had his legs up on the bench in front of him. Slow George and Mr Bridges were sound asleep and there were people nodding off in every row. Only Mrs MacAdams' huge arrangement of orange gladioli on the altar seemed to be standing up to the heat. Mum's fan stopped in midair and I noticed that her eyes were closed. In a second or two, I knew, the fan would fall. I touched her gently and it started up again. She looked down at me drowsily.

The best part of church was the pleasantries outside afterwards. They always continued for some time, no matter how hot the day was. Everyone was so busy all week that Sunday was by far the best time to socialize. And the services were attended by people from Mudoogla, the next community along the Lachlan, and Glen Hogan, through the hills. There must have been about forty people there under the blackwood acacia trees.

The Colonel talked briefly to Mr and Mrs MacAdams and then

galloped off down the hill. I saw the two magpies who nested in the big ironbark in the middle of Mr MacAdams' home paddock go for him. His cap went flying, and he had to circle, dismount, and pick it up, all under heavy bombardment. I smiled to myself with great satisfaction and made a bet that he would think twice before coming back to *our* church.

Brown appeared at the top of the woolshed steps. 'Let's help him down,' I said to Mum, but at that moment Mrs MacAdams came sailing up with something on her mind. Mr MacAdams followed her, his hands clasped behind his back.

Mr and Mrs MacAdams were the local aristocracy and lived a couple of hundred yards farther up the slope. Everybody else lived on rises barely above the floodplain, or on the low plateau where we lived, and scratched out rather precarious livings, but the MacAdamses were very comfortable indeed and looked down from the very highest point of the very best land in Billarooby. They had an artesian well, an electric windmill, and large water towers mounted high above their house. The house itself – almost a mansion – was built of Portland stone, with a grey slate roof and porticos front and back.

Mr MacAdams had a long, fleshy face, like those of the Border Leicesters in his creek paddock. He was also very tall. When he was talking to people he stood with his legs a yard apart so he didn't have to stoop. He was the only man to wear shorts to church; he wore them with brogues and long white socks. Mrs MacAdams, in her fifties, had iron grey hair pulled back into coils. At church that day she wore a wide-brimmed hat of Panama straw with a heavily dotted veil to keep the flies off her face. Her suit was of natural linen and well tailored for her body, which was more than a bit on the broad side. Mum complimented her on the suit.

'Well, thank you, Mrs Armstrong. So few people around here even notice. They have no style.' She lowered her voice a fraction and swept her eyes around the throng, who were not as oblivious of her scorn as she might have thought. Auntie Annabel said that Mrs MacAdams was never one to take into account the fact that she had more money than everyone who lived between Billarooby and Wudgewunda put together (and that included the Edgells, who owned the cannery).

'Just look at Annabel Douglass today,' she said. 'Frump. No wonder she never got a man. And all these cheap floral prints.'

'It's rather difficult finding anything nice with the war.'

'Oh, the war. It was the same before the war. Where did you get that hat? It's much too small for here.'

'My hat?' Mum was a little upset. Her hat was made of fine, pale straw and decorated with a bunch of silk lilacs. Dad had bought it for her in a fancy millinery shop in Frinton, a fashionable resort on the North Sea. She kept it for special occasions, like church.

'It's very nice, of course, but your skin is going to be ruined worse than it already is. Where's your makeup?'

Mum glanced nervously at Dad, talking nearby with Mr MacAdams, and said in a low voice, 'I'm afraid . . .'

Mrs MacAdams stared at Dad disdainfully and said loudly, 'Do it anyway. A little Pond's at least. As if he'd notice.'

'You don't know Dad,' I said.

Mrs MacAdams had trouble finding where my voice came from. Her eyes landed on Joan and Betty. The Reverend Pitts had them cornered by the pens. 'So that's them. You should have waited and got Italian POWs. Much cheaper. The Colonel says that they will be letting them out of the camp soon to work the fields. Might get some ourselves.'

'Both hard workers,' said Dad, coming over.

'Humph,' said Mrs MacAdams. 'You know what I think about market gardening, Jack. It won't work, this far out.'

'Irrigation – ' began Dad.

'Coast's a better place for you. Tasmania. Ever thought about Tasmania?'

Dad was at a loss for words, and Mum came to the rescue.

'I'm very happy the girls are here,' she said. 'Now I have some time to myself. My flowers, my dressmaking – '

'Yes,' interrupted Mrs MacAdams, 'that's what I came over for.' She took off one white glove and began to poke at Mum's pale yellow Sunday dress. 'May I?' She bent and lifted up the hem to squint at the stitching. Mum was taken aback about her petticoat showing and gave a polite little cough.

'Silk chiffon,' Mum explained, 'and it's lovely and cool. I made it up from a Grace Brothers pattern, but I brought the material out with me from England.'

'Well, aren't you the clever one,' gushed Mrs MacAdams in her Anglicized voice, which was meant to advertise her wealth and poshness. 'It is really rather well made. Can I trust you to make something like this for me one day? We will have tea together to discuss it. You would like that, wouldn't you?'

Mrs MacAdams began straightening her gloves and looking around.

'Brown Douglass. Now there's a man. Let's go and have another word with him, Bill.'

As Mr MacAdams went to follow his wife, I said boldly, 'Is the Colonel really a friend of yours?'

Mr MacAdams stopped and looked down from his great height. 'Plays a good hand at whist.'

'He beats his prisoners.'

'I should hope so. Keep those devils in order.'

'The magpies got him. It serves him right.'

'That's enough, Lindsay,' said Mum. Mr MacAdams raised his hat to her and moved away. 'We should go, Jack, Belinda's fretting.'

'Mum, I can't go until I meet Brown,' I cried in sudden panic.

'Oh, for heaven's sake, don't be so timid. Go and say hullo to him right now. I'm going to talk to Mrs Bridges here.'

Brown was with Slow George, Auntie Annabel, and some of the roughnecks who hung around the social scene at Mr Kelly's dump. They sat in the back row in the woolshed during the services and chewed tobacco.

Brown was leaning heavily on his crutches and putting up with a lot of chaff.

'Good to see yer back, mate. Kill any them fuckin' Japs?'

'Killed me, mate.'

'Now you can join the sewing circle.'

'Us old duffers.'

'Didn't shoot it off, did they, sport?' Blue Chapman called out. Auntie Annabel pursed her lips and looked to one side, but everybody else laughed.

'No bloody fear.' Brown jerked his thumb in the direction of Joan and Betty. 'Already got a couple there in my firing line.'

'Better get yer wick in quick, mate,' Blue Chapman continued, 'before the bloody Itis beat you to it. The bastards are gonna let 'em out as from next week. Take our jobs, fuck our women.'

'Quit it, Blue,' said Slow George. 'Annabel doesn't like to hear that sort of lingo.' Which wasn't true. She did, and they knew it.

'Yeah, Blue,' added Brown. 'Give the lady here a fair go.'

Brown gave Auntie Annabel a grin. She simpered sweetly and hit his arm with her hymn sheets.

Brown had a grin that split his face and lit up his eyes. He looked very much the way he did in Auntie Annabel's photograph, the one that Mum had not wanted to give back, although all the colours were different. His eyes were green, for example, and his face was rather pale instead of mauvy brown. He had a heavy forehead that reminded me of the crust on the top of Mum's bread, and there were two deep creases in it, like exclamation marks. His hair was dark brown and very thick. He had sideburns and a widow's peak, but what made him so handsome was his nose, which was the straight Douglass nose that was too long on Auntie Annabel but just right for him; and he had a moustache.

'We were almost in the war,' I suddenly blurted out.

Everyone looked down at me.

'Yeah?' said Brown.

'The *Esperance Bay*, the ship we came out from England on, became a troop ship and the Japs sank it in the Battle of the Coral Sea.'

'Close shave,' said Brown. Everyone laughed and I felt slightly mortified, but the way Brown kept grinning at me eventually made me laugh too. My heart opened, and I would have started up a conversation then and there if Mum and Dad had not come up to say hullo and take me home. Blue Chapman and the roughnecks drifted off at their approach. I think they found my parents a bit superior.

'Our dog had pups under the house,' I said to Brown. 'Six of them.'

'They Jojo's?' Jojo was the Douglasses' blue heeler.

'You must come and have a look at them,' put in Mum. 'They look so lovely.' I was surprised at Mum. Up until then, she had always said she didn't like to invite anyone back to the house because of the floor.

'Right-o,' said Brown, 'I will.'

Mum dropped her eyes.

'Them Landgirls of yours can come back in the truck with us, if you like,' suggested Auntie Annabel. 'A mite less crowded for you in the sulky.'

Mum and Dad both thanked Auntie Annabel.

'Keep lover-boy here company.' Auntie Annabel giggled, and, reaching up, she gave Brown's moustache a tweak.

'Brown's got the hots for Betty,' remarked Heather as we rolled down the slope behind Belinda.

'Brown's not interested in girls,' I said.

'Heather, where did you pick up such an expression,' Mum remonstrated. 'I wish you wouldn't use it.'

'It's true,' said Heather, 'just you see.'

'Nonsense,' said Mum, putting her arm through Dad's. 'It's so much better that the girls have gone with the Douglasses. What a kind thought that was of Auntie Annabel's, dear.'

6

OVER THE YEARS I have come to realize that this is more of a love story than I knew at the time, Mum and Brown being such souls of discretion and me being an innocent in such matters. I can relate the little I did know, however, and there is no better place to begin than with the time Brown came round to our house a few days after the church service. It was not under circumstances that anyone could have anticipated that Sunday.

Mad Meg, the Douglasses' crazy old roan cow, had eaten Heather's daisy chain. Heather hit her with a stick and Mad Meg saw red.

I was up in the mulberry tree at the time and no help at all. In fact, if I hadn't yelled for Heather to climb the tree, she might very well have made it to the fence. As it was, she half turned for the tree, then changed her mind. Her patent leathers slipped on the grass, and down she went. Mad Meg was on her in an instant. She butted Heather with her ingrown horn and kept up a continuous bellowing. Heather was rolled this way and that, and each time she tried to get up, the cow knocked her down.

'Lindsay, help!' she cried.

'Grab that stick,' I shouted. 'Hit her across the face.'

Heather did grab the stick, but it was Jojo who came to her rescue, not me. He appeared from nowhere and sank his teeth into Mad Meg's nose. She tossed him twenty feet into the air. Heather crawled for the fence. Jojo landed on his side, winded. In that moment a shot rang out. Mad Meg went down on her forelegs, rolled over, and then lay still. I saw Brown leaning against the open door of the Douglasses' feedshed with a shotgun. He slung it over his shoulder, grabbed his crutches, and came swinging over.

Heather wasn't hurt much, and she was never one to shock that easily, but she made a big fuss about her knee and not being able to walk.

'Hop on over to the dairy. Auntie Annabel will fix you up.'

'I have to go home. What do you think I'm all dressed up for?'

'We're going to the Cutlers' for tea,' I explained. 'Mrs Cutler has a book about the Japanese for me.'

Brown hesitated for a moment. 'I'll tell ya all about the bloody Japs you'll ever wanna know,' he said. My eyes went to his legs. He thrust his crutches towards me, grabbed Heather roughly, and had her up in his arms before she realized what he was doing.

'Put me down. I'm not hurt that bad.'

'Aw, come on, Heather. Haven't had a sheila in me arms since – before the war.' Brown laughed.

It wasn't much of a hill, but halfway up Brown was in difficulties.

'Betty home?' he gasped.

'She's out the back. Digging a new dunney hole.'

'Good-o. I'll give her a hand.'

Mum saw us coming from the verandah and came running out in alarm.

'It's nothing,' Brown called out at once. 'Just that crazy old cow. I been telling Dad to get rid of her.'

'Oh Brown, put her down. You shouldn't be doing things like this. She's a lump of a girl.'

'There,' he said, depositing her on the couch. 'All the way home.'

Mum rushed to the washroom for some antiseptic and didn't notice that Brown had gone green under his tan. He almost fell into Dad's armchair. He motioned to the footstool and I pushed it towards him. He lifted his bad leg on to it, leaned back, and closed his eyes. Coming back, Mum gasped.

'Brown overdid it,' I said.

She handed the antiseptic to Heather and fetched Brown a glass of water and a damp towel.

'I'll be OK in a minute, Mrs Armstrong. Taking a breather.' Brown opened his eyes, rolled them up so that only the whites showed, and closed them again. Mum stood uncertainly for a moment before turning her attention to Heather.

'Put that book down, for heaven's sake.'

I gazed at Brown in some wonder. I saw him as a fallen warrior, and was happy that he remain so if it meant he would have to stay in the house a while. All he had on was a pair of army trousers held up by a wide canvas belt. I moved closer and made a full inspection. There was a red puckered scar that disappeared down into his trousers, and the line of another scar, which went all the way from one shoulder across to below his ribs on the other side. I found myself tempted to trace the scars with my finger. I reached out.

'Lindsay,' came Mum's voice reprovingly.

I drew back and went over to where he had leaned his shotgun. It was well oiled, with the stock highly polished. I thought I might try it for weight and glanced back, but Brown was watching me.

'Ain't gun-shy,' he said.

'Dad has a double-barrelled shotgun too. It belonged to Grand-dad. Granddad used to let me carry it.' I pointed to the wall above the front door. 'That's it there.'

'That's quite enough, Lindsay,' said Mum from the other side of the couch. 'You'll excite yourself.'

It didn't take long for Brown to be up and about on his crutches again. As I stood by Mum with the bowl, I watched him come to a halt in front of the full-length mirror. He ran a hand through his hair and gave a hitch to his trousers, smoothed his moustache, and felt his chin. It looked as if he hadn't shaved since Sunday. He took a quick look over at us and then smelled his armpits. He looked back at Mum and I could tell he had decided to leave.

'I'll show you the pups,' I said quickly.

'Missus — ' Brown began, but Mum interrupted him.

'I'll be with you in a moment.' She didn't want him to go just then either. She cut the end of the bandage with a pair of scissors, sent Heather off to her room to change, and went to where he was standing. The grandfather clock began to strike four, and they listened together to the deep, melodious chimes.

'Ain't that a beaut,' said Brown.

'It's over a hundred years old,' said Mum, smiling. 'It was a wedding present.' She pointed to the miniature paintings in the corners of the clock face. 'See, the four seasons. Spring, summer, autumn, and winter.'

'Oh yeah,' said Brown, taking a closer look. 'Snow. Never seen it. They had some on Canobolas couple years ago, Mum said.'

'Well, it's beautiful, but you haven't missed anything. Turns to slush mostly.'

'You got this place looking real nice. It used to be a dump when the Bagleys were here.'

'Look at this writing desk. It's Jacobean.'

'Nice old wood,' said Brown, running a hand over it. He flicked one of the brass handles. 'Helen MacAdams got some of this.'

'It's mahogany, and the inlay is teak. I'm afraid it all looks a bit rickety at the moment. Jack never seems to get around to fixing the floor.'

'Jesus, missus,' said Brown, after she had taken him around the room — the oak chairs and table, the Queen Anne walnut bureau, the silver candlesticks. 'Nothing but antiques.'

'Well, not really. But there are some fine old things. It all came from Jack's father. Wonderful old man in his way. He quite took to me.' Mum looked out of the window for a moment or two and then caught my eye. 'A little potty towards the end. He forgot that children were children. Thought they were like him, only smaller.'

Something stirred unpleasantly in my head. I looked down at my left hand, and Mum reached out instinctively and ruffled my hair.

'We lived in rather a grand house. That's it there,' said Mum, pointing to the watercolour of the Armstrong farmhouse in Suffolk. 'I'm afraid I miss it.'

'The Old Country, eh?' said Brown. 'I'm just beginning to get the picture. You and Jack are a coupla real bloody Poms.' He laughed.

'I hate that word,' said Mum. 'We use that word back home only for a type of dog.'

'Missus, I'm sorry. I wouldn't offend you for the world.'

They were standing in front of the rosewood cabinet in which all her best china was displayed. They had both become embarrassed. Mum didn't have anything to say for a while, and I could tell from his forehead that Brown was thinking about a way to make up for his rudeness.

'I'm so glad that you're – ' Mum stopped and looked around helplessly. She gestured towards the cabinet. 'This is my china.'

'You're a nice bit of china yourself,' Brown replied, and gave his big grin. Mum went so red I thought she would burst into flame.

I decided to come to the rescue. 'Mum, I'm going to take this bowl and water the sweet peas.'

'That's a good little boy,' she said, as though I were about five years old. As I was going out the door she said to Brown, 'Try not to step on the carpet – with those feet.'

Brown wasn't wearing any boots.

I watered the sweet peas and hurriedly sneaked up to the side window.

'I'd make you a cup of tea,' Mum was saying, 'but we're supposed to be over at Mrs Cutler's. She is going to introduce us to Eddie.' She looked at the mantelpiece clock, and it struck the quarter hour.

'Eddie.' Brown gave a chuckle. 'Well, gee, missus. We gotta do it some other time. Gotta get back and skin Mad Meg. She had it coming to her, but Dad's gonna hit the roof. She was a good milker.' Brown seemed to have forgotten all about helping Betty, who was still out the back, digging. I could hear her around the corner going *ouf*.

'Brown, I can't thank you enough. Heather could have been badly hurt.' Mum held out her hand and smiled. I had never seen her look so pretty.

'Scared the shit outta me.' Brown wiped his hand on his grimy trousers, and then they shook hands. Suddenly he raised hers to his lips and kissed it. Mum drew her hand back quickly.

'Seen 'em do that in the pictures,' said Brown, with one last grin. He grabbed his crutches, picked up his shotgun, and hurried out the screen door. Mum stood stock still, gazing after him. She put her hand to her chest and then noticed my head in the geraniums at the window.

'Goodness' sake, Lindsay,' she said sharply. 'What are you staring at? Come in and do your hair. You look a fright. And I'll warrant your shoes are filthy. I told you to stay out of the dirt.'

'Mum, the dirt's everywhere,' I protested, but I came in and obediently began to polish my shoes with a rag.

Heather returned from her room wearing her old checked frock. She had missed all the excitement. She gave me a kick as she went by the shoe box. 'That's for making me fall and ruin my frock.'

'You fell yourself,' I yelled.

'Don't shout at Heather.' Mum was adjusting her hat in front of the mirror. 'She's just had a terrible experience. And I've told you a hundred times, don't raise your voice to girls.' She was ready. 'Hurry up. What sort of impression is Mrs Cutler going to get if we are so late?'

'Oh, Mum,' I said, exasperated, 'Mrs Cutler doesn't even have a clock.'

'Of course she does. She's a doctor's wife. She's used to people being spick and span and on time. She's not like the uncouth people around here.'

I exchanged a look with Heather. Mum kept up this pretence about Mrs Cutler just because she was English, like us.

'I think Mum likes Brown,' I said to Heather the minute Mum was out the door. 'I like him.'

'She wouldn't like someone like Brown. He's common. And he can't walk properly.'

'He can walk enough to carry you up the hill. And anyway, he got that in the war. He's a brave man.'

'So's Dad,' said Heather.

'You just say that because he likes you,' I said resentfully. 'Tell me one single thing he's brave about.'

Heather stared at me for a moment. Then she clouted me over the head and ran out after Mum.

7

Mrs Cutler lived half a mile away across the plateau in a dilapidated house perched on the edge of an eroding cliff of soft red earth, high above the Lachlan. When we arrived she was out on her front verandah, banging together a hutch for Willie, her pet wombat, who was asleep, half covered by a blanket. She spat out the nails she had in her mouth, threw down the hammer, and greeted us effusively. 'My dear Lillian, what perfect timing. Let's go round the back.'

She went ahead of us with a broom, sweeping away the droppings. Free-ranging hens moved off the verandah unwillingly at our approach. A large Berkshire sow, snuffling at some bran spilled in our path, was given a hard swat with the broom, and when that didn't work, a boot.

'Damn pig. Turning that into pork will be Eddie's first job.'

In the back yard there was a campfire burning. Over it were crouched Jennifer and Jimmy, the Cutler twins, and someone who had to be Eddie.

'Some yabbie, some yabbie,' Eddie was saying excitedly as we came up. There was a blackened pot on the flames with crayfish boiling in it. 'I cook, I cook.'

'Listen to that accent,' said Mrs Cutler. 'Say hullo to the Armstrongs, Eddie.'

Eddie stood up, bowed, and then shook hands with each of us. His real name was Eduardo Larguili, and he was an Italian prisoner of war. Three days before, Mrs Cutler had gone to the Control Center in Wudgewunda and chosen him from a line-up. She had been told he could sing, play the piano, and cut hair. In return for his work, he was to receive a pound a week plus room and board. Under no circumstances was Eddie to leave her property except with written permission from the authorities.

'I Scotsman, very Scotsman,' said Eddie, pointing to his fair hair.

'Sing for us, Eddie.'

'I no sing today. I eat yabbie.'

'Isn't he a treasure,' said Mrs Cutler, who seemed unable to keep her eyes off him. 'Well, what do you think, Lillian? Speak freely, his English is abominable.'

Well, he seems to have excellent manners, and apart from the accent, you'd hardly know he was Italian at all.'

Mrs Cutler laughed delightedly. 'Keep his mouth shut and I'll be able to take him anywhere. Get him out of that horrible uniform, find him a cap. Mr Eddie, my chauffeur.' Mrs Cutler had a Vauxhall Cabriolet (on loan from Mrs MacAdams) parked out front amid the dandelions and dockweeds. She loved the car but hated driving.

'Did you meet the Japs in the camp?' I asked. I knew the Italian compound was right next to the Japanese one.

Eddie's face fell a little. 'Japs? No like Japs.'

'Eddie's camp days are over, Lindsay. Lillian, sit down, do,' said Mrs Cutler.

Mum sat down on a plank laid between two kerosene tins, unpinned her straw hat, and set it down on a nearby stump. She shook out her hair a little. The acacia trees growing by the verandah spread a dappled shade and were full of twittering sparrows and finches. I helped Jennifer and Jimmy keep the chooks at bay while Eddie served the yabbies. Mum stretched out her legs, wriggled her toes. The worst of the day's heat was over. It was that quiet interval between the flies and the mosquitoes, and I could see that Mum found the company, the atmosphere, and the temperature very agreeable.

It hadn't been easy for Mum to get used to Mrs Cutler, who had failed to set much of an example since arriving from England. She had a husband called Alfred, who was a brain surgeon back in Torquay. He had sent her out to Australia just after the outbreak of war.

'Believe it or not, my dear,' Mrs Cutler had said when Mum asked her how on earth she had wound up in Billarooby, 'we met

Bill and Helen MacAdams when they were holidaying in Torquay seven years ago. Alfred operated on Bill. A small tumour of some sort and we've corresponded ever since. It was Alfred's idea and Bill agreed, so here we are. MacAdams owns this house. Bill's a bit of an old fogy, but I like him. Helen's appalling, of course. Although she has virtually given me the Cabriolet.'

To me, at eleven, Mrs Cutler was an overwhelming, easy presence, my first experience of someone both brash and free. She was in her late thirties and quite tall, with frizzy brown hair pulled back and fastened with a clip. She had large, kind grey eyes, a strong nose with big nostrils, and little gold rings in her ears. Her mouth was wide and horsy with a show of tombstone teeth. She always wore the same pink lipstick, smudged a bit, and her clothes were forever in need of repair somewhere. That day she was wearing a dress of sea green crepe, torn at the shoulder, and I have a vivid memory of her breasts swinging freely under that dress, the nipples clearly pointing.

'Listen to that screeching,' cried Mrs Cutler. It was the cockatoos in the sunflowers, down below the cliff (Alfred's Leap, she called it) on the floodplain. 'Kids, why don't you all take Eddie to have a look.'

Jennifer and Jimmy jumped up, and so did Heather.

'We can swing on the rope,' shouted Jennifer.

My heart sank. I was too scared to swing on the rope, which was the way they travelled from one side of a steep gully to the other before going down the cliff.

'I would like to look at that book you mentioned.'

'Oh, I forgot all about it. The fascist propaganda.' Mrs Cutler laughed. 'It's in the book room somewhere. Get it later, Lindsay. Have some fun with the kids. Help Eddie with his English.'

Jennifer's eyes were shining. Inviting me as always. But I was intimidated by the Cutler twins. It wasn't only the rope. Jennifer had been sent home from school more than once for not wearing any knickers, and Jimmy was the instigator of all the sexual games behind the lavatory block at the far end of the playground.

I set off with them, but as soon as I was out of sight of Mrs Cutler, I ran away around the back of the house.

'Cowardy custard, cowardy custard, poop your pants, can't cut the mustard.' Jimmy's derisory chant still rang in my ears as I dashed inside.

Mrs Cutler had mostly abandoned the house to the livestock, and lived in the back yard. The living room was full of dust and cobwebs, piles of old newspapers and chicken shit. Broody hens glared from the armchairs, and the pigs and the wombat wandered around at will. I liked the house, I decided, as I picked my way through the mess to the book room. It was like a menagerie, and so different from our atmosphere of fading gentility. Mum was always scrubbing and dusting and worrying about the earthen floor, but Mrs Cutler did not concern herself with anything like that. She had gone bush with a vengeance.

The book room was right next to the back yard, and I could hear Mrs Cutler's laughter as I entered and closed the door. It was one of the few rooms in the house to which the door was always kept shut. The room was whitewashed and lined with cupboards and shelves, which overflowed with new and old and mostly broken precious objects – footballs that needed pumping up, roller skates, a couple of eyeless dolls, cricket bats split in the dry air, half-built Meccano constructions, and all sorts of games. Mrs Cutler indulged the twins in anything they cared for, but their enthusiasms were short-lived and everything was soon cast wantonly away. Heather and I were both shocked by this carelessness. Of necessity, we were much more provident in our family.

There were so many books, I hardly knew where to start looking and felt a momentary despair. Most of them were very different from our serious works of literature at home and the limited choice in Mr Buchanan's school library. The Cutlers had such diverse things as *English Rainbow Comics*, *The American West in Pictures*, *The Illustrated London News* and *Picture Post*. There were *Lamb's Tales from Shakespeare*, *Little Lord Fauntleroy*, *The Boys' Own Annual*, *The Girls' Bumper Book*, and *British Birds and Their Eggs*, with over a thousand illustrations. That was one of my favourites, although the birds weren't the same as those around Billarooby, except maybe the sparrows.

As I threw aside one book after another, I began to get more and more excited. I felt that I was on the verge of a momentous discovery.

The book appeared.

The Knights of Bushido, it was called, and I still have that book. Illustrations by Yukiteru Kanoya, text by Helmut Hartmann, translated into English by S. V. Miller, and published in London in 1937. Those details I know by heart.

The voices from the back yard faded away. It wasn't often in my life that I had seen a book so sumptuous. The pages were made of soft, thick paper with ragged edges and the coloured plates were protected by crisp, translucent tissue. I was soon lost in a world of medieval oriental legend.

The knights of Bushido were samurai, said the introduction, members of a unique and elite caste who had ruled Japan in feudal times and whose moral traditions remained strong to the present day. The samurai were chivalrous and courteous in their behaviour, both at home and on the battlefield.

The pictures were filled with detail. The samurai armour was all glistening metal, bamboo struts, and silk-covered padding. Vertical flags with emblems of carp and falcons flew from quivers on their backs. Pennants fluttered above them. Samurai fighting on caparisoned horses, samurai with long, thick moustaches and topknots, devout samurai praying inside an elaborate mountain shrine, whole armies of samurai fighting for their Emperor on the slopes of a snowcapped volcano. It took only a few of these pages to have me seeing myself as a noble samurai, striding around the field between the house and the school, dropping from the yellow box tree on to the back of Eric Kiddy and other hapless foes. Mr Buchanan's evil poster, THIS IS THE ENEMY, suddenly swam in front of my eyes, and then his voice buzzed some kind of warning loud and clear, right in my ear. I jumped up and peeped into the back yard, convinced that Mr Buchanan was paying a call. He was not. Mrs Cutler was giving Mum a tour, showing her the rabbit skins that she had stretched, still viscous, red-veined, and beginning to turn a bilious yellow. They were encrusted with feeding flies. As Mum and Mrs Cutler moved back towards the fire, where a blackened billy was boiling for tea, their voices came clearly to me through the window.

'. . . this whole sordid war business. Alfred's a pacifist, you know.'

'Really? That was the trouble with the Armstrongs. They're all so warlike and self-righteous, when it gets right down to it. Those brothers of his. Presbyterians.' Mum lowered her voice when she said this, almost as though she thought Dad would hear her.

'The worst,' said Mrs Cutler.

'His father was disgusted with Jack when he was rejected for military service, as though it were Jack's fault. It was the final straw, really. I mean, it hurt Jack terribly. His father called him a coward up and down Haverhill. It was what decided us to leave England. And the Suffolk farmhouse was right between the Germans and London. We didn't want the children getting bombed or anything.'

'What was all that about the father's death? Buchanan was telling me – '

'Well, of course that had something to do with it. Those awful brothers, but Lindsay was there, and he stood up at the inquest and told the truth so clearly, just as it happened. We were both very proud of him.'

'Jolly good for him. What did happen?'

'If it hadn't been for his evidence, Elsie, things might have been very difficult. Not that Jack did anything wrong, of course, but he and his father had been drinking and quarrelling that day. I'm afraid they often did.'

'Thought he didn't drink.'

'Oh, Jack used to love a drink. You might not think it now, but Jack was quite a fellow.'

'So what happened? He got religion?'

'Well, he was very upset, of course, by his father's sudden death. They were so close, in a way. Not the healthiest way, perhaps. It made him get a better hold on things. Well, to be frank, yes, he stopped drinking and got religion. You'd have thought his brothers would have been pleased.'

'It can happen to the best of us,' said Mrs Cutler. I heard a squawk. She had thrown a stone at a chook. 'But my dear, don't let me scoff. Every man has to grow up somehow. Even if it's into a pokerface.' She laughed.

'It was very frustrating for Jack. He and his father never were friends, and yet somehow he could never break away. He tried Canada for a while, but it didn't work out. Going back to his father was the very worst thing he could have done. Jack got off to a bad start in life . . .'

I had heard how Granddad kept Dad in the big house just as a torment, and how he had turned Uncle Peter and Uncle Allan against him. And I had heard how they refused to believe that Granddad's death was an accident, despite my evidence, and had practically driven our family out of England. And how, when we reached Australia, we had kept going farther and farther west, to smaller and smaller places. Until we had wound up in Billarooby. By the time Mum had made a good friend in each new place to whom she could tell the story, Dad had got into one of his depressions and given up yet again. But she always managed to tell the story before we left, and I had become very familiar with her version. I turned back to the book.

'. . . and before he died, Kusonoki handed his sword, a gift from the Emperor, to his eleven-year-old son, Tadao Masatsura, and told him that he, too, must fight to the death for the Emperor . . . Tadao is still regarded as a gunshin (war god) and a model for all samurai.'

Tadao! His name! My eyes rushed on.

Each picture, I realized, was an illustration to a story from samurai mythology. The Sea of the Sacred Carp. The Flight of Minamoturi. The Shogun and the Seven Egrets. The Battle on the Steps of the Temple of Heaven. The Bell of the Three Freedoms. The Night of the Thousand Lanterns. The Great Captivity! 'Surrender is a disgrace. Capture is a shame the samurai will never bear. Heroes prefer to become gems to break into myriad fragments than to become roof tiles to live out lives in idleness – ' I closed the book with a bang and hugged it to my chest, suddenly too excited to read. I peeped out into the other world going on in the back yard. Mum was taking a puff of Mrs Cutler's cigarette.

'. . . withdrawn. He goes off alone and gets lost in his own little fantasies. Doesn't seem that interested in playing with boys his own age.'

'What's wrong with Jimmy?'

'Well, both the twins are much more rough-and-tumble than he is.'

'They're rough all right. Look at this welt. And I'm their mother.' Mrs Cutler laughed.

'Have they gone to that prisoner of war camp?'

'Good God no. Nothing there for them.'

'Lindsay's itching to get across the river and visit it. It's a very dangerous interest.'

'Get him a horse. Much better. You never know where you are with Orientals. Jennifer rode all the way to Bindialla Falls last year without telling me. I walloped her, of course, but spirit of adventure – I encourage it. Let them run free.'

It was time for some tea and damper. Mrs Cutler's damper was not as good as Auntie Annabel's scones, but she was much more generous with the jam. I ran with the book to the back yard.

Mrs Cutler lay in the dust, propped up on one elbow, drinking tea out of a wire-handled mug she had made from an Edgells can. Mum had out a needle and thread and was preparing to put a stitch in the shoulder of Mrs Cutler's dress. Conversation had moved on to Brown, and she was smiling up at Mum in a devil-may-care way. 'Helen MacAdams says that he is not the man he used to be, but he'll still be after those glamorous tootsies of yours. I hear he likes them young. The busty blonde. The shy brunette. Can't imagine the legs will cramp his style. They go for that, the young ones. Such a handsome beast.'

Mum looked at me nervously as I approached them. 'I didn't mean . . .'

'One of the few men around here. Can't count Buchanan. Thank God for the Italian debacle in North Africa.' Mrs Cutler gave a rather dirty laugh.

'I have to admit that he was very gallant this afternoon. Well, in that Australian way. He seemed to get on so well with the children.'

'Oh, he's gallant all right. Ask that schoolteacher from Mudoogla. He was having a fling with her before he went off to war. But seriously, my dear Lillian. He's changed since he went away. And I don't just mean the moustache. It was no picnic up there in New Guinea. Those psychotic Japs.' Mrs Cutler smothered some damper with butter and jam and handed it to me. 'Yum yum,' she said. 'I see you found the book, Lindsay. Food for the imagination, don't you think?'

I thanked Mrs Cutler very sincerely for the book and wolfed down the damper. Mum gave me permission to go for a walk to my secret cave, and I went off at a run, anxious to get away before the twins came back.

8

I HATED GOING for walks with Jimmy and Jennifer, for they brought along their catapults. They had even tried to kill Gus, the magpie who lived with his wife, Gertie, in the only tree still left in the field that stretched between our house and the Cutlers'. Gus had been vicious in the springtime, even for a nesting magpie, but nowhere near as bad as the ones in Mr MacAdams' home paddock that had gone for the Colonel.

The field played an important part in my life in Billarooby, and I accepted the fact that Gus was something I had to put up with. It was his field before it was mine.

I had spent one of my most industrious and happy weekends carrying stones from the Lachlan and placing them at various strategic locations in the field. And after my discovery of the camp, I had added a large construction, mysterious even to me, in its very centre.

The school, the Cutlers', and our farmhouse were all located at the edge of this field, a vast, Australian version of a village green, and each building happened to be equidistant from the others. The paths with which I had connected them were in the shape of a triangle. For one geography lesson I had drawn a map of my placements for Mr Buchanan, who said that the equilateral triangle was a powerful form and that my central construction was an ancient religious symbol known as a Celtic cross. He showed me a picture of one in the encyclopaedia. The idea that I had accidentally constructed something religious was so abhorrent to me at the time that I let Mr Buchanan in on the secret: I had copied the cross and the circle of stones enclosing it from the prisoner of war camp. 'That's how it looks from my lookout in the outcrop, sir.'

'Religion takes many forms, Lindsay. Ever heard of Stonehenge? Angkor Wat?' Mr Buchanan said I would grow up to be a builder of temples or cathedrals. I objected, and he said, 'Better cathedrals than prison camps.'

Anyway, as soon as I left the Cutlers', I ran to this pile of stones and paced around it for a while, my new book clutched to my chest, my head filled with some sort of raw and hazy iconography about the Japanese. I stepped on the special stone in the very centre of the cross and drew my compass from my pocket. Solemnly I took a reading, and then set off in a southwesterly direction. Gus understood perfectly and left me to my own devices.

As I approached the outcrop, a truck went by below me and I heard men singing. It was some Italians, crowded into the back and returning to the camp after a day of cutting asparagus for the cannery. Bloody Itis, everyone called them. Now that I had met Eddie, I felt I knew all about them. If Mrs Cutler could have an Iti for a friend, I could certainly have a Jap.

As I settled myself in the rocks, I had eyes for only the Japanese.

There seemed to be hundreds of them in their compound. Some were running, some were using a vaulting horse. Others were tending flower and vegetable gardens close to the huts. Most of them, however, had arranged themselves in a huge circle, six or seven deep in the middle of the softball field. Those in front sat on the ground. In the centre were two men, dodging warily. Suddenly they locked in combat, pushing and shoving. Then one of them cartwheeled through the air and landed heavily on his bare back. The other jumped on him. A great shout went up and then died. From the Italian compound came the sound of a saxophone and a mandolin. The wrestlers circled once more. Judo wrestlers, I found out later.

I looked hard for the man that the Colonel had so cruelly whipped. Mr Buchanan had said that he was transferred to another camp, but you can't always believe just because you are told, and I searched anyway. A couple of times I almost convinced myself that I recognized him.

'Samurai,' I said aloud to myself with great satisfaction.

Traditions live on, Mr Buchanan was always saying, they just

take different forms when circumstances change. All you had to
do, he said, was remember the origins.

The referee barked commands that came through the air harsh
and clear. His voice was high-pitched and rapid. It was an alien
sound, and I liked it. 'It's a sound that has been around for
hundreds of years,' I told myself. 'It's time-honoured. It's in the
book. It's the sound of Bushido.' I articulated the word for the
first time and had to push my elbows into my sides to contain the
thrill.

I don't know how long I watched the spectacle of the samurai
once more enduring the Great Captivity, but whistles blew, and
then a bugle. A number of guards appeared. The circle broke up.
The summer sun was heading for the horizon; shadows were
creeping across the plain. The smell of a meat-and-potato stew
came wafting on the breeze, and I realized I was hungry. As I
turned to go, a bright yellow electric light sprouted from each of
the tall poles along the roads quartering the camp. Against the
gathering pink of the sky, the effect was so eerie that I gave an
involuntary shudder. 'Be careful,' went a warning in my head, and
it was Mum's voice. I climbed down through the rocks and set off
for home. Far below, in the big river gums, the kookaburras
started up their sundown laughter.

It was almost dark by the time I reached the flats, and I suspected
that there was going to be trouble. As I raced up the final hill,
Dad emerged from behind the rocks that surrounded the dunney.
Instinctively I veered away and ran a little harder.

'Come here.'

I stopped and walked back.

'Where have you been?'

'I've been in my secret cave.'

There was a long pause. 'What's that under your arm?'

'It's a book. Mrs Cutler gave it to me.'

Dad reached out a hand for it. He opened it up but in the
darkness he was unable to see what it was.

'Come with me.'

I followed him into the dunney and he lit the hurricane lamp. I
tried not to be apprehensive, alone in the dunney at night with
Dad, while he turned the pages of *The Knights of Bushido*.

As dunneys go, it wasn't a bad one. There was a smooth wooden bench to sit on and the deep hole was well covered. It smelled of quicklime more than anything else. Mum hated it because it was on the hillside in front of the house and visitors had to pass by it. Not that we ever had any.

'This is a book glorifying the Japs. That woman has no business letting you have such a thing. I've a good mind to drop it down the hole.'

'She wants it back,' I cried in a panic. I made a grab for it and Dad held it out of reach.

'You went to that camp.'

'No, I didn't.'

I could sense Dad's anger rising even before he yelled at me to get out and bend over.

Outside in the dark Dad unbuckled his belt. I waited, but no beating came. It never did. We had often got to this point, but never further. He wanted to but couldn't do it. I even felt I deserved a punishment, both for my lie and for the fact that I liked the Japanese.

I despised Dad for his weakness. Despised him, but still there was that fear, fear that someday the throbbing vein in his temple would burst and the beating of beatings would come.

'I will not be lied to.'

The merest bat's flicker of my nightmare went across my brain, and under my breath I said, 'You're the one who makes me lie.' My head jerked down in sudden shame.

'What is there about that camp to attract a normal young boy?'

Dad moved closer and hustled his body against mine in a kind of frustration about not having the nerve to thrash me.

'That Chinaman of yours was an escaped prisoner. You're a little Jap-lover.'

My head dropped even lower.

Heather's voice came calling from the yard. 'Dad, dinner's ready.'

Dad flapped at the night air a couple of times with his belt and then put it back on.

'Go clean yourself up. There's no pudding for you tonight. And I'm keeping this book.'

The garden smelled of honeysuckle and geraniums. As I

splashed water on my face from the kitchen tank, I speculated both on what I might be going to miss for pudding and on where he might hide the book.

When I walked in through the screen door, I almost collided with Mr Kelly.

'Here is the little snowdrop, Mrs Armstrong, your tiny tearaway. You can ease your mind.'

Mr Kelly reached out to grab me and I twisted away. I might have known it was he who had ratted on me.

'Once more, dear ladies, farewell. I will see you in appleblossom time.' He raised his hat and gave a sinister smirk all round. How they could all be smiling at him was beyond me. 'Or even sooner,' he continued, winking at Joan.

'Dad's out waiting for you,' said Heather, the minute Mr Kelly was gone. 'You're going to get it.'

'I already got it.' I automatically kept up the pretence of Dad beating me, and then lashed out about Mr Kelly. 'What's he doing in the house? He's a murderer.'

'It was manslaughter,' said Heather.

'He paid his debt to society,' said Mum. 'You can't judge him now.'

That night Dad read a bloodthirsty passage from Deuteronomy. It seemed to be all about stoning me to death, and wearing the right clothes, but everyone knew it was just the Bible. Dad was always reading something horrible from the Old Testament. I waited impatiently for it to be over.

' " . . . and the woman shall not wear that which pertaineth to a man, neither shall a man put on a woman's garment: for all that do so are abomination unto the Lord thy God . . ." '

Smack! Dad got a fly. He kept a swatter beside him at meals, and any old time he could pick it up and lash out with a deft stroke.

The room was very hot from the cooking. The smell of mutton chops made my mouth water. Their slow sizzling from the stove seemed to grow louder and louder. I could hear the dying buzzes of the flies trapped on the sticky yellow flypapers, the ticking of the clocks, Joan at her nails and Heather breathing, the flutter of the moths against the tall white glass of the Aladdin lamp, and the soft hiss of the lamp's incandescent mesh as the oil burned. My eyes fell on *The Knights of Bushido*, which Dad had left on Mum's rosewood desk.

Tadao, naked but for a loin cloth, swam out of the darkness and from behind wrapped a red cloth around Dad's neck. I saw Tadao's scar and Dad's scar, both together. I gasped and sat up straight in my chair. I rubbed my eyes. Tadao did not go away. As he pulled tighter and tighter, Dad's voice began to come from a great distance, and then it disappeared completely. *Blip!* The samurai disappeared with the voice, but as I watched Dad's lips continue to move soundlessly, I became convinced that Tadao had broken his vocal cords. In a panic, I reached out to Mum.

Smack!

'Miss Cash, will you stop that sacrilege?'

Dad had killed another fly, an inch from Joan's plate.

'Stop what?' Joan had not even jumped. Dad was scowling at her.

'Your fingernails. Not at the table. And never while I am reading the Good Book.'

'The Good Book.' Joan turned her mouth down and put her nail file away.

'She didn't realize, Mr Armstrong,' said Betty.

'I never realize,' said Joan.

'Enough!' Dad resumed his reading. Joan and Betty looked at each other. Joan opened her red mouth in a big O and rolled her eyes to the ceiling. They both began to suppress giggles, and suddenly I found myself doing the same. Mum unfolded her napkin and kept it to her lips because of the disrespect. I managed to stop myself and decided Joan was a bad influence.

When Dad had finished, he rested his fingers above his closed eyes for a moment or two and then handed the Bible to Heather, who returned it to its stand. Dad said grace briefly; Mum removed the vase of Canterbury bells from the table and began to bring the food. She took forever, and by the time I sank my teeth into my chop I felt like a starving wild animal. I began snarling at Dad for confiscating my book. That samurai would get him again.

Everyone ate in silence. After a while Heather said, 'Mr Kelly saw you going to the camp. There's a No Trespassing sign and you went right past it.'

'What camp?' I asked, my mouth full of mashed potatoes. I stared belligerently at Dad.

'Oh, you fibber. Mr Kelly says the Japs are going to get you, and good riddance.'

'He must be thinking of someone else. I wouldn't go to the camp if you paid me.'

'I wish you would stop playing this silly game,' said Mum.

'I didn't go to the camp. I didn't.'

'Leave the table at once,' said Dad, 'and go to bed. Tomorrow when we get back from town, you're going to spend all day doing the beans.'

As I left the room, he called out, 'Don't forget to say your prayers. Even as we will all pray for you.'

I consoled myself by calling Dipper and the pups into my room and lifting them all up on to the bed. I don't know why playing with them made me burst into tears.

Later, alone in the dark and listening to the thin, high whine of the mosquitoes, I heard the door creak open. It was Mum, with a piece of queen's pudding for me. It was one of my favourites – a bread concoction, soaked in milk and cream, stuffed with lemon peel and raisins, topped with jam and golden peaks of meringue.

Mum put her lamp on the dresser and sat beside me on the bed while I ate. Her hair was out, brushed and ready for bed, and she wore her long white nightgown. She looked like an angel. After I had finished my pudding, I began to cry again.

'If it hadn't been for me after Granddad died, he would have been in serious trouble.'

'That was all a long time ago.'

'What's the matter with me?'

'There's nothing the matter with you.'

'Then why doesn't he like me?'

'He does like you. It is for your own good. Any father would want to stop you from going to that camp. You didn't see any other boys playing there, I'll be bound. It's very dangerous to be anywhere near the Japanese. You read the papers.'

'Japs rip out your toenails and if they come here they will turn the church into a whorehouse.'

Mum was horrified. I smiled to myself.

'Mr Buchanan told us that.'

'He has no business saying such things to his pupils. All the more reason to stay away. Now are you going to promise me never to go there again?'

'I promise.'

I was too glib. She didn't believe me.

'Deceiving your parents is one of the worst things you can do. You'd get along much better with your father if you told the simple truth.'

I liked the sound of that. A surge of affection for Mum had me up on my elbow, planting a kiss on her cheek. 'You look so pretty in the light.'

'Don't be cheap. I want that promise.'

'I promise.'

'That's better.' She brushed the hair out of my eyes. 'We'll get Eddie to give you a haircut. Did you have a nice time at Mrs Cutler's this afternoon?'

'Oh yes, I like Eddie.'

'You see? There are plenty of people around, much nicer than the Japanese. Jimmy and Jennifer say they will teach you to ride.'

'Mr Kelly's not nice, and you let him in the house.'

'Didn't you see the kangaroo skins Mr Kelly brought round? He wants to be a friend of the family. A good neighbour.'

'He's covered in hair. He's the Bunyip.'

'People can't help their hair. It grows quite naturally. You might have hair like that when you grow up.'

'I'd shave it off.'

Mum sighed and picked up the pudding plate. 'I want you to try and like your father a little more.'

I sat up in bed. 'I love Dad,' I protested vehemently. 'It's him who doesn't love me.'

Mum paused a while and then said, 'You remember how hard Granddad was on your father. That makes him a little hard on you. I don't say it is right. But he is under a lot of pressure just now. Nobody has ever done before what your father is doing in Billarooby. It is very important that the farm is a success. For us all. And for the memory of Granddad. You know how he honours his father, and you should do the same. It's in the Bible. When you are down in the fields tomorrow, straighten your shoulders and do it like a little man. That's what he likes.'

She kissed me good night. 'When the strain is off and the crops start coming in, you'll see how much your father loves you.'

The minute I heard Mum and Dad go to bed I sneaked into the living room and rescued my book. I lay in the dark with it clutched to my chest for a long time. The sound of laughter and music came distantly from the Landgirls' room. Joan had bought a wireless in Wudgewunda. It wasn't until well after they had switched it off that I heard the quarrelling and the sound of Mum crying. When the clocks struck midnight, I was standing outside their bedroom door, which had been left ajar. In the moonlight flooding the room, I could see the white sheet covering Mum and Dad swaying and shuddering. I thought at first they must be having a nightmare. The more I looked, the more the sheet seemed to acquire a life of its own. Mum was gasping in pain, and my puzzlement at what was going on began to turn to fury.

'It's no good, Jack, you know it's no good.'

'I want that son, Lillian,' Dad said loudly. 'I mean to have a real son. Our prayers will be answered. They will.'

I felt as though I'd been kicked in the chest. I ran back to my room. I almost ran into Heather's. I was beside myself. Suddenly I was back at their door.

'I'll kill you,' I screamed. I shoved the door open as hard as I could and ran off into the night.

9

I WAS AWAKENED by the dawn chorus of the kookaburras in the trees above my head. From where I lay, I could see a line of six of them against the bright orange of the early sky. I wriggled and stretched luxuriously under my blanket. Around me the riverbank was alive with the twittering of zebra finches. The sunshine came flooding in and I smiled as I recalled my headlong flight through the night. Imagining Dad in full pursuit had given wings to my feet, and I'd outfoxed him as we left the flats and reached the river, my territory rather than his, the trails I knew backwards and he scarcely at all. I had escaped, and the spirits of the bush all around exulted with me as I tumbled breathless and triumphant into my cave. I did a forward roll to celebrate, and as I fell asleep, my one thought had been for Mum, a wish that she not worry about me.

My cave was in the grove of majestic river gums that I had discovered the day I chased the Chinaman. The cave was really a large hole, almost ten feet square, gouged by floodwaters from where the great tree had fallen across the river. The back wall was formed by a flat grey boulder. There was a ledge on which I had placed my galah wings, a lacquered box containing my marble collection, a kangaroo skull, and other valuable items. There was straw from the Douglasses' feedshed, bedding, a tin of biscuits, a tin of tea. It was my home away from home. A refuge from Dad.

'Dad just wants to get rid of me,' I said in my own defence as I squatted on the platform at the mouth of the cave. Above me was the tangled crown of tree roots; below flowed the river. I was wearing the Japanese's white cap with the chrysanthemums as a symbol of my defiance. Beside me was *The Knights of Bushido*, which I had brought with me. 'He says he believes in God, and

God will punish him,' I muttered. A blue-tongued lizard warming himself on the corner of the platform flicked his tail and disappeared. As the sun rose a little higher, I took off my clothes and had a swim. It was a baptism, in a way, for I had never thought to swim naked before. Dragonflies appeared, hovering and darting above the water. I was excited by my nakedness and dashed about the bank playing with myself, something absolutely forbidden. It filled me with intense satisfaction. I climbed in and out of the cave, courted disaster by cartwheeling on the fallen trunk far out above the water, and was like some mad little god or goblin. My blood pumped and I trembled with a kind of crazy, careless freedom. I had discovered a power, realized for the first time that there was a world that was mine and no one else's. I began to shriek like a parakeet.

Then I remembered that it was Saturday and that we were going into Wudgewunda that morning.

'I spent the night in my cave.'

'We thought you must have done that.'

I stoked up the fire and Mum warmed the porridge. Then she cooked a potato pancake from batter she had kept just for me. There was also fried bread and a fresh pot of tea.

Mum was very tired. She looked at me and then at her hands resting on the tablecloth in front of her.

'Such a noise you made leaving.'

I looked at the floor but in my new mood did not feel any need to apologize. Dad was the one who should apologize.

'Come here.' She gave me a hug and rocked me like a little boy. 'There's no baby going to replace you.'

'Dad . . .'

'Dr Abercrombie has told us that it is impossible for me to have any more children. Your father is very unrealistic about these matters.'

I pulled away roughly from Mum, and to hide my confusion about babies and how they happened, I poured myself some more tea in my most adult manner and changed the subject.

'What's Mr Buchanan doing here?' His little red Morris was parked out front.

'He's out with your father at the back tank.'

I stared. It was no small thing for someone to be with Dad when he was in the middle of his big wash for going into town.

'He had wonderful news for your father. His friend at the camp, Sergeant Duffy, told him that there is a shortage of vegetables. So many new prisoners are arriving, they can't keep up with the demand. Your father is going to see if he can supply them with lettuces.'

'The Japs will be eating our lettuces?'

'There's nothing wrong with that,' said Mum sharply. 'It will be good money for us.'

'When he goes to the camp, can I go too?'

'Mr Buchanan's already talked your father into it. After we drop Joan and Betty off in Wudgewunda this morning, you can ride over to the camp with him. But get those romantic notions about it out of that head of yours.'

On the way into Wudgewunda we stopped by to pick up Brown, who was having trouble with his legs and had to go in to see Dr Abercrombie. He sat in the back with Heather and me and two crates of lettuces and a cloth-covered box that he set down beside him. The Landgirls squeezed into the front with Mum and Dad.

Alone with Brown for the first time (Heather was reading and did not really count), I felt very shy, and stared out at the passing scenery. My mind was full of the visit to the camp coming up, but that didn't stop me from watching his every move. The first thing Brown did was prop his leg up on one of the lettuce crates. Then he took a packet of Turf from his trousers, extracted a cigarette, and lit it in the hot wind by cupping his hand around the match. He took a deep draw, looked around at Heather and me, and said, 'Jesus, can't tell you how happy I am to be back in Rooby.'

Dad hit the pothole at the end of the poplars and Brown's leg fell off the crate. 'Fucking Christ.' I thrilled at the profanity as he took his leg in both hands and carefully lifted it back. 'Same old road.'

'It happened on the Kokoda Trail, didn't it,' I said, showing off my knowledge.

'Yer dead right.' Brown grimaced. 'Japs hit 'em for six.'

'Dad's taking me to visit the Japs today.'

'Some blokes get all the luck.'

A squealing came from inside Brown's box.

'Want a decko?'

The box was really a cage and inside were two animals.

'Weasels,' I said.

'Stinkeroos.'

They had white fur and pink-rimmed eyes. They kept twitching their orange snouts back to reveal little needle-sharp teeth.

'Stick yer dick in. Bite it right off.'

I let the cloth drop back quickly, and Brown laughed.

'Me dad's ferrets,' he said. 'He's selling them. Getting another two.'

'Disgusting smell,' said Heather.

'Scares the bejesus outta the bunnies.'

'Why are you called Brown?' I found it a strange name, although I knew that if you had red hair you got called Blue.

'Never wear a hat, never wear a shirt, that's why.' Brown looked very tickled by my question.

'You're wearing one now.'

At that, Brown hauled the tail of his khaki shirt out of his trousers, seized the shirt at the open neck, and pulled it apart. The buttons went flying. Heather looked up and Brown stripped the shirt right off.

'How about that?'

Brown's body was lean and strong like Dad's. He began running his hands over his torso, then flexed all his muscles so that they rippled.

'Couple more days out in the paddocks and I'll be back to me full colour.'

Brown then yanked out a few of the hairs that were growing around his nipples, and laughed when he noticed both Heather's and my interest. Perhaps we looked scandalized. Dad's grooming never went so far.

And that wasn't all. In the very next second, he suddenly picked up his shirt, bundled it loosely, and threw it up into the air with a shout. 'Bloody army!' The wind sent it sailing off into the dust and out of sight.

'That's a terrible waste,' said Heather. 'What are you going to wear in town?'

I have never forgotten that ride into Wudgewunda with Brown.

He treated me like an equal, and it made me feel heroic just to be with him. As I knelt in front of him in the wind and dust, I found out all sorts of things. When Brown's mother had upped and left Slow George in the great drought of '27–'28, she had gone to live on a cherry orchard near Mount Canobolas with a younger man. Auntie Annabel had given up her life in Coonabarrabran, where she had been hoping to marry a clergyman, to come and look after them – Brown and his young brother, Roy. Roy was one of the surviving rats of Tobruk in North Africa. Unlike Brown, he loved the army and had no intention of ever coming home. Brown had lived most of his life in Billarooby, but he had some property near the coast on the Nepean. He loved the Lachlan when he was a boy my age, and still did. He knew all the good places along the bank and was sorry he wouldn't be able to get to them anymore. There was nothing about Billarooby he did not like. Even all the ring-barked trees. 'Where else the bloody galahs gonna sit.'

A flock of parakeets burst out of the blue gums no more than twenty yards from the road, and Brown wanted to bet me money they were lorikeets.

'All right,' I said boldly, looking at Heather. Dad strongly disapproved of any form of gambling, and we were forbidden to play cards or any games that required the use of dice, at least on Sundays.

'I'll tell Dad,' said Heather, turning a page.

By the time we went by the cannery, we had run out of things to talk about, and Brown craned his neck around to have a look through the back window at the Landgirls. The girls were staring straight ahead. Conversation between them and my parents did not seem to be flowing. Brown tapped on the window and Betty turned and flashed a smile. Brown gave her a flutter with his hand and Joan too looked round. There was an old blowfly crawling on the inside of the glass. She picked it up between her thumb and forefinger and squashed it, threw it out the door, and then wiped her fingers on the glass.

'Yuk!' exclaimed Brown, and made a face.

Joan laughed and put her tongue out at him. The tongue was just the sort of nasty thing that Heather did to me, but it made Brown grin from ear to ear.

'Christ, see all that?' he said, turning to me. 'Bloody sheilas.' His eyes gleamed, the heavy forehead came to life.

'Now you wouldn't get yer mum doing things like that, wouldya. Your mum's a real lady.'

We dropped everyone at the post office. Brown had some time before his doctor's appointment and decided to come and have a look at the camp too. We both climbed into the cabin with Dad.

It was three miles out along Plurry Creek Road, and as the terrain grew more rugged, my excitement mounted. Brown pushed up the window with one hand and pressed down on my head with the other. 'Yer gonna fly out, me young kooka.'

An army convoy approached along the road, and we travelled through dust so thick I could see nothing. Then we went through a cutting, the dust cleared, and there on the plain stretched a great jumble of buildings and barbed wire. We came to a halt outside a huge log gate on which was written simply 'POW CAMP.'

'What are you waiting for?' said Dad. 'Go and have your look.'

'This isn't it,' I said.

Dad ignored me and disappeared into a nearby Fibro building. There was a sign above the door which read 'OFFICE — AUSTRA-LIAN MILITARY FORCES.'

'It isn't,' I insisted.

'Ain't no other,' said Brown.

I found it hard to let go of my disbelief. All was silent, still, hot, and dusty. There were no red uniforms to be seen, there was no singing, no exercises or martial games.

'Don't wait for me,' said Brown. 'Reckon I've seen enough Japs.'

Still I hesitated.

'Shake a leg,' said Brown.

I got out of the truck and walked past the big entrance gate towards the first of the guard towers. I looked up at the outcrops surrounding the camp and tried to orient myself. After a while I decided that I recognized the one where my lookout was. I saw where Tadao had been knocked down and measured the distances with my eye. The slope began some thirty yards from the outer ring of barbed wire, and the rocks themselves began another twenty yards above that. It wasn't far to the kurrajong trees and my lookout at the top, but from this side it was a very steep climb. That gave me some satisfaction. The Colonel wouldn't be catching me up there in a hurry.

I put my hands up on to the barbed wire and gazed through to the first row of huts. I couldn't understand where the Japanese were. Could they still be asleep at nine in the morning? Did they have work to do inside before they were allowed out into the yard? Perhaps they were at desks, learning English. Or underground, digging a tunnel out. For several moments I was convinced that that was what they were doing. Then I saw a row of them in the shade of a concrete building that looked like the lavatories. Some squatted on their haunches, others leaned up against the wall, others were doodling in the dust. Cigarettes were going from hand to hand. They were plotting, I told myself, they couldn't be just sitting there; those doodles were diagrams. I ran farther around the outside wires and saw other Japanese lounging in the shade of their huts. One or two were strolling about. Three barbed wire fences separated me from them.

It was all a great disappointment. I had pictured myself inside the camp, going along a line of Japanese until I came to Tadao. We would have recognized each other, shaken hands, and then talked about freedom. Around us there would have been restless, angry pacing, faces turned sad-eyed to the dry northern plains. I would have overheard mayhem being planned against the despicable Colonel and his officers. Tadao would have put his fingers to his lips and together we would have sworn secrecy.

Feeling suddenly that my thoughts were being read, I looked up and caught the eye of the sentry in the nearest tower. I took my hands off the barbed wire and ran back to the truck.

'Got yer fill?' Brown flicked a butt out the window. 'Guard up there's got some hot lead in his pencil for you.'

I looked around quickly, and Brown laughed. In fact, none of the guards seemed to be taking the least notice of us. At the far end of the compound a group of soldiers were in a circle having a smoke and keeping out of the sun, just like the Japanese. But unlike the Japanese, they were all middle-aged and saggy, more like Mr Buchanan. There was one soldier lying with his head in his hands, as though he were sick, or drunk, and a little black and white dog sniffing at some garbage.

'Security's tight,' said Brown, and laughed again.

'It's a horrible place,' I said as I climbed back into the cabin. 'How can anyone be happy here?'

'Never known a prison that wasn't. End of the line, mate. Failure of humanity. That's what a prison is.' He was shifting about uneasily on the seat.

'What is Dr Abercrombie going to do?'

Brown pulled a bottle out of his trouser pocket. 'Give me more of these.' He shook two tablets out into his hand and dropped the empty bottle on the floor. He washed the tablets down with a swallow from his canteen. 'Swig?'

'It's whiskey.' I pulled a face. Brown laughed and put the canteen away.

Dad came out with an elderly fat man in bifocals and a sweatstained uniform. He had a pencil behind his ear and a notepad in his hand. He inspected the crates briefly and nodded. Dad began carrying them inside.

'Hey kid, looking for a pet?' asked the fat soldier as I went back to the barbed wire for another look. 'Take one off our hands. Take two. They're small.'

'They'll buy anything I can get to them,' said Dad as we drove away.

'Now that you're bloody rich, you can shout us a beer at the William.'

'Rich?'

'Feeding the Japs, eh, mate? What they call that, collaboration?'

Dad did not smile. Mrs MacAdams, who always had a low opinion of Dad for some reason, once said that if Dad only knew how to chaff, he might make a real friend or two in the district, instead of just Mr Buchanan.

'Joking, mate.' Brown laughed and clapped him on the shoulder. 'Just make sure you get your bloody quid.'

As we skirted Henry Kendall Hill and made the descent back into Wudgewunda, Dad said, 'Glad I made that connection. Want to do my bit. If there was more I could do, I would. I tried to enlist, you know, but they wouldn't have me.' He looked across at Brown anxiously and then tapped his chest. I had seen him do that many times before when this vexing topic came up. 'That's why I came out here. Better weather.'

'You look pretty A-1 now. For a bloody Pom.' Brown winked at me. 'Worse places than Australia for a TB case, mate.'

'The farm's my war work,' Dad went on hurriedly. 'Somebody's got to keep the home fires burning. My produce will be going straight from the cannery to the front lines.'

'So that's what they told you. Make a quick killing *and* do good.'

'We'll get you to that doctor,' said Dad, turning too sharply into Bell Street. 'After what you went through in Burma . . .'

'New Guinea.' Brown took another swig.

'Of course.'

'Flaming Yanks. Never did come.' Brown reached down and gave his left knee a feel.

I was ashamed of Dad's ignorance about the war. He would often throw the *Sydney Morning Herald* down rather than face the news. These days Dad didn't read anything really, except the Bible.

It was always busy in town on Saturdays. The shops closed at noon and everything had to be done at a gallop. Wudgewunda was a wartime boomtown. The population of three thousand had been almost doubled by the presence of the camp garrison and an infantry training battalion. The fortunes of war, said Mr Buchanan – the camp created animosity, but along with it business, both legitimate and black market.

Lawson Street was tarred, but the side streets were not, and the town was usually dusty as well as hot. There were a few plane trees, but most of what shade there was came from the awnings and railed verandahs in front of the shops and pubs. The Lachlan flowed by at the bottom of the main street and was spanned by two bridges, one for trains, the other for everything else. The attractions of Wudgie were the Showground, with its track for trotting races; the aborigines who lived in shanties under the railway bridge; Bingham Park with paved walkways, caged emus, waratahs, and a bandstand; and Henry Kendall Hill with its fine view, coolabar trees, mimosas, white cedar, and wilderness of rocks. But it was mainly the bustle of the main street and the crowds that I liked. It was a big change from the quiet of Billarooby. The only noisy things out there were the cockatoos, and sometimes the cows, when Slow George separated the new calves from their mothers.

Dad and I went into the Ritz Milk Bar and Café and took places opposite each other in a booth. The Ritz was full of the smell of fried egg, tomato, and sausage. When Mrs Andronicos came to take our order, Dad said I could have anything I wanted. I asked for an ice cream sundae and a Coca-Cola. Dad ordered a pot of tea and a custard tart. We avoided each other's eyes. The fan directly above us circled slowly. The ceiling had once been cream-coloured, but it was now thickly coated with grease and speckled with flyspots. The only decorations were the sticky yellow flypapers that were alive with the buzz of trapped and dying flies. The café was busy, mostly with soldiers. The door to the kitchen was out of alignment and banged every time Mrs Andronicos or the waitress went through.

Dad looked up at me as he readied himself to talk. The silence continued until a terrible tension had built up.

'The heathen Japs. Did you see the heathen Japs?' he suddenly rasped.

I nodded slowly.

'A scourge sent by God to test the Australians. And the world. It has nothing to do with us, nothing whatever, do you understand?'

'I was hoping we could go inside.'

'What we do is stay away.'

'Mr Buchanan's friend, Sergeant Duffy – '

'You had a good ten minutes. That's enough to satisfy anyone's curiosity. From now on, I order you to forget about the camp. Is that clear?'

He glared at me and immediately started to talk about the farm. I got the feeling that he did not want me to get a word in edgewise, that he was nervous about my running away, about what had happened the night before. Perhaps he could sense my newfound power.

I was powerful but a bit dazed as I listened to his explanation of how he had fixed the pump the day before. Would I like to learn how to set up the liquid manure? Had I noticed how

successful his method of staking the tomato crop had been?
Would I like to hear how he had managed to keep the insects
down without any spraying? He was getting some bees from Slow
George and setting up hives out by the wattle tree . . .

Mr Buchanan and Mum must have given Dad a good talking-
to, I thought as I tried to grasp what was going on in his mind. If
I started running away and hanging around the prisoner of war
camp, it might reflect on him as a father and affect his standing in
the community, with the Reverend Pitts, his future as a church-
warden. My mind drifted.

'You never listen. I'm going to make you knuckle under on the
farm if it kills me,' he suddenly said in a loud voice. I jumped in
fright, and then almost without a pause he continued, 'Why do
you play girls' games at school? Hopscotch. What's the matter
with you?'

'I'm the best of anybody at it,' I said. 'Even better than Jennifer.'

'Jennifer!' said Dad scornfully. 'Your report card was much too
good. Is Buchanan up to something?'

'I'm not very good at arithmetic,' I said hopefully.

'It runs in the family. Your granddad couldn't add two and
two.'

It was a cue. Suddenly I wanted desperately to tell him all about
my nightmare, get it settled, have the truth out in the open. It
would be man to man between Dad and me.

'Did you say anything to Mr Buchanan about me and
Granddad?'

Dad's eyes slid away, then came back with that glare. 'You
know the story, better than I do. You're the one who liked
Granddad. You're the one who was upset when he died, not me.
You're the one who has that nightmare about him. It's about him,
isn't it?'

'It was a different nightmare last time, Dad. It was a flood, and
Granddad and Uncle Peter and Uncle Allan were all drowned. We
let them get swept away over the weir – '

'That's enough. Remember something pleasant about Granddad
for a change. What about that time he took you and Heather on
the barge to Oxford? The blackberries by the canal. You got his
hat back for him . . .' Dad gave an encouraging smile.

I couldn't handle the smile, and looked away. Dad smiling at

me wasn't the real Dad. It was just because Mum and Mr
Buchanan had ordered him to. Mr Buchanan had said that Dad's
abrasiveness was just a manner of getting by in a harsh world,
and that I should go beneath for the real person. But that was the
problem. I took a look back into Dad's dark eyes and all I could
see was Granddad. There was a flash of red behind my eyes, a
crawl on my scalp, and I looked down quickly to my hands on
the table. My resolve to get to the bottom of things drained away.

Dad doesn't care about me at all, I thought moodily. What he
had said the night before in the heat of the moment was the truth.
He wanted another son because I couldn't cut the mustard, didn't
love the land.

I decided to excuse myself and go out to the lavatory in back.

'Why don't you like me?' Dad asked suddenly, just as I was
about to get up.

How could he get it so wrong? It was the other way round. I
said nothing, and we were still staring at each other in a kind of
belligerent misery when Mum and Heather arrived.

When we left the Ritz, it had gone twelve and the shops were
closed. We walked to where Dad had parked the truck, at the
intersection of Lawson Street and Bell Street, which was the centre
of Wudgie. On each of the four corners there was a pub. The
Imperial, the Lachlan, the Royal George, and the Prince William.
Mr Buchanan drank in all of them, but it was the Prince William
that always had the biggest and most boisterous crowd.

'Wudgie's overrun with soldiers,' said Heather.

'I wonder where Brown is,' said Mum.

'In the pub, where else?'

'Oh, Heather, why do you assume that?'

I looked for him. It was hard to see, there were so many men
drinking. They were draped lazily against the fluted iron columns,
they were standing on the pavement, and they were sitting on the
two long steps that led down to street level. From the cavernous
main doorway came the smell of sweat and stale beer. There was
the roar of male voices and the sound of the first race being
broadcast from Randwick.

'Blast it! Elsie Cutler.' Dad swore before he could stop himself,
and moved round to the other side of our truck. I had heard him

saying to Mum that Mrs Cutler was no better than Joan. He disapproved of Eddie and made it clear that he believed it had been very irresponsible of her to give me the book about the Japanese. Heather said he didn't like Mrs Cutler because of her pigs. 'Pigs are unclean. It says so in the Bible.'

'Come on, Jack,' called Mrs Cutler in her heartiest manner as she approached. 'Take us up to the Ladies for a drink.'

Dad ignored her. Respectable women, even with escorts, did not go into pubs, even upstairs to the Ladies' Lounge at a new one like the Lachlan.

'Oh dear,' said Mum, 'he looks so forlorn.'

'It's tough being a teetotaller out here.'

Dad made a point of avoiding the Prince William. That morning we had crossed the street rather than walk along its beery verandah. He had wanted to thank Sergeant Duffy for the tip about the lettuces but couldn't bring himself to go in, even though Mr Buchanan was in there too.

'He doesn't look a mess like they all do,' said Heather.

I had to admit Heather was right. Dad's blue shirt was stiff with starch, and Mum had freshly steamed and blocked his Stetson before we left home. She had put a crease in his cavalry-twill trousers and Heather had polished his elastic-sided boots. Mum would never have him looking like the men at the Prince William, with their grimy trousers or shorts and singlets, open shirts or bare chests.

Suddenly there was Brown, vaulting across the street on his crutches. Dad immediately made to leave.

'Aw, come on, Jack, came over to get you. Shout you one. Yer mate Fred's over there.'

'I don't drink,' said Dad curtly.

'Christ. Keep forgetting.' Brown's face fell momentarily. Then he looked around at all of us with that grin that always had Mum smiling back. It was all right for Brown to be barechested and look like the men in the William. 'Well, here I am. Reckon we'll go.'

'There's no hurry, Brown,' said Mum.

'I could go home with Fred, but you know what he's like. He'll be hours.' Brown put his crutches in the back of the truck. 'Where's the girls?'

'Betty and Joan have the day off. They are making their own way home,' said Mum quite rosy in the face with Brown's decision.

Heather and I piled into the back and Dad cranked up the engine, but some time was to elapse before our shark-nosed, round-fendered old Ford left that parking place.

'Look, Brown,' I called through the window. A convoy of buses, painted a military green, was coming from the direction of the railway station. A charge animated the lethargic street. The men loitering outside the Prince William called to others within. Two sulkies pulled into the cross street. Some trucks hurriedly parked and others roared away. A group of girls on ponies galloped off towards Bingham Park.

I remember Mum's face looking through the back window to check that Heather and I were all right.

Dad had plenty of time to leave if he wanted to, for the approach of the convoy was excruciatingly slow. Waves of heat rising from the bubbling pavement distorted the buses' outlines. The first one stopped at the intersection and the driver began a conversation with someone outside the Prince William. I stood up in the back of our truck and found myself eye to eye with the passengers. They were Japanese prisoners of war on their way to the camp.

My blood surged through me. The Japanese were all wearing the red-dyed uniforms. Some of the men were smoking, and there was quite a lot of chatter. The bus was packed. Ferocious, sardonic, heroic samurai, imperial knights of the sun, fallen eagles. I looked eagerly towards the other two buses, stopped behind. Hundreds more. My racing eyes finally rested on the profile of one of the men closest to me. He was leaning his head against a bar across the window. He was a swarthy yellow colour, with a sharp little flap of skin covering the corner of his eye. Was it he? I was disappointed that he wasn't even bothering to gaze out at the sights of Wudgie.

Oh, please look out, I pleaded silently. Look at me. I dared not voice my passion aloud and held my breath.

The seconds passed, and then he did look at me. The pleasure was great. For a few moments we were alone together, I in the mulberry tree, he in the gully, I on the tree trunk, he swimming the Lachlan, I in the outcrop of rock, he below being beaten by the Colonel. His scar had healed. Up close I saw that it went from beneath his hairline, past his right eye, and raggedly down his cheek to the corner of his mouth. He was being transferred back to the camp. He must be a rebel that no one knew what to do with. Like Eric Kiddy at school.

I found my voice. 'Your cap. I've got it.' He looked down at me and raised his eyebrows. I had a doubt. 'Don't you remember? Lindsay.' I was in a panic, sure the bus was about to move away. 'Lindsay,' I repeated, pointing to myself. 'You Tadao.'

Finally he smiled a smile of recognition. It was broad and friendly, I am sure, but at the time it alarmed me, for his mouth seemed to expand and travel grotesquely along the scar up to his eyes. The devil himself! I stepped back hurriedly and tripped on the groceries. He laughed, and the laughter was like the high-pitched clang of the school bell. I was up in a trice. 'Escape,' I whispered, making my mouth form the word very clearly so he might understand. 'Escape.'

'Lindsay!' Dad's voice came from his window. He stuck his head out to see what I was up to. 'Come away from there.'

'Lindsay! Lindsay!' mimicked Tadao, and laughed once more.

Dad stared up at the bus window, and I saw their eyes meet. Tadao passed his hand over his face, and when he lowered it his smile was gone.

'Dad's right,' said Heather, pressed back against the cabin. 'Come and sit down. Japs spit.'

At that moment there was a tremendous crash, and from the roof of the bus came a shower of beer and glass. Tiny shards stung my face. The remains of a bottle of Tooth's KB hit the street. Heather screamed. I dropped to the bed of the truck and looked up to see a second bottle hurtling down from the upstairs balcony of the Prince William. It went right through one of the open windows at the back of the bus and smashed. There was great consternation among the Japanese. A babble arose, and Tadao's and all the faces nearest to me disappeared from my sight. Dad was out of the cabin and lifting Heather to the pavement. 'Get down from there,' he yelled at me. I did not move, and neither did the bus.

'Kill the cunts,' came a bellow from upstairs at the William.

Almost as if in answer, there was the sound of glass smashing on the other side of the bus. It was beer glasses being thrown by the men from the William. A woman ran into the road and hurled a potato. 'You'll pay. We'll make you pay,' she screamed.

From all sides rose shouts and swearing. 'Bloody Japs!' 'Fucking Japs.' 'Murderers!'

'What's the matter with that driver?' shouted Brown.

A group of men from the William ran to the back of the bus and began to rock it up and down. At that moment it jerked forward into the crossroads and a third bottle sailed down from the balcony. It crashed on to the roof of the bus, near the front this time, farther away from us.

'Come off it, mate,' came voices from here and there in the crowd. Now that the bus was moving off, there was a sense that things had gone far enough.

'Take a hint,' yelled the hidden voice. 'Get the fuck outta here.'

The driver accelerated and the bus was suddenly down the street and away. The buses following did not even stop at the halt sign but barrelled through at high speed, swinging wildly as they made the turn into Plurry Creek Road and headed out towards the camp. There was the smell of petrol and beer and something else I had never smelled before. A crumpled newspaper was burning in the street.

I was blooded that day. I did not even know it until Mum climbed out of the cabin and gave a cry. I knelt down and she wiped my face with her handkerchief, then I looked in the rearview mirror. There were several tiny cuts on my cheek and forehead from the flying glass.

'It could have gone in your eyes. Jack, let's get out of here at once.'

It wasn't that easy. The entire population of the town suddenly seemed to be there. I had never seen anything so dramatic in Wudgie. Dad picked pieces of glass out of the truck. Employees of the Prince William came out with brooms and buckets and began sweeping up the glass; water was sloshed over the beer spills. A policeman strode into the evil-smelling entrance to the pub. Bruce Kelly appeared on the upstairs balcony, waving to the crowd.

'Bruce Kelly,' said Mrs Cutler. 'I'm not surprised.'

'Jack, I knew we should not have had that man in the house,' said Mum, still dabbing at my face.

'Come on down, Bruce,' yelled someone. 'Beer for Bruce.'

Mr Buchanan hastened over from the Prince William, smelling strongly of booze. The policeman who had gone into the pub reappeared and went back around the corner to the police station.

'Forgot his notebook,' said Mr Buchanan sarcastically.

Mr Kelly came out on to the street. Several people clapped him on the back, and there were congratulations on all sides. Someone handed him a cruiser, a schooner appeared in his left hand, and he drank from each in turn, swaying back and forth as he began to smirk and then to expound. Dad moved a little closer to listen.

'King of the William,' remarked Mr Buchanan.

'Jack, it's time we went.'

'They're all in it together, that William crowd,' said Mr Buchanan. 'And the bus driver.'

'What could have possessed him to do such a thing?' asked Mum.

'Mob of racists,' said Mr Buchanan. 'We're going to see more of this.'

'Looked like an act of war,' said Mrs Cutler. 'I come thirteen thousand miles to get away, and I can smell it all around me.'

'What were you talking to that Japanese for?' demanded Heather as we finally drove off towards the Old Billarooby Road.

'He's called Tadao. I'm going to write him a letter.'

'You're not allowed. It's fraternization.' Heather glared at me. 'They don't have names. They have numbers.'

'This is a free country. Mr Buchanan says.'

'You little traitor. We are at war with the Japs. They look like insects. Ugh!'

'They're prisoners. It's different.'

'There's still blood on your face.'

I rubbed my cheek with my fingers and then licked the blood off them.

'Use the handkerchief. Some of it might be theirs. You'll get infected.'

TWO

Dance

10

THAT SUMMER in Billarooby was a scorcher ('Never knew one that wasn't,' said Brown) and the Christmas holidays were burning weeks that seemed endless. There was a grass fire that swept over my central stone and threatened, for a while, both the Cutlers' farmhouse and the school, and there were so many brown snakes that Mum insisted I wear shoes and long socks if I went walking. Dad killed at least two a day, and hung them on the fences as a warning.

Slow George said that it was the hottest summer in Billarooby for fifteen years, and that we might be in for trouble. The water at the ford was only ankle-deep.

Dad bought Heather a bicycle, and when school began again, she pedalled the three miles through the hills east of Billarooby to the siding at Glen Hogan, where the train picked her up and took her on the single track into Wudgewunda to attend the high school there. Gordon Morrison accompanied her on the journey. Mr Buchanan said he was very sorry to see the two of them go.

In deep secrecy I composed a letter.

Dear Tadao,
    When you escape from the Great Captivity, come and visit. Our house is about three miles from the camp, across the river in a northwesterly direction. It is on the plateau above the mulberry tree, which you have seen before. It is the only mulberry tree in the district. Usually they don't grow this far out. There is food in my room if you need it for your journey to rejoin your Emperor. Come in the back way if I am not there, so as not to disturb Mum and Dad. Particularly Dad

as he got off to a bad start in life. If you think it is too dangerous, there is food also in my cave, which is by the big fallen tree you crossed the river on last time. I hope you are taking the English lessons and can read this.

Your secret friend,
Lindsay

I wrote this on brown paper, wrapped it around a stone taken from my circle in the field, and tied it up well with string from Mum's kitchen ball. When Dad went next to the camp with a load of vegetables, I accompanied him. As soon as he went into the quartermaster's store with a crate, I ran along the wires to the Japanese compound. I heaved the message as high and as far as I could, and had the satisfaction of seeing it fall just inside the innermost wires.

'Hey, clear off,' yelled a guard from one of the towers. 'Hey you,' yelled another, and they called out something to each other. Then there was laughter. It sounded pretty mirthless to me, and I ran for dear life back to the truck, half expecting them to start shooting. But I knew that they were not smart enough to know that there was a message around the stone.

When Dad came back he asked me what was the matter, so hard was I panting.

'I threw a rock at the Japs.'

These were glorious days for the farm. Dad's vegetables kept coming in and coming in, enough to fill the horn of plenty. We were all down on the flats from dawn until after dark. I got so caught up with the excitement of the harvesting that I made sure I didn't miss a single moment.

From my perch on a branch high up in the pepper tree, I could see Dad below consulting his pocket watch. The Landgirls had not appeared for porridge and were still in their room, presumably getting ready for work. I knew they would be late, because I had been awakened in the early hours of the morning by the sound of Mr Kelly's truck dropping them off.

The pepper tree was very sticky and sweet from its ripening clusters of pink, papery-shelled berries, and round me hummed thousands of bees, with whom I was on excellent terms. The sun had come up that morning in a skywide blaze of scarlet. I had watched from my bed as the colour changed to yellow and then to grey, the clouds from cirrus to cumulus. Now, the sky was completely covered with a layer of grey. It felt like rain. The flies were less insistent and the garden was full of late-summer sparrows looking for seeds. They fled in a whirr of wings before Dad's pacing feet, but the next second they were back as though he hadn't been there.

Dad made a move towards the Landgirls' room and then hesitated. He was shy about their room. Heather came by with water for the chooks. Since starting at Wudgewunda High School, she had changed her hair style to a single plait wound tightly around the top of her head, and Dad had taken to calling her 'princess'. He followed her to the chook run to make sure she did not spill a drop.

'Princess, tell Joan and Betty if they are not here in the next minute, they'll have to walk down, and I'll dock their pay.'

Heather went skipping around the verandah. 'Any excuse to go to the Landgirls' room,' I said to the bees.

'And tell them to turn that stupid wireless down.'

Heather and I were in agreement about the Landgirls' room. It represented the sins and excitements of the city, right there in our own home, and we both loved it. We followed the mysterious comings and goings of the girls and studied with interest the walls of their room, which were covered in pictures, mostly pinups of Hollywood movie stars and soldiers, taken out of *Star Dust, Film Fan, Yank,* and the *Army Weekly.* The smells in the room existed nowhere else in the house. It wasn't just the cosmetics, but odours I realize now had specifically to do with being young, vibrant, and female. It was always Joan with the strong smells, never Betty.

Mum came out the front door and watered the violets.

'Don't the flowers look lovely,' she said. There were late-blooming marigolds, African daisies, zinnias, and snapdragons, as well as the straggly banks of geraniums and nasturtiums. By the tanks were blue hydrangeas, and around the side a row of sunflowers.

'Too lovely,' replied Dad sourly. 'How much water have you been putting on them?'

'Jack, I have to have a few flowers. Brown says we are sure to get good rains this winter.'

'Brown, Brown, Brown! What does he know?'

'Well, he's lived here a darn sight longer than you have, for one thing,' said Mum. She went back into the house and let the screen door bang behind her. Dad looked surprised.

'Heather!' he shouted. She had not reappeared, and the wireless was still going. Dad picked a few tomato seeds off his overalls, glanced at the door, and then charged off in the direction of the Landgirls' room.

I shinnied down the pepper tree and raced around the house. I could look through the back window and no one would see.

By the time I got there, Dad had created a scene. Joan and Betty were rushing round pulling on their work shorts, looking flustered. They didn't even have their blouses on, and even now this remains my clearest memory of the great size of Joan's brassiere. Dad was concealing his embarrassment by taking it out on Heather, who was seated at the mirror – a mirror that Mum, and even I, had also surreptitiously sat at with the lipstick and rouge.

'Get that muck off your face, and go help your mother.'

'Lay off, will you,' said Joan. 'I spent a packet on that stuff.'

'It's good quality, Dad,' said Heather. 'It's hard to get.'

'Your mother doesn't paint her face.'

'She would if you weren't such a prig and let her,' said Joan. She tucked her blouse into her shorts and Dad turned away from the sight. It filled me with nervous glee to hear Joan stand up to Dad. Sometimes I thought he might take a swing at her, but he never did. Joan had a hold over him, that's what it was.

'You were never lovelier,' sang a man's voice on the wireless, 'never lovelier than today . . .'

'We're teaching Heather to be a young lady,' said Joan. 'Nobody else around here seems to be doing it.'

'Lady? You're turning a child of fourteen into a tart.'

'Girls start young these days, I'm sure you have noticed.' Joan showed him the tip of her tongue.

'You're a disgrace.'

Joan giggled. She took remarks like that as a compliment.

Her hair was freshly peroxided, the tight little curls swept up high and kept in place with a cotton headscarf. She picked up her gum from the dressing table, put her Capstans in her breast pocket, and headed for the door. Betty had already gone. As Joan went past Dad she stopped. She looked up pertly, cupped her hands underneath her bra, and pushed up her tits. 'New Perma-Lift,' she said, and let herself fall against him.

'Come on, farmer, follow me.' As Joan sashayed past, she caught sight of the top of my head in the window corner and said, 'Snooper.' She thrust her bosom towards me with a little shake and was out the door. I ducked down so quickly Dad had no chance of seeing me.

That day was the last of the tomato harvest, and we were drunk on the smell of them, the Landgirls drunkest of all. How else could they have been so hysterical at the mice they discovered when they were picking down in the river rows? They ran screaming for the packing shed and nothing could persuade them to return. Joan flopped down beneath the awning. 'I quit.'

'They're everywhere,' said Betty, her chest heaving from the run. 'Big ones, itty bitty ones . . .'

'Go down there with the dogs, Lindsay, and get rid of them,' said Dad.

'Take Jimmy,' said Mum, who was so pleased that finally I had made a friend that summer.

Jennifer and Jimmy Cutler were working for us that day. And so was Brown, for Dad needed all the help he could get. Twice already, Brown had driven to the cannery, and then to the railway station in Wudgie, with a full load of tomatoes.

When Jimmy and I got to the rows near the river there was nothing to be seen at first. Dipper stood around wagging her tail, waiting for instructions, and I looked back to the packing shed, thinking for a second that a trick was being played upon us. April Fools' Day was not far distant. The plants were growing in a luxuriant tangle along the ground, the tomatoes bright red against leaves that were yellowing and turning to rot as the season climaxed. They had been the last to be planted, and Dad had not had time to stake them.

'You're scared,' said Jimmy.

'No, I'm not, you are.' I went forward boldly and lifted up a bush with both hands. Mice scattered in every direction. Dipper and her pup were on to them at once, and there began a carnage I have never forgotten. We beat at them with our sticks, and tiny shriekings filled the air. Each time we lifted up another bush, we found more, and our killing frenzy grew. 'Sic 'em, Dipper, sic 'em!' Jimmy began to stomp on them with his bare feet as well. That seemed to me to go too far. I tried to work up to it, for friendship's sake, but failed.

I paused for breath. We were smashing more tomatoes than killing mice.

'Stop, Jimmy, stop!'

It was just then that he found the nest of baby ones. We kept the dogs away and knelt to look at them. They moved about slowly on wisps of grass and fur.

'Let's save them.' Jimmy took off his old straw hat and in it carefully placed all nine of them. Dipper snarled and crunched nearby. The pup rummaged for more. I watched Jimmy tenderly stroking the little creatures with his forefinger, and I have to confess that the accommodation with him that had grown all summer turned, in that single instant, to love. He was the tough, dirty, shaggy towhead he had always been and as contemptuous of me as ever, but magically these terrible drawbacks were now transformed into attributes. I knelt to look at the mice and put my cheek so close to his that I felt the warmth of his skin. Out of the corner of an eye I looked at the fine white down on his cheeks and was within a split second of planting a lusty kiss right then and there.

'Let's take them back and show the others,' said Jimmy, suddenly jumping up.

Interest in the baby mice back at the packing shed was marginal. Mum thought we should put them back and let nature take its course. Dad said to give them to the dogs and to go back and get rid of the rest of them. 'The broadtails love 'em,' said Brown.

Jimmy ignored all the advice and sat down with the mice on the running board of Brown's truck. I followed him, but almost immediately Jennifer said they had to go: Eddie was driving the Cutlers into the pictures in Wudgie. I was disappointed that Jimmy was leaving so soon. It was as though he were leaving forever. I wished it was of some use asking Dad to let me go too, but he disapproved of the pictures even more than he did of Mrs

Cutler. I had yet to attend a picture show. Mum decided to leave with them and to take Heather, who had been listless all afternoon. Mum was worried that she might have got a touch of sunstroke.

'That's not what's the matter with her,' said Joan, pulling a knowing face.

'Joan!' said Betty.

Mum and Joan stared at each other and then at Heather, who pouted, close to tears. 'Heather is getting so developed,' I had heard Mum say to Mrs Bridges one day after church. I knew that it had something to do with that, but I didn't know anything about periods in those days.

Mum's final words before parting, as she adjusted her fly veil, were for Brown. 'I wish you'd put some boots on.'

'No shoes until after the rain comes, missus.' He looked down and laughed. He was up to his ankles in red pulp.

'June, am I right?'

'Not until June, even for you.'

Mum smiled, put up her parasol, and moved off through the irrigation channels.

That was the end of the workday, really. Brown chewed on a twig for a moment, watching Mum's back, and then got some beer, still cold, from the truck. Joan and Betty were only too happy to help him drink it. Dad worried for a moment about time wasting, but then gave in.

'All right. We've had a good day. Except for the mice.' Dad smiled and walked off to collect the kerosene tins that Joan and Betty had abandoned in the sun.

'Jack made a joke,' said Joan. She glanced round and then did something to the back of her bra, which caused her tits to fall down.

'His hard work's paid off,' said Brown. 'I'd be joking too.'

'Hard work and no play makes Jack a dull boy,' said Joan, taking the beer.

When Brown and the girls got going, I usually made a getaway, but this time something made me stick around. It might have just been the heat, but more likely that near-kiss with Jimmy had aroused something that hadn't been aroused before.

Brown stretched out lazily under the awning with his hands

behind his back, and Joan and Betty lay down on either side of him. Betty put a cigarette in the side of his mouth and lit it for him. She blew out the match prettily and gave a giggle. The beer went from hand to hand. I noticed that Brown still managed to keep an eye on Mum, who had reached the orchard and was about to ascend the hill. Jimmy was up the mulberry tree. Betty waved the swarms of little flying insects away from Brown with her hat, and when he spilled some beer on his chest, she smiled up at me, shrugged, and then licked it off. Betty loved to do things for Brown.

'What a clean girl.'

Betty looked at her thighs and blushed. They were caked with dirt and pungent juices from the tomato plants. She spread out her hands. They were green and black from the picking. Brown suggested that we all go swimming in the river to clean up. I thought that was a terrific idea, especially since the river was so close, but Betty was pretty hesitant about it at first – she wanted to go back to the house for her swimming costume. Brown said it would be all right just to wear shorts, and he had soap and a towel in the truck. It was as though he had planned the whole thing.

'What about Jack?'

'Jack loves a swim.'

Betty still looked doubtful.

'Let's do it,' said Joan, 'seeing the "ladies" have gone.' She cast a mocking glance in the direction of Mum and Heather. 'Bloody Queen of England. Too proper for us poor Aussies.'

'Joan!' said Betty again.

I wondered what had put Joan in such a nasty mood. Brown wondered too, and suggested that it might be jealousy.

'Like hell.' Joan got to her feet, unstuck her shorts, and took the scarf off her hair. 'Jack wouldn't know a good time if you laid one on his face. I'll give her jealousy.'

She stalked off to where Dad was returning with the tins.

'I'm gonna take his ferret for a swim. You watch.'

11

I TOOK MY SWIM and washed off all the tomato stains.

'Aw, come on, Jack, how about a lesson?' Joan called. 'What's one little lesson?'

Dad ignored her and swam steadily around the waterhole a few times before seating himself on a log, where, much to Joan's annoyance, he began whittling at a piece of willow. She halfheartedly scooped some water over him and then lay down on a strip of dun-coloured river sand nearby and watched, her mouth turned down in a pout, her legs stretched wide. Brown and Betty were the ones who had all the fun. They soaped each other down, splashed about, and made a lot of noise. Finally they ducked each other. Brown might even have given Betty a kiss under the water. Anyway, by the time they lay down on the bank next to Joan, they were both laughing and quite out of breath.

Joan and Betty had taken off their brassieres to swim, and wore only their blouses with their shorts. The pink of their nipples showed clearly through the thin wet cotton.

I was very uneasy. I knew very well that it wasn't the correct thing for women to be half-dressed like this. When Mum went swimming she wore a costume that covered her almost to the knees, and she wore a bathing cap to protect her hair. If Dad had said to go away, I would have done so at once, but he seemed oblivious to the fact that very unusual things were going on. I moved away up the bank, above the willow tree, and felt a little better. Dipper found a fresh burrow and began digging furiously.

Dad hadn't whittled for years but was an excellent carver. Back in England, before Granddad died, and when Dad didn't really do much of anything except tend the kitchen gardens, he carved

many little wooden animals for Heather and me, all of which had
been left behind when we made our sudden emigration.

Dad was looking at Joan out of the corner of his eye. A memory
flashed into my head of a woman coming to the door of our house
in Suffolk and making a scene. It was something that Dad had
done with that woman. She didn't have a baby in her arms or
anything Victorian like that, but she had been shown into the
sitting room, and Granddad had a long talk with her while
Heather and I were kept out of the way upstairs. Heather said
Dad was going to run away with that woman and leave us. Mum
had cried all evening and Granddad had been very angry. After
the woman had left, he went out to the barn and did something
to Dad that gave him the permanent scar by his left nostril. Dad
had to be driven to the doctor in Haverhill. He came back with
his face all bandaged, and he was forbidden to go to church for a
month. It all happened not that long before Granddad died.

For Mum's sake, I decided to keep a close watch on Dad.

Mr Kelly appeared on the other side of the river, and Brown
swore under his breath.

'Why doesn't he stay up by his dump, where he belongs,' I said
to Dipper. Since Mr Kelly had revealed his true colours in Wudgie
and thrown the beer bottles, I hadn't spoken a word to him.
Neither had Mum.

'I believe I am going to come over and join in the fun and
frolicking,' Mr Kelly called out, and walked across the river above
the swimming hole. The water was so shallow he didn't even
bother to take off his boots.

'What happened to the rain, Brown?' Dad called from his log.
He threw some shavings into the river. 'I thought we might get a
few drops today.'

The promise of the early morning had lingered until about
noon, but then the sky had cleared.

'Some years it don't rain at all, mate.'

'You told Lillian we'd get lots of rain this winter.'

'Gotta keep yer missus smiling.'

'I don't want the Lachlan to die on me.'

'Don't worry. I don't see no drought pattern developing yet.
There's months of pumping in these waterholes.'

Dad continued his whittling.

'This is Australia, mate. We get it all here, all or nothing.'

'Weather's OK by me. Heat gets me going,' said Joan. She spread her legs wider and, arching her back, thrust her magnificent breasts skyward. Dad and Mr Kelly exchanged glances. Then she stuck her legs straight up into the air and exercised her feet and ankles. I began to giggle. I really didn't know anything about young women like Joan and Betty in those days, but I imagined that the streets of Sydney were crowded with others exactly like them. Mostly I just accepted Mr Buchanan's comment that they were overgrown schoolgirls, and his advice to give them a wide berth at all times, and left it at that.

'Hey, farmer,' Joan called to Dad. 'How come you're sitting so far away? Married man's safe with me.' Dad frowned. 'Come down here, why dontcha?'

Joan put her legs down and got to her feet. She walked slowly through the shallow water to where he was sitting on his log and whispered something in his ear. Her arm went round his bare white shoulders, then down his back. When she ran a hand over his chest, he pushed her. She fell over into the water, causing Brown and Betty both to laugh.

'Very funny.' Joan turned on to her back and drifted away. One of her breasts came right out of her blouse and floated above the water. I had never seen a naked breast before. Dad was staring at her as her legs went in and out, and so was Mr Kelly. As Joan went out of sight around the willow tree, I looked more closely at Mr Kelly. I knew enough about what went on behind the dunney at school to know that he was playing with himself in his shorts. I was shocked.

'I'm going to my cave,' I whispered to Dipper. 'Who knows, Tadao might have left a message.'

At that moment Brown called, 'Hey, Lindsay, let's do the willow tree.'

'It's too high.' I had never had the nerve to do it, and now, with the water level so low, it was more intimidating than ever.

'Aw, come on. We'll do it together. Even with me gammy leg I can do it. First jumped out of this tree fifteen years ago.'

'Brownie, no,' said Betty, sitting up. She brushed sand away from his shoulders, which were as brown as Dad's were pale. 'It's too dangerous.'

Joan came out of the water and made a halfhearted attempt to pull her blouse over her tits. 'Yeah, commando, do it.' She lay down once more, dripping wet.

'Wanna do it with me?' asked Brown, touching Joan on the thigh with his toe.

'I'll be down here waiting for you, soldier.'

Betty giggled and helped Brown to his feet.

'Getting a bit steamy down there,' said Brown when he joined me. 'Time to change the subject.'

There was no denying I was scared. I hoped that Dad would forbid the jump, but when no sign from him came, I realized he didn't care whether it was safe for me or not. It was up to me to decide. Suddenly there was nothing I wanted to do more than jump out of the tree with Brown.

The weeping willow was the most majestic of any along that stretch of the Lachlan. Its long fronds had not begun either to shed or to yellow for the autumn, and hung in graceful green parabolas from a great height. Two of its main branches stretched well out over the river.

As Brown climbed from the sand to the earth of the higher bank, I noticed that his legs were very stiff. His wet khaki trousers did not make it any easier for him. Brown never wore shorts, and it always made me itch to see what had happened to his legs.

I scrambled up and waited.

'Ah!' Brown grunted as he began to climb. It was awkward for him and when he reached me he gave a rueful smile. 'The old legs. Wanna go higher?'

'No,' I said at once.

He looked at me and we both laughed. It was the sensible height for both of us. He squeezed the back of my neck. 'OK, mate, let's give 'em a show. Coupla daredevils, eh?'

The thick foliage hid us completely from below. We edged carefully out along the limb until we were above the waterhole. Brown parted the fronds and looked down at the upturned faces.

'It's a long way down,' I said, looking up at him.

He put an arm around my shoulders and smiled. 'Twenty feet. Don't think about it. I'll be right behind.' He gave me a pat. 'Go on. Hold yer nose when you hit. Show yer dad.'

I closed my eyes and jumped, hitting the water with a great

splash and then kicking vigorously as I felt myself going down into the depths. I hated the bottom of those murky river pools. Quickly I was on the surface, spluttering, getting air. I grinned up at him, very pleased with myself.

'Good jump, Lindsay,' cried Betty.

'OK, you sheilas, watch this.' Brown grasped a handful of the pliant willow fronds, pushed off with his better leg, and swung out over the river. Out, back, out once more he went. Then he tensed himself and dropped into the water, far beyond the centre of the pool. He disappeared from view with scarcely a splash.

Brown didn't surface for a while, and when he did, his face was contorted with pain.

'Help me to the bank, mate,' he gasped. I swam towards him as fast as I could, but Betty was there before me. We got him to the bank and he dragged himself up on to the sand.

Brown pulled up his trouser leg to inspect the damage. We drew close to see. There were cries of concern from Joan and Betty, followed by silence. Blood poured down from his knee and above it.

It turned out that he had been unable to kick hard enough and had torpedoed down deep into the pool, slamming into a tree near the bottom. A branch had torn through his trousers and scraped down his bad leg, and he had had to extricate the branch.

'It's nothing, just a scratch. Gimme a towel.' Then Brown noticed our silent faces and looked back at his leg. He gave an offhand laugh. 'Lemme give you a real decko.'

With both hands he ripped the trouser leg all the way up to the thigh, and I saw for the first time the injuries he had received in New Guinea.

'I can explain just about everything that's wrong with it,' he said as he dabbed at the fresh blood with a towel. 'Me and the doc were good mates.' He calmly pointed out the details, and the leg became less terrible. He didn't have a calf or a kneecap, and the leg was held together by metal pins. Below the knee it had been shattered in seven places, and there was a great hole where flesh and muscle had been entirely torn away. The ankle had a strange bone sticking out. There were red weals and jagged scars all the way down.

'Tracer bullets,' he said, rolling up his other trouser leg. I gasped. 'It looks worse, but it's the other one gives me the problems.'

'It's a miracle you've got legs at all,' said Betty. 'Here, let me tie that.' The bleeding began to stop.

'Betteran the pictures, eh?' Brown said to me, pushing my head away. 'Pair of beauties.'

The tight, hot crawl in my groin would not stop. I caught Dad's eyes and he looked away. Without warning, part of my nightmare welled up in my head, the dreadful recurring vision of Granddad's shattered jaw, of blood gushing down over his shirt, blood spurting out over a tobacco-stained white beard. It was everywhere, the vision, and I could no longer see the people in front of me, the river, or the trees. I closed my eyes to make it go away and shook my head violently. A shudder went through me. An arm was put round my shoulder and Betty's voice said kindly, 'It's all right, kiddo. It looks bad, but he's OK.' The vision faded, and the first sight I became aware of was Dad's eyes boring into me. 'Brown will be able to walk again and everything. Nurse McCaddie will fix him up better than new.'

'Me ballroom days were already done, Lindsay,' said Brown.

'Oh, Brown,' said Betty reproachfully, 'you mustn't say things like that.'

'I'll dance for you,' I cried, and my voice cracked.

'And I'll tell you the story of me legs, how about that? New Guinea.'

Dad thought I should go home, and I immediately became suspicious. Why should I be got out of the way?

Brown saved the day.

'I'll keep it clean, Jack. There's nothing a boy of eleven can't know about. And it certainly ain't no romance about the Japs, if that's what's worrying you.'

I don't remember all the details of Brown's great adventure, but I know he started the story off in a way that he thought would particularly interest me – full of monstrosities out of a Grimm fairy tale. There were spiders as big as dinner plates that fell on them from the trees and gave them fevers, giant grasses that cut like swords, phosphorescent swamps and mushrooms that glowed in the dark, leeches that clung to their balls and made their way into their arseholes.

'I know about leeches,' I said. 'I got one in Mr MacAdams' dam. On my leg. It was horrible.'

Brown rolled a smoke from his tobacco tin. 'You sure you want to hear about the Japs, Bruce? Don't want ya to die of boredom.'

Mr Kelly laughed. 'Excite me, Douglass. Pour on the pain.'

Brown didn't like that. He shrugged and lit up.

I remembered Mr Buchanan saying that Mr Kelly was nasty simply because he was nasty, and not to inquire beyond that, because it was a can of worms. Maybe the seven years he had done for manslaughter had embittered him, but it was his terrible temper that had got him in jail in the first place. Mr Buchanan didn't know why Mr Kelly hated the Japs more than anyone else, but he hated anyone who wasn't pure white. Even Continentals were suspect, although he didn't mind the French. Everyone else was mongrel. Black mongrel, yellow mongrel, Jew mongrel. Mr Buchanan said that Mr Kelly was a man who had come from a good family and had a good education but, through disappointments in life not faced up to, had gone bad. Now he relished his badness, which was a dangerous thing.

I listened to Brown with rapt attention, although he took a long time getting to his legs. Port Moresby, he said, was a dump, but it was paradise compared to the Kokoda Trail. The rain turned the jungle to slime, the ridges of the Owen Stanleys were like razor blades, the ravines had no bottom, the mountain passes were freezing cold, and his mates were dying of pneumonia.

'I had dysentery the whole time.'

'What about the Japs?' I asked. 'Did they have dysentery too?'

'Didn't have no time for Japs, mate. Too busy shitting.'

Mr Kelly lifted his leg and made a loud farting noise.

'And spewing.' Brown imitated the sound. 'That's how I met my first live Jap.'

Brown said that he and his mate, Booker, knew that there were two Japs on the other side of a clearing. They threw grenades. When it was safe, Brown crossed the clearing. The Japs had both been blown apart, and it was then that he vomited.

'It was the guts, the bits and pieces, the bloody stench. If Booker hadn't been covering me that would have been the big shut-eye.'

'You were choking to death?' I asked.

'Third Jap jumped out of a tree. "Aussie, you die!" he yelled. I was still chundering. Booker shot him in midair. He got in a swipe with his cutlass as he fell.' Brown pointed to a scar on his forearm. 'Booker ran up and finished him off with his bayonet. He didn't look like a Jap. He was a fatty in goggles with flowers and leaves in his helmet. Green paint all over his face.'

Brown took several more puffs from his cigarette and then threw it away.

'You don't want to hear about the suicide charges, and yer Dad would send you home if I told you about when they tried to stink us out with the rotting corpses.'

'Barbarians,' said Mr Kelly. 'No respect.'

I can still conjure up that afternoon on the riverbank – lanky Betty hunched up, sad for Brown; plump Joan spread out, her blouse dried and nipples hidden; Brown's thick hair plastered down, his forehead alive, his leg oozing; Dad doggedly whittling away at his piece of willow; Mr Kelly growing increasingly morose as Brown's story proceeded; Dipper swimming round and round the waterhole with the pup watching her from the bank. A kingfisher speeding back and forth over the pool, a bright flash of turquoise and orange in the late afternoon. Sunlight filtering warmly through the trees on the western bank . . .

'. . . the Maroubras had been pretty lucky up to that point. We reckoned we could hang on at Isurava until the Yanks arrived. There was no way the Japs could get to the bloody place except along the bloody track. The track was one at a time and the jungle was impenetrable.'

Brown didn't use many big words. 'Impenetrable' was one I learned that afternoon. He made Isurava into the most eerie, terrifying place, a festering, steaming mudhole in the jungle, where they waited day after day with nothing to listen to except the drip of the trees and the griping of their insides – until one morning when the jungle became full of the sound of the chik-chak birds, when their curiosity and delight at the sound turned to alarm, when every chik-chak bird turned into a Japanese jungle fighter and all hell broke loose in Isurava.

'How the fuck those bastards do it?'

'Samurai,' I said excitedly.

Brown flicked a look at me. 'I tell you, mate, they caught us

plaiting poop, those bloody samurai. Booker was the first to go.
Ah, Dave Booker.' Brown raised his arm in a farewell gesture.
'Saved my life one day, lost his own the next. Saw it happen. He
didn't feel a thing. Blew his head right off. I ran for the hut and –
kabooey! The ground exploded and down I went into the mud. It
was the mud that saved me. The Japs were screaming all around
us. "Banzai! Banzai!" I saw blood rising up through the sludge,
felt the pain in the old pins – and that was the end of me tropical
holiday.'

'You were dead?'

'Dead to the world, mate. I closed my eyes and kept still.'

'Hidden in the mud, like a crocodile.'

'I was lucky. Anyway, we got the hell out of Isurava after that
first wave of Japs. Us wounded were taken on stretchers all the
way to Ioribaiwa. Through the Gap. Don't ask me how I made
it.'

'It was silly to risk your legs jumping out of that tree,' said
Betty.

'Dr Dunstan was the bloke who decided I could keep them. I
thank that man every day.' Brown stared down at his leg and then
took a look under the blood-stained towel. He gave a laugh. 'I
don't know about this one. It might have been better to let it go.'

'Then you would be like Long John Silver,' I said.

'Looked like Moresby was going to blow, so they flew us to
Brisbane. Nothing but the best.'

'I'm glad they gave you the best,' I said. 'Otherwise you might
have died.'

'And otherwise we mightn't have met each other.' Brown smiled
at me and I became shy. 'Or Betty Boop here.' Betty blushed.
Brown grinned and there was silence except for the faintest ripple
from the river. In the big gums above the ford a kookaburra
tentatively began its song.

'Pity you didn't manage to kill a few more of those fuckers,'
said Mr Kelly, hurling his beer bottle into the waterhole.

'I did my best.'

'Some best.'

Betty helped Brown to his feet. His torn trouser leg was red
with blood.

'There's thousands of them right over here,' said Mr Kelly. 'We can blow them all sky high. Snap their necks. Cut their bloody balls off. Have them fuckers singing soprano. Disembowel them! If they can get out of that camp, we can get in.'

'Shut up, Bruce,' said Brown. 'Nothing you can do about it now.'

'All's fair in love and war. Particularly war. There's nothing I want to do to a Jap that is not thoroughly deserved. What do you think about that, my friend?' Mr Kelly tripped and almost fell as he climbed the bank towards the ford. 'Revenge is sweet. God help me, and the sweetness of my tooth.'

'There goes trouble,' said Brown, palming his forehead and then giving it a good rub. Betty combed his hair back with her fingers.

'It was the jungle got the Japs in the end. You read what happened, Lindsay. By the time they got to Moresby, they were so beat they turned round and went back again. Croaked on the way. We didn't have to lift a finger. Bloody Kokoda. Rather drown in me own dunney any day.'

'They all died?'

'Except a few who wound up here.'

'The Japs who blew you up are here?'

'Maybe.'

I could not help feeling sorry that the Japanese had not managed to capture Port Moresby. They merited it after their heroic feats on the Kokoda Trail. I rubbed Dipper on the belly and kept this thought to myself. It was a terrible thought, considering what they had done to Brown. But the Japs did not mean it personally. It was just war, wasn't it? It wasn't in the family, like when Granddad died. It wasn't like the Colonel attacking Tadao, was it? I was confused. I picked at a scab on my elbow until it came off. There was still a little blood, so I rubbed mud on it.

The entire time Brown had been telling his story, Dad had sat on his log, whittling away. As we moved slowly towards the lorry parked at the ford, he presented what he had made to Joan and Betty. It was an Indian canoe. The inside was carefully hollowed out and had little seats at both ends. A centre bench had been slotted into grooves along the side, and under the bench were two little paddles.

'Art,' said Brown.

'What am I going to do with it?' Joan had snatched it for herself and then refused to be pleased.

'Wedding present, Joan,' said Brown.

'It's too big for me. I wouldn't know where to stick it.' She made a face at Dad.

'Joan,' said Betty reprovingly, looking at me. 'We're giving it to the boy.'

Silently I took the canoe. It wasn't balanced right, as it turned out, and tipped over in the water, but it found a place on my chest of drawers. 'Dad made it for me,' I later told Jimmy Cutler.

'Ever see a Jap pray?' asked Dad.

'Can't say I ever did,' replied Brown. 'But how would I?'

'What about you?'

'Me? Some blokes prayed. The chaplain was the first to go. Skidded off the Golden Staircase second day up.'

Those were the first of several questions Dad asked. Having become accustomed to his not ever wanting to know anything about the war, I scowled at his sudden interest. The Japs belonged to me, not him. Suddenly I could not stand to be near him.

'I'm going home,' I shouted. 'Come on, Dipper.'

By the time I reached the pumpkin patch, I had a stitch in my side. I sat on a large pumpkin and looked back. The lorry had arrived at the packing shed. Dad and the girls began clearing up while Brown sat on the running board, doing something with his leg. Then Brown got them laughing, and the girls began kidding around with him and Dad. The smell of the dead pumpkin leaves became sour in my nose. I was jealous. I wanted to spirit Brown away and have him sitting in the pumpkins with me, telling me more of his story. I wanted to cure his leg for him. I wanted to confess to him about Tadao, and tell him I was sure it was all right to be friends with a Jap and encourage him to escape. I wanted to show Brown my book so he would know what the Japs were really like. But I couldn't possibly. He would point to his legs and we would be friends no more. There are some things you cannot be, and I was one of them. A little Jap-lover. I pulled Dipper towards me for comfort, but I was rough and she yipped in protest.

'I'm sorry, old lady dog, I'm sorry.'

Dipper forgave me and licked my face all over, but I felt very lost and lonely there, sitting amid the patch of Queensland blues. My thoughts meandered along a back road in my mind until they turned to Jimmy Cutler. I looked around and there was our farmhouse on the hill glowing in the light of the setting sun. Home. I began running hard and left the others to their grown-up silliness down there by the packing shed. I did a quick circle around the mulberry tree. What a harvest that had been. Mum had sold pots of jam in Wudgie and everyone in Billarooby had had mulberries from our tree for weeks.

I remembered that Jimmy had gone to Wudgie and that there was no chance of seeing him that evening. But my darkness had cleared. As I ran up the hill, I got the dogs jumping and thought about all the fun we had had with the mice. Tomorrow, I said to myself, I would go round to the Cutlers' and Jimmy and I would play with the ones we had saved. I would even swing with Jimmy on his rope across the gully.

'Good dog, Dipper, good dog,' I shouted, throwing a stick. She and the pup went for it and I raced for the farmhouse gate, determined to get there before the dogs caught me up.

12

IT MUST HAVE BEEN six weeks or so after I heard the story of the Kokoda that Mr MacAdams held his big dance in the woolshed. It was the autumn of 1943 and the nights had become rather cold. There had still been no rain and it did not look like rain. As Mum kept pointing out, there had not been a single drop since our arrival in Billarooby. Dad's irrigation system had ensured a good year for our family, but for the majority of the farmers in the district it had not been easy. The high temperatures and hot winds had withered the crops, and Slow George said that the yield from his alfalfa was the lowest it had been for years. All was dryness and dust, and finally everyone was talking about a drought. The first of the winter frosts only made it seem more ominous.

Mr Buchanan was inclined to look on the bright side. The weather was one thing, he said, the war was another, and women were something else again. There was much to celebrate. The Germans had been driven out of Africa; the Battle of the Bismarck Sea was the beginning of the end for the Japs; Brown Douglass was home for good; local boys Tom McCaddie and John Gunn, and John Corish from Glen Hogan, were home on leave; and my dad's tomatoes had been the sweetest he'd ever eaten.

'On your feet,' Mr Buchanan shouted the day before the dance. Ever since it had become too cold for swimming, our recreation on Thursday afternoons had been ballroom dancing. We had been dragooned through the Barn Dance, the Canadian Three Step, and the Gypsy Tap, and there had been an attempt at the foxtrot.

'One two three, one two three . . .' he shouted as he banged out the waltz from *The Merry Widow* on the piano.

I whirled Nettie Bridges around in front of the desks. Jennifer and Jimmy Cutler glowered from beside the fire. They hated dancing.

'Stop being miseries,' Mr Buchanan yelled at them. 'It's not every day there's a party in Billarooby, for God's sake. All you little bastards are going to have a good time if it kills you.'

When our family arrived, the woolshed still smelled of antiseptic and was rather empty. Dad Packman was sitting on one of the benches used for the Sunday church service, tuning up his fiddle with trembling fingers.

'It looks a bit stark,' said Mum, but that was mostly the effect of something I had not seen before in Billarooby – electric lighting. The big generator used for the shearing had been hooked up, and strings of naked light bulbs bathed the interior as brightly as the midday sun. The platform on which the bands were going to play was festooned with red, white, and blue bunting and flanked on either side by two large Australian flags. Around the walls were arranged huge bouquets of fresh gum leaves. Mum, Mrs Bridges, and Nurse McCaddie had helped Mrs MacAdams decorate the shed, and Dad was one of a team of men who had scoured the floor and swept away dirt and cobwebs from the walls.

Dad Packman was joined by another fiddler, and then a man with a banjo appeared. They all stepped up on to the platform. After some tuning up and a couple of false starts, the banjoist shouted, 'Here we go, something to warm us up – Jigging on the Jindabyne,' and at a fast clip, off they went. Almost at once the shed began to fill. Everybody headed for the kegs and the beer was soon flowing freely.

For a few minutes we stood up close, listening to the music. One of the fiddlers played the spoons as well, and the fat lady from the grocery store in Mudoogla started up with a button accordion. I loved the music, but it wasn't until Dad took us through to the shearers' kitchen, where Mr MacAdams was providing brandy, whiskey, and Bundaberg rum for everyone who had helped with the preparations, that I realized the woolshed dance was going to be an occasion to remember.

Mr MacAdams was wearing a tam-o'-shanter. He stood in front of the big range, warming the seat of his trousers and talking to Brown, who had his crutches that night. The accident at the waterhole had caused complications with his leg. The kitchen was warm, crowded, and friendly, and over by the biscuits I saw Lorraine and Margaret, Mr and Mrs MacAdams' snooty daughters, who were back for the dance. Heather and I hardly ever saw them, for they spent most of their time down in Sydney at an exclusive private school, where they were taught everything from Latin to piano and Highland dancing.

'Got your shirt on tonight, Brown,' Mr MacAdams was saying as we came up.

'Bloody oath,' he replied. 'Colder than a shark's arsehole out there.'

Mr MacAdams agreed and rubbed his hands over his trousers.

'Gonna dance with me, Lillian?' Brown waved his crutches and hopped up and down on one foot. 'The one-legged woolshed waltz.' It was the first time I had heard Brown use Mum's name. He always called her 'missus.'

It wasn't until I went over to the punch bowls, where Dad was being ribbed about asking for lemonade, that, in the midst of a group of other soldiers, I saw the Colonel. I stared and then caught Brown's eye. Brown opened his mouth wide and showed his teeth in a grin of mock terror. There was worse to come, for a few minutes later Mr MacAdams came over and introduced him to Mum and Dad.

Close up, the Colonel seemed extremely old, although I know now that he was in his early sixties. His moustache was waxed and his complexion was red and shiny. I looked for signs of viciousness but could see none. He was wearing an immaculately starched and ironed uniform and was with his wife, Edwina, who lived on the coast at Bulli and came to see him only from time to time. Beside him she looked a bit rumpled, maybe because she had a bad cold. Behind her ear there was a pink rose that suddenly dropped a petal. She was the only woman, apart from Auntie Annabel, who was wearing a full-length gown that night. It was made of yellow taffeta, and over it she wore a woven shawl with long black fringes. There were murmurs of admiration.

'Austerity Ball,' said Mrs MacAdams, and everyone laughed.

'Hear you got Japs coming out of your ears,' said Brown affably.

'Yes,' said the Colonel with irritation. 'Nothing I can do about it. Sydney's fault.'

'Al, here,' said Mrs MacAdams to Brown, with a laugh, 'is one of the few people not rejoicing about the Japanese defeats in the Pacific. I don't think anyone else could make the Battle of the Bismarck Sea sound like a major disaster.'

'If I had my way,' barked the Colonel, 'they'd all be shot. The whole bloody lot of them. Take no prisoners. They don't appreciate it.'

'Jack here's one of the blokes that keeps you in veggies,' said Brown, making another effort. 'He's got the magic touch.'

'Ah,' said the Colonel, calming down.

'Yes,' said Mr MacAdams, 'Jack beat the Chinks at their own game. I've never seen anything like it.'

'Luck,' said Mrs MacAdams.

'It was the superphosphates,' remarked Dad modestly, nodding thanks to Mr MacAdams, who had been instrumental in getting them. It hadn't been easy because the Japanese had cut off Australia's usual source of supply, which was Nauru in the Pacific.

'Think nothing of it, Jack. I congratulate you. If this shindig is to celebrate anything at all, how about we celebrate what you did down there. A first for the flats.' Mr MacAdams raised his glass and drank to Dad. Everyone did the same.

There was a silence while they all waited for Dad to say something. Dad looked embarrassed by the attention, and when he spoke he stammered a bit. Social situations were not easy for him. Mum gave him a nudge.

'If the Lachlan keeps flowing, I can build up a big system here. Vegetables will thrive in the heat as long as they get plenty of water.'

'Blood and bone,' said Mr MacAdams. 'Blood and bone.'

'Cauliflower cheese,' said the Colonel, 'that's what I like. If only Edwina would come out here more often . . .'

'We've got some good cooks here in Billarooby,' said Mr MacAdams. 'We'll pass you around.'

The Colonel handed his glass to his wife for refilling without looking at her, and he began a discussion with everyone about food and farming, mostly food. I refused to be proud of Dad and left the kitchen, disgusted with them all for being friends with the Colonel.

Outside, cars and trucks and sulkies were arriving. The sky was clear with a quarter moon, and the stars were dazzling. Everyone was cold and hurrying to get to the woolshed. The entrance steps were decorated with Christmas lights. The horses stamped their feet, ate from their feed bags, and snorted steam into the still night air. I saw the Cutlers going up the steps and excitedly I ran back towards the shed. Jimmy Cutler had long trousers on.

The noise inside was thunderous now. Saxophones were blaring, drums were beating. The fiddlers had gone; up on the platform it was the Town & Country Swingers, an eight-piece band that Mr MacAdams had hired from Bathurst. A middle-aged man in a spotted bow tie stepped forward and blasted the air with a trumpet solo. They were playing a song I had heard on Joan's wireless, 'Sweet Georgia Brown,' and everyone was doing the quickstep. The woolshed was packed. Clouds of dust rose from the floorboards and hung in an incandescent haze about the dancers, thickest at about shoulder level.

I found all the boys from school standing on the sorting tables and climbed up to join them. I had become Jimmy Cutler's right-hand man, and that night we were all part of his woolshed gang. Jennifer Cutler ran with us. We were like foxes slipping lightning-fast in and out of a chook run, or fish gliding through a crowded pond. We climbed in and out of the wool presses, snatched sips of beer, and were outside as much as in. Jennifer ripped her dress rolling down one of the chutes to the holding pens, but she didn't care. We ran obstacle races through the maze of sheep yards, and when we were cold, stood around the big fire that had been lit round the side.

Once I found myself alone with Jimmy out in the dark under the acacia trees, I started up a wrestle. As we struggled and rolled, I kissed him again and again on his face. I could feel him trying to stop me, but I kept going anyway. When we crashed up against a fencepost, he broke away and wiped his face with his sleeve.

'What did you do that for?'

I did not say anything but just grinned foolishly in the moonlight. I wanted to do it again.

There were some difficult moments, and I thought perhaps

Jimmy was going to hit me, but he just said, 'You're drunk.' He stood up and brushed off his new trousers. 'Let's take some beer to Eddie.'

Eddie was spending the evening shivering under a blanket in the back of the Vauxhall Cabriolet. He had arrived in style on Mrs Cutler's arm but bolted when he saw the Colonel and all the soldiers. Mr Buchanan said that Eddie was right. Italian POWs discovered publicly socializing with their employers would be sent back to the camp and locked up in the calaboose. Mrs Cutler argued that Eddie was unrecognizable in his tuxedo. Regulations, Mr Buchanan continued, were that Eddie had to wear his red uniform at all times. I agreed emphatically with Mr Buchanan. 'If the Colonel sees him,' I said to Mrs Cutler, 'he'll beat him black and blue. That's what the Colonel's really like.'

'I've already fed him,' said Mrs Cutler when she caught us one time. We were headed out with a glass of whiskey from the kitchen and a piece of pie.

Eddie said we were his only friends that night. 'Thank you, Mister Jimmy. Thank you, Mister Lindsay.'

In the middle of the evening Mum grabbed me out of the crowd. Jimmy and I had just fallen off a rail. 'You're getting much too giddy,' she said. 'It's that cold of yours.' I was sneezing, but Jimmy had been right: I was a little drunk. She shooed me up the steps that separated the main floor from the baling area and took me to where she was sitting with Dad and Brown. Someone had unscrewed the lightbulbs there, so it was out of the glare. Trestle tables had been set up and it was a good place from which to watch the dancing.

I calmed down almost at once. I reached for a piece of pumpkin pie, and Mum poured me a glass of lemonade. On the table were jugs of beer, a bottle of rum, and lots of glasses.

'Brown is glowing in the dark,' said Mum, who was a bit lit up herself. I hadn't seen her laugh so much for a long time. 'Oh, Jack, just look at him.' She clutched Dad's arm. 'Can you believe how civilized he is tonight?'

Brown was an unusual sight. He was decked out for the evening in a double-breasted dark blue serge suit with a white shirt and a red-and-green-striped tie. His hair was cut. One curl had escaped from the brilliantine and fallen over his forehead. I looked under the table to see if he had shoes on. He had.

'. . . in the mood . . . da de da da . . . in the mood,' he sang along with the band. 'Can't sing for nuts. Come on, Jack, you can sing.'

Dad was in good spirits after meeting the infamous Colonel and being complimented by Mr MacAdams, but he just sat there, wearing his best suit, keeping his arms folded, and sort of smiling.

'You look like someone from a city,' I said to Brown, 'a detective or even a gangster.'

'Don't be fooled by the fungus,' said Brown, stroking his moustache.

Mum laughed happily once more.

'Wore all this for you, missus.' Brown gave Dad a big wink and leaned up against him. 'Hey, Jack,' he urged, 'just one beer.'

I saw Mum and Dad both hesitate.

'One beer wouldn't hurt,' said Dad.

'Right,' said Brown, reaching for a jug, 'one beer's not going to kill you.'

Dad looked at Mum, who smiled and shrugged. 'All right, Jack, just one beer.'

'Hooray!' Brown shouted, and Dad let out a laugh. Brown poured full glasses of Tooheys for each of them and said, 'Here's to beer.'

I knew it was a serious thing, for someone who has given up drinking, to have even a drop. Dad took only a sip at first. Then it was to hell with it, and he began to drain the glass. Brown joined him, and they both looked at Mum while they were doing it. I could see Brown's grin through the glass even as he drank. They banged their glasses down both at the same time. Mum clapped and put her hand fondly on Dad's arm. Brown wiped his moustache and clasped Dad around the shoulders. 'Hey, if God hadn't wanted us to drink, he would have made life a bit bloody easier.' He refilled the glasses. 'Here's to a wet winter and another good year for the best bloody farm on the river.'

The Town & Country Swingers finished with Golden Wedding and announced a break, but the cheers and applause would not stop. The dancers stamped their feet for more and the trumpeter jumped off the platform and gave an encore. A circle formed around him, and Tom McCaddie and his girlfriend did the jitterbug. Finally the crowd streamed away for more beer. The tables and benches filled up. The sound of banjo and accordion, and sticks beating on tin cans, came from the bonfire outside. I saw the Colonel and his wife going into the kitchen for a refill.

The Landgirls appeared with their partners, young men from the Wudgewunda Recruit Training Center. Joan wore a fluffy white sweater, Betty a blue one.

'See those overgrown schoolgirls a mile off,' Mr Buchanan had said caustically, and Mr Bridges called them a pair of blinking lights, the sort of thing that the young recruits had come to the woolshed ball for. That and the farmers' daughters whose boyfriends were away at the front. Even Heather was getting attention. It had been all over Wudgie that there was a free-for-all out at Billarooby for those who had the petrol to make it that far.

Betty sidled in on one side of Brown, and Joan plumped down heavily on the other, in between him and Dad. They each put an arm through Brown's and gave him a big kiss. Joan's and Betty's partners hovered for an instant, uncertainly, and then disappeared. Soon there was lipstick all over Brown's face.

'Oh, Brownie,' Betty said with a sigh, 'I wish you could dance with me. Are they really so bad tonight?'

'How about the pictures next Satdee?'

'Ooo, yes,' said Betty, snuggling up. Joan buried her face in his armpit. They were both in such a sentimental mood, I couldn't look.

'Rum?' Brown reached for the bottle. He poured rum for everyone. Joan downed hers at a gulp. Even I could see that she had already drunk enough. Earlier she had been boozing with the recruits out by one of the fires and had fallen over and torn her nylons. 'She was out in the pens with Mr Kelly,' Jimmy had whispered in my ear, 'making babies.'

'Ladies and gents, take your partners for the Old-Time Waltz,' shouted the band leader.

Heather came running out of the crowd and stood in front of me aggressively, hands on her hips. 'We can do this.'

I hesitated, shy about dancing with her in public. It wasn't like waltzing to the wireless in the Landgirls' room. And suddenly she looked grown-up. Her long hair, released from its plaits, cascaded down her back in a golden mane. A wide red velvet band across her forehead held it in place, and she was wearing a new party frock that Mum had finished just in time. She didn't have her glasses on, so I knew she was blind as a bat.

'I'm not going to wait all night.' She stamped her foot and took a sip of beer. Already the couples were whirling by in a dusty glow.

It was Mum that got me up really. I saw her staring at Brown. When she caught his eye she looked away and said to Dad, 'Jack, you're going to dance with me whether you like it or not.' She was as sick of Brown's smooching as I was.

'All right,' said Dad. He reached for a glass of rum and drained it. Mum didn't even blink. She straightened his tie and took his arm. They moved through the crowd and down to the floor.

'If Dad can dance, so can you,' said Heather.

In the first minute I saw Jimmy Cutler jeering at me from beside the platform, but Heather said he was just a wallflower and to take no notice. So I jeered right back at him and soon I was having such a wonderful time out there on the floor, I wished I had been dancing all night.

Mr and Mrs MacAdams spun by. She had her eyes closed and her head back, a picture of trust. Then Auntie Annabel and Slow George noticed us and smiled down benignly. He was wearing a cravat, and she was in gloves and an oyster satin heirloom that Mum had refurbished for her. Her nose was powdered and her glasses hung precariously on the end of it.

'You look so youthful, Auntie Annabel,' said Heather. She had said the same thing to Mrs MacAdams. It was her word for the night.

'Who have you been dancing with?' I wanted to know.

'Gordon,' Heather replied. 'He's a good dancer,' she went on defensively. She was always defensive about Gordon because he was so gawky and had only one front tooth. 'Better than you. My Gypsy Tap with him was my best so far.'

'Well, why aren't you dancing with him now?'

Heather spun me round and bent me over backwards. 'I had to slap him.'

Mrs Cutler and Mr Buchanan waltzed right into us.

'Watch where you're going, Fred. It's all these handsome men,' she shouted at us as they got going again. 'He's swooning.'

'It's you, you battle-axe,' said Mr Buchanan, who was dancing with a cigarette in his mouth. 'Look out, kids.'

'Hullo, Mum,' I shouted as Dad whirled her by. She was a shining blur of auburn hair and pale green silk in the haze. She had time to give me a smile and a wave over Dad's shoulder, but the very next instant she and Dad collided with the Colonel and Mrs Smith. It was Dad's fault, and it was a bad collision. Both the Colonel and Edwina went down. There were some moments of dreadful confusion and several couples had to stop. The Colonel was twitching as Mum and Dad assisted them to their feet. I could tell that Mum was quite mortified. It was a terrible thing to knock over an elderly couple, let alone two of the guests of honour at the dance.

'Oh, I really am so sorry, Mrs Smith,' she said several times as she helped Edwina find her shoes. Rose petals were scattered everywhere. Edwina was not hurt. She checked her stockings and her gown and took the opportunity to blow her nose. She seemed not to be worried at all, but the Colonel, on the other hand, used some terrible language on Dad.

'You should watch what you're bloody well doing, you clumsy fool,' he shouted. A little foam oozed from the corners of his mouth.

Dad not only took the remark in stride but stepped up very close, saluted, and said, 'If you ever need any help handling those Japs, Colonel, just let me know.' He did it right in the middle of the dance floor. Mum looked amazed, and so did the Colonel. 'A volunteer,' Dad continued in his best British accent. 'The army turned me down, but I'm handy with a shotgun, believe me. I know how to deal with a bloody Jap, if that's what you have to deal with.'

'Well,' said the Colonel, recovering. 'We have the situation well in hand, Mr Armstrong. I think it would be better if you just stuck to your vegetables. We can always use a few more of those. Now if you will excuse me . . .'

The Colonel steered his wife off, and Dad gazed after him. The passing dancers bumped us this way and that. Dad looked down at Mum with a triumphant grin.

'Jack, if we're not going to dance, we should get off the floor. I don't know what has got into you.' Mum gave Heather and me a push. 'Enough of your stares. Get dancing!'

It wasn't the last of the Colonel that night. During a Barn Dance, much later, I saw that he had forgiven Mum for her part in his fall. He kept throwing his head back and laughing maniacally. 'Ha ha!' He even took her out of the circle and danced with her for an extra turn. 'Ha ha! Ha ha!' At one o'clock in the morning, when Mr MacAdams appeared on the platform with a bagpipe, there was the Colonel at his side, with a glass in his hand, still laughing but swaying sort of diagonally.

Mr MacAdams announced that in memory of his friend Major Jim Dawson, who had been killed in the moment of victory at Gona six weeks before, he was going to play 'The Skye Boat Song.' As he played there was a profound silence everywhere, except for drunken singing from the soldiers around the bonfire outside.

'Such a dreadful thing, the war,' said Mum, standing arm in arm with Mrs Cutler. As she wiped away a tear, the Colonel took a step off the platform and fell flat on his face. His wife hurried forward, and so did a couple of officers. I watched with great satisfaction as he was carried off to the kitchen.

It wasn't long after that that I ran into Mum and Brown. I can even recall the tune the band was playing at the time, 'Dancing in the Dark,' a song made famous by Artie Shaw. Neither Mum nor Brown saw me, and I thought for a moment that it was Betty that Brown was holding so closely, there in the gloom between the trestle tables and the wall.

'You've had too much,' I heard Mum say as I went by. 'Let's just dance.' Her hair was dishevelled and shone red-gold in the half-light. They were moving slowly together in the one spot, and after a moment or two I realized that Mum was holding Brown up. It was his one-legged woolshed waltz again.

I hid behind a stanchion and watched for a while. I would have liked to watch forever. It filled me with happy wonder to see them like that, but I slipped away to look for Dad, who had been all over the place since his encounter with the Colonel, not like his usual self at all. He had danced with Joan, and then with Betty, and then with the fat lady who ran the grocery store at Mudoogla. He had been out by the bonfire, roasting potatoes and singing with the soldiers. He had challenged Mr Buchanan and Sergeant Duffy to jump through the fire with him, but Mr Buchanan had fallen and set his trouser leg alight. Sergeant Duffy had pulled out his dick and pissed on the flames. It really was a mess out by the fire. There was a soldier with a bloody nose, and another who was lying in a pool of vomit, snoring loudly.

The night ended in the best possible way. Heather came running out to get Dad and me for the final waltz. There on the floor was Mum with Mr Bridges, who had a bottle in his hand and was having trouble standing up. We rescued her, and Mr Bridges walked off into the wall and slid to the floor. We Armstrongs all got together and did a sort of foursome waltz. Dad swung me off my feet and put me on his shoulders. 'There you are,' he shouted, and started galumphing around with Mum, with me up there, high above all the other dancers. I felt that Dad had seen the error of his ways and had taken me back into the fold. I knew that Mum and Heather were proud of him that night, and so, I realized, was I. I felt his roughened hands holding firmly on to my bare legs, and remembered, from out of nowhere, an occasion back in Suffolk when Dad plucked me out of an apple tree that I had become stuck in. Back in the good old days, before Granddad died. When Dad let my legs go, to swing Heather with one hand and Mum with the other, I squeezed my knees tight around his neck and gave his head a little massage, as I had seen Mum do. And when he said to slide off, I gave him a hug on the way down.

The dance came to an end. Dad helped Nurse McCaddie get Dad Packman up on the platform, so he could join the Town & Country Swingers in the Maori Farewell. Dad Packman could still play the fiddle at three o'clock in the morning better than he could hold the church collection plate, which he continued to drop just about every Sunday. The band played a two-verse national anthem and then packed it in for the night, but everyone stood around talking and drinking beer, in no hurry to leave. I began yawning wide enough to split my face and went into the kitchen, where it was warm and quieter. I lay down on the bench beside the ovens.

There were several babies on the floor there, all wrapped up and sound asleep. Mothers were coming in to get them, but I must have fallen asleep also, for I remember nothing more until Mum woke me up to go home.

THREE
Cherries

13

THE WINTER WAS entirely dry. With the coming of spring, the weeping willows along the Lachlan seemed reluctant to bud, and when they did, they soon lost their green under a layer of dust even thicker than Joan's face powder. The river itself was down to a trickle. Our house tanks still held water, but without rain they would be empty by Christmas.

The crisis had mounted during the winter months, but Dad behaved as though nothing were wrong. He mended the holes in his rabbit-proof fences and had the pump fully overhauled. He planted cold-weather crops of beets, swedes, broccoli, and cabbage. He carefully cleaned out and enlarged his entire system of irrigation ditches and prepared the ground for the spring plantings. Yielding to the entreaties of the Reverend Pitts, he joined the Wudgewunda Combined Churches Choir, and two evenings a week he drove through the crackling frosty air to rehearsals for a springtime concert, which was cancelled for reasons having to do with the personal life of the Reverend Pitts.

The winter mornings were sometimes so cold I refused to get out of bed and Mum had to haul me. The flats were a sea of green-white diamond glitter, with frost so heavy it did not disperse until mid-morning. Mum knitted thick gloves and socks, but Heather and I still got chilblains. After I had thawed out by the school fire, my ears would burn bright red for hours. Mr Buchanan said he could warm his hands by them.

Mum spent some time up at Moorellen fitting Mrs MacAdams for a tweed suit, and Mrs MacAdams professed herself delighted with the result. She said she had friends who might also be interested. Mum was very happy to have brought in some money on her own.

There were jolly nights around the big open fire when the
Douglasses, the Cutlers, the Bridges, Mr Buchanan, or various
combinations of them came over. Brown came to flirt with Betty
but really, I hoped, to see Mum. Mr Buchanan came to play chess
with me, and to give extra coaching to Heather, but really to see
Dad. The Cutlers came round with their Monopoly game on those
nights when Dad went singing for the Reverend Pitts in Wudgie. I
discovered that Jimmy Cutler would cheat rather than lose.

It was only the frequent visits of Mr Kelly that I did not enjoy.
He managed to ingratiate himself with Mum again and spent a lot
of time in the Landgirls' room around the side. Heather said he
was courting Joan. I was at a loss to fathom Mr Kelly's appeal,
unless it was that he always had so much money to spend.

Walking along the river one morning above the cradle, I came
upon an eroded gully full of junk – old tyres, derelict cars, rusting
drums and cans, rolls of twisted wire, an old white bathtub . . . It
was Mr Kelly's dump. There was the smell of burning rubber, and
a thin, almost invisible line of smoke rose from the centre
somewhere. His broken-down house stood on the bank high
above it, raised on pilings in case of flood. The early morning
quiet was suddenly broken by a shriek of laughter. Joan came out
the front door on roller skates, wearing a dressing gown and not
much more. She rolled out of sight around the side verandah, and
I heard her crash into the wall. There was another shriek, and Mr
Kelly appeared in his long johns, also on roller skates. He pinned
her against the wall. It was the strangest sight, the two of them. I
should have enjoyed the chance to laugh at Mr Kelly, but instead
it disturbed me and was on my mind for days. I mentioned it to
Brown, who just laughed. 'He's good on the pogo stick too.
That's the secret of the old bastard's appeal.'

Twice near the ford I encountered the Colonel. He had taken to
riding that route to visit Mr MacAdams. The second time, he was
watering his horse in the river. I really wasn't interested in being
nice to the Colonel at all, but I had *The Knights of Bushido* in my
satchel and decided to show it to him. I handed it up, and he took
a pair of glasses from the breast pocket of his uniform and put
them on. He leafed through the book.

'Very nice. Do you know something, little fellow? I'm colour
blind.'

'That doesn't matter. It's about your Japanese.'

'Really?' The Colonel was surprised and looked again.

'They have a Code. You don't have to treat them badly.'

The Colonel made no reply and handed back the book. He put his glasses away.

'It says the samurai are like a swarm of wasps.' I pointed to the paragraph.

'Really? Bees are better. They die if they sting.' The Colonel's horse was champing at the bit and backed away into the mud by the waterhole.

'But the wasps sting and sting again. It is the Code. Don't you know anything about the Japanese?'

'Sullen bunch. Sitting out the war.'

'You have a samurai with a scar,' I shouted, suddenly angry. I traced with my finger from forehead to mouth. 'He'll have your head. You'd better watch out.' I ran off but stopped at the top of the bank and looked back. The Colonel was galloping in the direction of the camp.

One cold Saturday morning I took a secret trip there. I knew I had promised Mum, but Jimmy Cutler was always saying, 'Once is never,' so I did it. I could go with Dad around by the road any time he delivered vegetables, but it wasn't the same at all. It wasn't my very own camp that way.

The plain was covered with a ground mist, and the Japanese huts rose out of it like a mountain hideout lost in the snows. It was colder there than at the Billarooby flats; the frost still lay thick. The prisoners walked around their compound in big red overcoats, swinging their arms around and banging their shoulder blades to get warm. Steam rose into the air from their mouths. I had Brown's binoculars with me, but no matter how hard I looked, I could not see Tadao.

Another morning, I went for a trek almost to Mudoogla with Dipper, who discovered, half in and half out of a hollow log, a swaggie huddled up in blankets. She rolled in the body and the smell was terrible. The crows had been at him. I hastened home to tell Mum, and in the *Wudgewunda Star* the following week it said that he had died of natural causes.

Dad Packman died of pneumonia in his own bed.

The swedes and the beets got blight, and the broccoli was killed by a frost that was the worst late frost that Slow George could remember, but it wasn't until one morning in mid-September, a little more than a year after our arrival in Billarooby, that I really understood that things were going very wrong indeed for Dad.

The morning was warm and sunny. Heather had gone off on her bicycle to catch the train, and I had been kept home because I had sandy blight. It had been frightening to wake up and find I could not open my eyes. Mum bathed away the sticky yellow pus with warm water until my eyelids parted. She blamed the dust. And the flies. They had been back for weeks.

We knew something was amiss when we saw the truck speeding back up the slope from the flats even though it was only ten in the morning. The truck skidded as Dad pulled up in front of the house. Dust enveloped him as he emerged from the cabin. He came over to where Mum was toiling in the smoke and steam from the copper.

'They've just posted the pump. Petrol ration's cut.'

We did not know what he meant.

'Hargreaves, from the Shire Council,' he shouted angrily. 'No more pumping from the Lachlan. It's illegal.'

'Oh, Jack,' said Mum, alarmed. 'What does this mean?'

'It means we're done for. It means I've failed. It means I'll have to let Joan and Betty go.'

'Couldn't you reason with him? You're a farmer. You have to pump.'

'He says I'm the wrong kind of farmer for here. I'm not wanted.'

'Nonsense. The cannery – '

'I've been arguing with him for an hour. It's hopeless.'

'Let's get out of here while we can,' said Mum suddenly. 'Go down the coast where there's rain.'

This was not the first time Mum had brought up this subject. There had been long and serious discussions about it during the winter as the pattern of drought had established itself, but Dad prayed every night for rain and believed firmly that it would come.

Dad went to the pepper tree and banged his head against the trunk several times. 'Are you mad? You want me to give up?'

'Jack, don't start that up again. You'll hurt yourself.'

Dad strode back to the copper. There were red marks all over his forehead from the tree. He glared at me. I squeezed my eyes shut and turned my head. 'Why aren't you at school?'

'I'm helping Mum with the washing.'

'You're going to cut down all the thistles around the pump. Take the machete.'

'Jack, he's chopped down more thistles than anyone.'

'Not where it counts. And he leaves the biggest.'

'I kept him home because he's sick.'

'There's nothing wrong with him. Red eyes. We have to get rid of these bloody thistles.'

That is what really precipitated it, I suppose. The thistles. Apart from the yellow bursts of the wattles and the enormous increase in the number of rabbits, the most dramatic sign of the end of winter had been the appearance of noxious weed, the variegated Scotch thistle. Before we fully realized it, the weed had spread from the river's edge through the entire farm. It grew thickest and tallest where Dad had done his most intensive cultivation. No spot on the farm escaped. The thistles thinned out halfway up the hill, but they were six feet high in the orchard, and it was impossible to get anywhere near the mulberry tree.

'It's just me,' Dad had shouted at dawn one morning. He was standing outside the shed looking down over the flats. 'It's a plague of Egypt visited upon me.'

'Jack, everyone's got the thistles,' Mum said. 'Even Mr Mac-Adams has a few.'

Dad took no notice of her and became obsessed with getting rid of them. Wherever he could, he ploughed them in and had Joan and Betty hacking away for days without much apparent effect. The nightly Bible readings began to come from the Lamentations of Jeremiah, but I was not convinced that the thistles were a manifestation of the wrath of a righteous God. Even so, every day after school, I had to attack them. Even before school and sometimes at lunchtime. They became people to me, the thistles, enemies, and I went to war, tirelessly slashing with the machete for hours at a time. My greatest feat was to hack a path from the driveway to the orchard, a distance of fifty yards.

My fantasies about them reflected the confusion in my loyalties.

Sometimes the thistles were rival samurai, in the employ of an evil shogun, but more often they were the soldiers who guarded the prisoner of war camp. They were always drunk and vomiting as at the woolshed dance, and it was easy to hack and thrust my way into the densest thickets and rescue Tadao from his Great Captivity.

Sometimes I was Brown on the Kokoda Trail, fighting for Australia and the British empire, but even then, I would spare the tallest thistles. They were the noblest of the samurai and did not deserve to die. Sometimes I would fight Tadao himself and hack him down, but he would always be resurrected in the form of the next thistle, and ultimately I would stop at the very largest and spare him. I would raise the machete to my lips and bow to his majesty, and he would bow in return.

One day, playing warlord in the thistle forest, I recruited Jimmy Cutler. He said he enjoyed swinging machetes.

'Follow me,' I shouted. 'Take this, take that. Fall, fall, fall!' I quickly worked myself into a frenzy of hatred for them. 'Run, Tadao, run. You're free. Freedom!'

When I paused for breath and looked around, Jimmy had gone. His machete lay on the ground. I observed a few minutes of calm for Jimmy, and then went back to the thistles. I didn't really care anymore. Jimmy had taken to showing me his hard-on, and a few times he made me rub it, but he had never let me kiss him again, although I ached to do so. Then Dad had caught the two of us together in the dark of the hen shed with our trousers down and our dicks sticking out. It was a Sunday and he had beaten both of us. That was the first time Dad had ever actually laid a hand on me. Afterwards Jimmy threw half of a house brick and hit me on the head. 'It's all your fault!' he screamed, and ran home crying to his mother. Mrs Cutler got Eddie to drive her round in the Vauxhall Cabriolet, and she and Dad had a terrible row – a row made worse by the fact that Mrs Cutler and Eddie were both drunk on grappa, the home-brewed Italian wine, which Eddie had taught Mrs Cutler to make.

The brick was pretty bad, but it was a couple of other things, really, that caused the romance to sour that winter. Jimmy had thrown the baby mice down the big covered well behind his house, and had killed Gertie the magpie wife with a stone. The

Cutlers had eaten roast magpie for dinner. Mr Buchanan put Dave Bridges between us at school because of the bickering.

My blood lust that day was ended only by Mum's coming all the way down the hill after dark. She said she had been calling for twenty minutes. I stank of thistle juices and could not eat for exhaustion.

'I don't have to do around the pump.' It was after lunch, and Mum was bathing my eyes a second time. 'That's the Landgirls' area.'

'This is one time you can really help him, and I don't want to hear any nonsense. Off you go.'

It was hot. The pump was situated in a depression where once there had been an oxbow lake, and was sheltered from the wind by a stand of red gums. I waved at the flies, then noticed Dad's double-barrelled shotgun leaning up against the side of the pump. I was surprised. As far as I knew, it was the first time the gun had been taken down from its hooks above the front door.

Some paper wasps had begun to build a nest in the cabin of the old Model T pump. I had been stung by paper wasps and knew not to go anywhere near them. I moved to where the thistles grew thickest and prepared to do battle.

That was when I heard the noises.

I half suspected what it was all about and I should not have gone looking for trouble, but it was one of those times when more than simple curiosity is at work. Stealthily I made my way through the thistles towards the sounds. A narrow path led to a clearing, and in the centre of it were Dad and Joan. I had a glimpse of Dad's white naked buttocks and legs with his blue overalls pushed down, the red slash of Joan's mouth, and one of her great breasts. I was no sooner there than I was backing away. I ran, but I knew they had seen me. I heard Joan hiss my name and felt Dad's eyes upon my retreating back.

I was in a paralysis of fear. I remember being poised at the pump, machete in hand, unable to make up my mind. I wanted to run home to Mum. I heard a paper wasp. My eye fell on the shotgun, and suddenly I was off towards the river instead, running as hard as I could go. I didn't stop for breath until I was at the waterhole with the great willow tree. The cattle were using it now and it had become a smelly quagmire. I started up again almost at once, sure that Dad was in pursuit. The river was a dead serpent, its skeleton of fallen trees and stumps exposed and bleached, like dry bones in the sun. I reached my cave and jumped in, panting. Safe.

I must have huddled there for ten minutes or more. I had seen Dad doing something I should not have seen him doing. It seemed that something more than just punishment was due. All my fears of Dad returned in one big rush. I would have to run away.

I emerged cautiously and headed blindly across the river. The dry mud flakes crumbled under my feet. I was just about to race up the hill when I saw four soldiers coming over it. I dropped like a stone and crawled back towards the shelter of the trees. I hid and watched the patrol go by no more than thirty yards away.

The crunch of feet on bark made me whirl round. There were two more soldiers emerging from the trees. One had a rifle, and the other who lunged forward and grabbed me by the arm, carried a pick handle.

'Gotcha,' he said. 'Ha, ha.' They were big, beefy men, sweating in their baggy uniforms and smelling of booze.

'What are you doing here, you little fucker? Army territory. Can't you read the bloody sign?'

'Let me go,' I said. His grip tightened.

'I could shoot you dead, right between the eyes, mate. You know that? And why shouldn't I?'

'You're hurting my arm,' I cried.

'I'll hurt more than your fuckin' arm, mate. What you doin' snooping round the camp? This is a war zone, ain't it, Pete?'

'Too right. It's a bloody war zone.'

The two men laughed. Neither of them had shaved for several days, and Pete had a fat lip and two teeth missing.

Mr Buchanan had told me not to be so hard on the garrison soldiers. They were the old codgers who had been found unfit or born too soon for active duty overseas and they were doing their best. But still I couldn't help thinking how horrible they all were. Sergeant Duffy, Mr Buchanan's friend, was the only nice one I had met.

'I'll tell my mother.'

'Your mother!' The two soldiers laughed again, but I was let go with a shove.

'You can tell yer bloody mum that you're in big trouble. This place is top secret.'

'I didn't know it was secret.'

'Now you do. And you'll keep it that way, won't you, sonny?'

'Of course,' I said quickly. Too quickly.

The soldier took a couple of steps forward and grabbed me once more.

'You fuck around and Pete's gonna pop yer buttons, pull yer trousers down. That's what Pete likes to do, don't ya, Pete? Remember, top secret. Loose lips sink ships.' He gave my arm another twist and pushed me away. 'Now get the fuck outta here.'

I began to run, but I wasn't out of the woods yet.

'Hey you, stop.' I stopped and looked back. Pete, the soldier with the rifle, had unshouldered it and was aiming it right at me.

I wanted to scream, but no sound came out. Instead I heard Dad's voice.

'Drop that rifle, soldier.'

I looked round. Dad was below us on a cow trail, his shotgun trained on the two soldiers. Their grins died.

'Dad, they're shooting me.'

Pete lowered the rifle hastily, and the one with the pick handle raised his arms high. 'Don't shoot, mate. The boy was trespassing.'

Dad lowered his shotgun and climbed the remaining few yards to the top of the bank.

'What do you mean, trespassing? You're the trespassers. This is Bruce Kelly's property.'

'It's OK, mate,' said Pete. 'We were only having a bit of fun with the kid. We didn't mean him no harm. I got kids.'

The man with the pick handle delved in his pocket and brought out a white paper bag. He fumbled it open.

'Here,' he said, holding it out to me, 'licorice.'

I shook my head.

'What are you doing out here?' Dad demanded.

The soldiers looked at each other. Then Pete said, 'Two prisoners went over the wires just before dawn. Nips. One of them's a real nasty bugger. Been out before. Regular Houdini. We think they're hiding along the river. Might be heading out towards Condoblin.'

'Are they dangerous?' asked Dad.

'You betcha, mate. Vicious. All them bloody Japs. When we ran into your kid we were jumpy.'

'Did one of them have a scar?' I cried. 'Like this.' I traced up from my mouth and pulled a face.

'They all got horrible bloody scars, mate.'

'Are they armed?' asked Dad.

They seemed to find something funny about Dad. I think it was the English accent.

'Search us, mate. They got knives. One thing they won't have is rifles. Even we don't have rifles.'

'How can you guard the camp without rifles? No wonder they're escaping.'

Pete pulled out a packet of Players. 'Wanna smoke?'

Dad accepted a cigarette and introductions were made. The man with the pick handle was called Ron. Soon all four of us were sitting in the shade of a tree. Pete produced a flask of brandy and that went round. Since the woolshed ball Dad had got into the habit of drinking once more. It was partly the influence of Brown, partly those long winter nights when Mr Buchanan had come by so frequently. And Mr Kelly always had a bottle to pass round.

'Is the camp safe?' Dad asked.

'You gotta be joking, mate. There's thousands of them Japs in there and more arriving every week. I don't like it. None of us do.'

'Only good Jap's a dead Jap.'

'You think more of them will try to escape?'

'The whole bloody lot of them. It's just a matter of time. We can't stop 'em. I tell you, mate, it's just a couple of barbed wire fences between you and a fucking army of them. You live round here?'

'I have a farm across the river.'

'If I were you, mate, I'd evacuate. Get out while the going's good.'

'I can't get up and leave. Just like that.'

'Don't envy you, mate. Japs get out, they'll kill Wudgie. Go through the town like a dose of salts. Women and kids first. That's what the Japs are like. Glad the missus is down in Sydney. They'd have her well fucked, they would. Flaming war.'

'The Japs are not like that,' I cried. 'They have a Code.'

Pete stood up and took a leak in front of everyone. His pee stank and was bright green. He said he had been eating asparagus from the cannery.

'Slit yer throat, bayonet up yer bum. That's their code, mate. They'd eat you for breakfast.'

Those were Pete's parting words. The soldiers moved off towards the ford and the little party on the riverbank was over.

Suddenly I was alone with Dad, and terrified again. I thought of falling behind and making a dash for home along the other bank before it was too late. I would tell Mum about Dad's betrayal with Joan and she would protect me. Go, go, I told myself, but my feet seemed to refuse me.

My imagination began to fly. Dad had come looking for me with the shotgun. He had rescued me, but the shotgun was the one that Granddad had used that stormy day. The day Granddad had insisted I carry it. The day he had died. The day that was nothing but fragments and nightmares. When Dad fell back a step and let his hand drop on my shoulder, I cried out in fright.

'If two can get out, they can all get out.' His hand tightened on my shoulder like a vice. 'We have to get home to your mother. She's alone at the farmhouse.' His fingers dug in deeply and I squirmed in pain. I didn't believe him, he didn't care about Mum, he was going to push me into a Bunyip pool.

He propelled me across the dry bed and up the other bank. We approached the trunk of the fallen giant, and I looked up the slope to where the roots raised their crown above my cave. Tadao might be hiding there.

'Your cave is here somewhere, isn't it?'

His fingers in my shoulder blade were like a knife. I was eager to please him – anything to get rid of the pain. But there is also the possibility, I realize now, that I told him out of a half-conscious premeditation; that it was part of a trap I was already laying.

'It's up there. You can climb the trunk or go along the side.'

Dad immediately relaxed his grip and glanced upward then towards home. For a moment he seemed satisfied with the information.

'It's not really much to look at,' I said, already having second thoughts. 'It's a very difficult climb.' I was too late.

'I'll take a quick look,' said Dad, beginning to scale the trunk.

I watched him climb, feeling torn. I didn't want Tadao to be there and get caught, but if he was there, I wanted him to deal with Dad. I imagined them wrestling – Tadao throwing Dad over his shoulders, slamming him into the back wall of the cave. Tadao would come leaping down the tree trunk; he would take my hand and we would run run run . . .

Dad was peering into my cave. There was no one there. In horror, I dismissed my thoughts. I scrambled up, pushed past Dad, and snatched the machete from where I had hung it on an overhanging root. I held it vertically in front of my face. 'Those who enter the cave of the samurai – ' I began.

Dad shoved me aside. 'That's enough of that,' he said, and jumped down into the cave.

I could see that he was impressed by my blankets and layer of straw, my water canteen and my supply tins. And the bottle of citronella for the mozzies.

'There's that damn book.'

I had to do something. I dashed forward, opened the book, and cried, 'Dad, listen to this.' I began to read. ' "The sacred warrior never surrenders. Capture is a shame unendurable to bear, and the true samurai is forever at war with his enemies. If by circumstances beyond his command, he is captured, he will rise against his tormentors and renew the eternal struggle. He will not hurt the innocent, but will kill all those who dare to oppose him. If shed, his noble heart's blood will water the field of battle. Death is the final privilege. A thousand followers will spring from the earth and carry his soul to the Shrine of Yasukini – " '

But Dad's mind was elsewhere. 'Those guards are right. We have to get going.'

It was too much for me. I cried out, 'Why do you love Joan more than Mum?'

That surprised him. He had completely forgotten about Joan and what had brought him to the river in the first place.

'Joan?'

Dad took a step towards me, then stopped.

'Joan is an evil woman. The Lord will punish her in his good time.'

I remember thinking that it was an unsatisfactory answer, but I said nothing.

'Let's get out of here.' Dad put his hands on my shoulders and looking down into my eyes said, 'Don't worry. I'll keep your cave a secret. I won't tell a soul.' He sounded sincere, and as I looked up at him I almost felt I knew what made Dad tick.

'Honest to God, Dad?'

For a split second I understood the struggles depicted in his troubled face, the rocky road that had led him to Billarooby, the hidden thing that was wearing him down, but then his eyes went elsewhere and he gave me a squeeze that made me cringe.

'You follow me? We all have secrets. Only God need know.'

Dad's truck was at the ford. I could see neither Joan nor Betty as we drove past the flats. The sense of foreboding that had Dad rushing home so fast began to affect me also. As we gunned up our driveway, we saw Brown's lorry coming down. He pulled up beside us.

'Escaped Japs,' he said. 'They were here. Lillian's OK, considering. I'm going over to Moorellen to telephone.'

Mr MacAdams had the only telephone in the district. A private line all the way to Wudgewunda.

'Jack, thank God you're back!' Mum rushed forward and clung to him. Joan was making a cup of tea. Betty had brought a bottle of brandy from her room. Dad put his arms around Mum and I could see him looking at Joan at the same time. Joan avoided my eyes. The room was filled with the smell of freshly baked bread.

'We saw them run up the hill,' said Joan. 'We went for Brown and got up here as soon as we could.'

'Joan was terrific,' said Betty. 'She did the right thing.' Mum sat down again, almost knocking over her teacup.

Dad stood there with the shotgun in both hands. 'What happened?' Mum was in the middle of swallowing. 'Lillian!' he barked impatiently.

'I was in the bedroom, Jack. I heard a bang on the door. I called out "Hullo?" and then there was another bang. The screen door creaked, and when I walked into the living room, there they were. Oh Jack, my legs went to jelly. I had to lean on the desk.' Joan applied a wet handkerchief to Mum's forehead. 'Thank you, Joan.'

'Go on!'

'One of them clicked his heels, bowed, and gave his name.'

'Bowed?'

I could contain myself no longer. 'What name, what name?' I shouted.

'Oh, Lindsay, I have no idea.'

'He had a scar on his face, didn't he?'

'Yes, he had quite a scar.'

'Did he go to my room?'

'No.' Mum looked at me very strangely. 'He had a knife, but somehow he was quite the gentleman.'

'Gentleman!' Joan threw her cigarette end towards the stove. 'I'd have told them to beat it quick smart.'

Mum glanced at her. 'You weren't in the house with them. I was so frightened I thought it best to give them what they wanted, which was food. They drank all the milk, and then I took the cover off the mutton chops left from lunch. He said, "Bread." I handed him a loaf. I had taken it out of the oven only ten minutes before. He tore it in half, stuck the chops in between, and put the whole thing into a little bag he was carrying.'

'Then what?'

'They made themselves at home. One of them moved around the living room talking to himself, and the one with the knife tried your chair, Jack. And he did his hair in front of the big mirror. Then he handed me the clothes brush, and – well, I brushed him down. After I had finished, he pressed his hands together and put them to his chin. It was his way of saying thank you. Then he sat down at the table and stared at me. He was very young. He couldn't have been more than twenty.

'I don't know what would have happened next if they hadn't heard the truck coming up the hill. The one who had been wandering around the room looking at everything panicked and rushed at me. I screamed and ran behind the table. He came very close and traced his finger across my throat. "Woman, talk, you die," he said. The one with the knife began yelling at him in Japanese. I think he was telling him to stop.'

Mum began to cry, but almost immediately she wiped her eyes with her apron and continued.

'The one with the knife gave me the most awful sort of smile and put his fingers to his lips, and then they ran out. I jumped up and bolted the door. I couldn't see them through the window and realized they had gone round the side. I ran and bolted the back door. Then I saw them heading out into Lindsay's field. They were following the path towards the school.'

'When we saw them,' Betty put in excitedly, 'they were stopped in the centre of the paddock where Lindsay has all those stones.'

A thought exploded in my head. The power of my magic stones had saved Mum. Their presence nearby had reminded the prisoners – well, at least Tadao, for it was surely he – that they were samurai, not thugs, and they had no business disturbing innocent people like Mum.

'What happened to Dipper?'

'She was dozing around the side.'

I was disappointed in Dipper.

'I'm going to the camp,' said Dad, who was pacing up and down the room.

'Oh, Jack, I'm all right now. It was very frightening but they won't be back. It will just be a waste of good petrol.'

'They stick out like a sore thumb,' said Betty. 'They'll be picked up in no time. Brown will catch them.'

I didn't want Brown or anyone to get them. I imagined Tadao and his friend flying over the plains, always one step ahead of their pursuers. The Colonel would be swinging at them with his whip and missing by a wider margin every time.

'That's enough,' came Dad's angry voice. He looked round at us all. 'They've been out since dawn. That's almost nine hours ago and they still haven't caught them. I'm finding out a few things about that camp. Lindsay, you're coming with me.'

'Not with his eye condition,' said Mum.

Dad and Joan exchanged another glance. I was being got out of the way. I sensed Dad's guilt about what he had done with Joan, and his fear that I would tell. That was why Dad was making such a fuss, or so I thought at the time.

'Brown's already telephoned from the MacAdamses',' said Mum, but nothing she said was of any avail. I was hustled out. I didn't even have time for a cup of tea. As he left, Dad picked up the clothes brush and threw it out into the yard.

During the entire drive to the camp, Dad spoke only once. Just past the cannery he pulled over to the side of the road. 'See that?' There was a red-bellied black snake that someone had killed and hung on the barbed wire. 'You tell your mother and that's what God will do to you.'

We jolted to a stop in front of the quartermaster's store, and a soldier sitting on the step looked up from his magazine. Dad strode over to him.

'I demand to see Lieutenant Colonel Smith,' he shouted.

The soldier did not get up. 'The Colonel's not here. What's up?'

Just then the Colonel came round the corner of the barracks on his horse. He was about to set off on his afternoon gallop.

'Colonel Smith,' said Dad, once more giving a salute. 'You remember me?'

'Yes, Mr Armstrong. Always remember people who knock me down.'

'My wife was molested this afternoon by your escaped prisoners.' Dad's eyes were blazing. 'One of them made her brush his clothes.'

The horse pranced sideways and the Colonel cleared his throat.

'Well, I am very sorry to hear that, sir. Is she OK?'

'She is recovering. I want to know what you are going to do about it.'

'I presume you are talking about Ugaki and whatever his name is. Couple of fools, both of them. They were picked up on the Condoblin road and brought back here half an hour ago. They will be suitably and severely punished, believe me. The matter is closed.'

'Where are they?' I called, but the Colonel did not seem to hear me. He attempted to move his horse by. Dad reached out and grabbed the bridle.

'You can't ride off just like that,' Dad shouted. 'I have information your camp is unsafe.'

'Get your hands off my horse or I'll call the guards. If you have anything to say about the camp, put it in writing.'

'I'm going to report you to the police in Wudgewunda.' Dad turned to walk away and the Colonel spoke.

'Mr Armstrong, I would be glad for you to make a statement.' His tone was conciliatory. 'Major Brent of D Compound will see you. The prisoners were under his control and are his primary responsibility. Once that has been done, I will deal with anything you have to say. Private Simms, take Mr Armstrong to see Major Brent.'

The Colonel spurred his horse and galloped off.

'You wanna see the Major?' asked Private Simms, who sat down once more on the step.

There was no crisis at the camp. It seemed just another sleepy afternoon. I could hear the voices of the Japanese, calling to each other as they exercised in their compound. I could hear Dad's teeth grinding. He stared after the Colonel and ignored Private Simms.

'Hey,' said Private Simms, 'taking it a bit hard, ain't you?' He looked both ways and drew a flask from his pocket. 'Here, mate, have a tot.'

Dad reached out and took the flask. He uncorked it and began to swallow.

'Hey,' said Private Simms again. He got to his feet and forcibly took the flask away from Dad's mouth. Dad threw the cork at him and got back into the truck. We drove away without a word. I looked back. Private Simms had sat down again and was taking a swig himself, watching our departing truck through the dust.

We did not go straight home. Instead, Dad drove to the office of the *Wudgewunda Star* in Broome Street and informed old Mr Sullivan, the editor, of what had happened.

Mr Buchanan had told me all about Mr Sullivan, but this was the first time I had seen him. He had been editor of the *Star* since 1922 and was in his declining years. He had a full head of grey hair, brushed straight back, and nests of hair in his ears and nose. He seemed to have only one tooth in his lower jaw, and was wearing a thick scarf around his neck, despite the heat.

Mr Sullivan was very helpful. He said he would come and talk to Mum himself the very next day. He had been looking for a good story for the next week's edition.

After some hesitation, I told him about the Colonel whipping Tadao.

'Very interesting,' said Mr Sullivan. 'I'll have Mr Tappley look into it.'

14

MUM TOLD HER STORY to Mr Sullivan exactly as she told it to
Dad and me, but the article that appeared in the *Wudgewunda
Star* was headlined, 'ESCAPED JAPS ASSAULT BILLAROOBY HOUSE-
WIFE,' and in it Mr Sullivan commented that it was the sheerest
good luck that rescue arrived in the form of two brave Australian
Landgirls, who saved helpless English immigrant Mum from
certain rape and possible death. Mr Sullivan said that Colonel
Allan Smith, the commandant at Prisoner of War Camp No 24,
had assured him that security at the camp was in no way to blame.
It was tight. The Japanese who escaped were criminal escapolo-
gists, and standard measures, perfectly adequate for normal
prisoners, just pandered to their true nature. These two would
have escaped even from maximum security at Long Bay.

'We have to remember that the Japanese temperament is vicious
and autocratic. We Australians are, by contrast, good-hearted and
democratic in our dealings. We assume the same in others, and
thus, in our naïveté, have been taken advantage of. I am happy to
report that the overly kind treatment accorded to these two
prisoners up to now is over. They have both been sentenced to six
months' solitary confinement, hopefully on nothing but bread and
water.'

'Army leaned on Sullivan,' said Mr Buchanan. 'Old fart.'

'He's distorted the truth,' I said.

I cut out the article and pasted it in my scrapbook. I read it over
and over again and couldn't make any sense out of it. I told Mr
Buchanan so, and he agreed that newspapers were not to be
trusted, but said to stop worrying. Mr Sullivan was in cahoots
with the Colonel, but he also had a point. The Japanese were not
to be treated lightly and we had to believe some of the accounts

that were coming out about them – the atrocities at Changi, for example, the treatment of the Indonesians, the bayonet practice massacre at Rabaul.

'Who's Mr Tappley?' I asked.

'He was Mr Sullivan's partner. Died ten years ago. Why?'

I told him.

'It's a device he uses to put people off. War is war. It can bring out the worst in everyone.'

I began to count the days until Tadao would be out of solitary confinement.

Everyone was relieved at Mum's narrow escape, and the Reverend Pitts made much of it in his sermon and prayers up in the woolshed the following Sunday. Mum was embarrassed by all the attention and was careful to correct (although Dad told her not to) the many inaccuracies in the *Star*'s story. 'One of them was the perfect gentleman,' she insisted.

The escape of the prisoners was very disturbing to everyone in Billarooby, particularly after Dad recounted his conversation with the guards on the riverbank. Sergeant Duffy confirmed most of the information, and as a result, many things happened.

Mr Buchanan marched the school out to the slit trench dug behind the lavatories and put us through an air raid drill. The Packmans began building booby traps. Mr Morrison threw up extra pens on his poultry farm and installed Bogan gates at unlikely corners, creating a maze around the house. 'Buggers will need a map to get in here,' he said.

Dad started carrying the shotgun around wherever he went. He drove to Mr Kelly's dump and came back with rusty iron stakes and rolls of barbed wire. Within two days we had a double row of barbed wire right around the house.

Mum thought the wire was an eyesore. 'The great Australian ugliness,' she complained at breakfast as she plonked my oatmeal down in front of me. Dad was outside with Mr Kelly, who had come round to help finish the staking. *Clang, clang, clang!* went the sledgehammers. 'And why we have to see so much of that man Kelly, I don't know.'

'The barricade is all completely unnecessary,' I insisted. 'The Japs are not like that. My book – '

'Oh, your book! Mrs Cutler should never have given it to you. Get off with you. You'll be late for school.'

It wasn't just my book that was irritating Mum. It was Dad. Ever since Mr Hargreaves from the Shire Council had shut down the pump, he had scarcely visited the flats, except to parade around with the shotgun or sit moodily under the stringy bark tree and stare at the lettuces. He had instituted a hand-watering system and upped Joan's and Betty's wages on account of all the extra work it was going to be, but it was soon apparent that just about everything would die unless he started up the pump again.

Even Heather noticed changes in Dad. 'Dad's got a bottle of whiskey in your china cabinet,' she told Mum.

Mum said she was afraid that one of Dad's depressions was coming on and we would have to do everything we could to avert it. Everything had gone so well since our arrival in Billarooby that Heather and I had forgotten all about Dad's depressions.

I saw Mum doing Dad's hair for him through the bedroom door one morning. Generally she began giving him all sorts of extra attention. We had a roast beef dinner midweek as well as the usual Sunday, and for Dad's birthday, which normally we never celebrated, there was a sultana cake with bright pink icing.

Mum decided to tackle Dad's weakness in the face of authority, and rallied everyone around to help.

'Hargreaves is a bastard,' said Brown. 'Take no notice, Jack. Pump away. Nobody's going to put you in.'

'Problem's so bad for everyone,' said Slow George, 'Council will turn a blind eye. That's the reality of the situation.'

'Fuck 'em,' said Mr Kelly. 'I'll get the petrol on the black for you.'

It was Mr Buchanan who finally did the trick. He just went over Mr Hargreaves' head, and the Wudgewunda Shire Council told Dad to apply for special consideration. Dad applied, and two weeks later he was granted a variance.

The crisis was over. Or so we thought. In fact, it was just beginning, and a lot of it had to do with Joan and Mr Kelly.

I walked home from school in the hot, still afternoon, over a hundred in the shade. A mirage of shimmering water hung over

my field. A flock of Mr MacAdam's sheep was slowly making its
way in its own little haze of dust towards the shade of the yellow
box tree. The sheep walked into the mirage and turned upside
down. Bad omen. I decided not to visit my circle. By the time I
got home, the wet handkerchief I had knotted round my head was
long dried, and I was feeling faint.

I went to the back tap and found Joan there, running the water
to wash her feet. I just barged right in, stuck my head under the
water quickly, then turned it off.

'I'll tell Dad you're not using a bowl.'

'You just warn yer mum I'm coming in there any minute.'

I looked at her blankly. I hadn't liked Joan since the episode in
the thistles, and she knew it.

It was as hot inside the house as out. I padded silently along the
back corridor into the darkened living room. The curtains were
drawn against the heat and I gave Mum a fright. She was kneeling
on the floor in front of Brown, who was leaning back on the
couch with his hands behind his head, his leg up on the stool. The
hair in his armpits was curled with sweat. A bowl of water was
on the floor, and Mum was just about to change his bandage.

Mum half rose, then settled herself once more. Brown had a
silly grin on his face.

'Brown's leg is giving trouble again.'

I went to have a look at it. The tight feeling in my groin came.

'You're home early,' Mum said.

'Mr Buchanan let us off because it was so hot. And he was
feeling crook all day.'

'Feeling sick,' Mum corrected. 'Leave the slang for Brown.'

Brown laughed. 'I know where he was last night.'

'Is your leg getting worse?' I asked.

Brown reached out with a friendly swipe.

'It's yer mum's tea and bikkies I like.'

Mum quickly finished bandaging Brown's leg, and we took our
places at the tea table.

Brown was looking very proper. He wasn't wearing any boots,
but he had on a fresh shirt and clean, well-pressed trousers. I
knew he did not have so much work to do on the dairy. Slow
George had sold off all his dries and replacement stock, and was
hoping that he had enough feed in his shed to see him through.

Mum was out of her apron and wearing her pale green tea dress. Her hair was tied back, but loosely, so that it fell over her ears.

The best cups were on the table, white bone china with a delicate blue and gold floral pattern around the rims. There were only four of them left. Mum did not believe in keeping things just for display, no matter how valuable. 'You never learn to appreciate fine objects if you don't use them,' she would say, and was always prepared for breakage.

'I ran around my stones five times six,' I lied, 'to make sure that if the Japs escape they won't bother us. Not that they would.' I had been doing it, even if I hadn't that day. Mum didn't believe it worked anyway.

'Oh, Lindsay, it's sweltering. You must keep out of the sun.'

There was a heavy footfall on the verandah and Joan walked in. Her shirt was undone, and so was the top button of her shorts.

'How many bad legs you got, soldier?' she said, even though the first aid was over, 'to need so much fixing up?'

'Is Jack coming up for tea?' asked Mum.

'He'll be here any second,' said Joan, throwing a peculiar look at Mum and Brown. She flopped down in Dad's chair, put her feet up, and lit a cigarette. She blew two jets of smoke out of her nostrils. Joan's large nose pores were exuding beads of perspiration.

'I'm going to cook again tonight, Mrs Armstrong,' said Joan. There was a pause. 'If you don't mind.'

'Thank you, Joan, but I will manage tonight.'

'Suit yourself. You're missing a chance to take it easy.' Joan tossed her head and dislodged her hat. She caught it and then threw it expertly on to Dad's peg.

Brown, Mum, and I all looked at one another.

Mum carried the bowl of water over to the sideboard. 'With these hot nights, it would be lovely to eat outside.'

'Too many flaming insects,' said Joan.

'I'll get Jack to screen the verandah.'

'Jack hasn't the time to do things like that,' said Joan. 'Give the bloke a break. He works like a dog all day long.'

'It might be a good idea if you got yourself out of that chair before my husband sees you.'

Joan ashed her cigarette on the carpet.

'Use the ashtray.'

'Horrible old carpet. I'd get rid of it if I was running this place.'

'If you are insisting on helping with the dinner, you can start by killing the white chook. We're having her tonight.'

'Get Lindsay to do it.'

Joan pulled a face at me. She knew I couldn't kill a chook.'

'Come on, Lindsay,' said Brown, coming to my rescue. 'We'll do it together.'

As Brown and I went out the door, Mum was saying, 'Well, if you're not going to kill it, Joan, you are certainly going to pluck it. The water in the copper is almost boiling. All you have to do is stoke the fire.'

'In this heat? Jack doesn't even like chook.'

Outside Brown began laughing. 'Let 'em slug it out.'

'Joan's taking over the house,' I said as Brown unlatched the gate to the chook run, 'and the farm as well.'

'Increase in wages has gone to her head.'

'It's not just that,' I said darkly.

When Dad came in for tea he brought Mr Kelly with him. They had been drinking, and Dad hadn't been at the table five minutes when he knocked one of Mum's best cups to the floor. Mum didn't say anything, she just went about picking up the pieces.

'Bring us some glasses,' Dad said thickly, going to the china cabinet. 'Bruce and I are going to have a drink.'

Mum brought the glasses, and after a little while she said, 'The children would like to go to the pictures tomorrow. There is a matinée. Elsie Cutler is taking Jennifer and Jimmy.'

Dad did not look up from his glass. He ran a hand over his stubble. Dad had not shaved for three days. Which wasn't remarkable, except that Dad was someone who used to shave sometimes twice a day.

'They've never been, Jack.'

'It's a good picture, Dad,' I said nervously. I had been keeping my distance from him since the episode of Joan in the thistles. 'It's *Snow White and the Seven Dwarfs.*'

'You and Bruce could have a drink in the William. You seem to like doing that these days. And Eddie is singing in the Ritz afterwards.'

'Oh, is he indeed?' said Mr Kelly. He snickered and then clapped Dad on the back. 'Kids go to the pictures, we let Signor Eduardo Larguili entertain us. Sounds like a good idea, Jack.'

'The kids can go to the pictures every bloody week for all I care.'

'Jack, I won't have you swearing like that in front of them.'

Mr Kelly smiled at Mum. 'Everyone bloody well swears, my dear Lillian.'

'We're in Australia now,' said Dad, taking another drink.

'You might pour me a small one too.'

'No wife of mine is going to drink whiskey.'

'Come on, Jack, that's no way to talk to a lady.' Mr Kelly took the bottle and poured Mum a drink in her teacup.

There was such a bad feeling in the air I decided to leave and see how Joan was getting along with the plucking. I found it hard to believe the influence that Mr Kelly seemed suddenly to have over Dad. There was a time when he wouldn't even speak to an Irishman. Nothing but boozers and brawlers, he said. Roman Catholic to boot.

Jennifer and Jimmy Cutler were old hands at the pictures. They had seen dozens, but *Snow White and the Seven Dwarfs* was my debut. I must confess that from the very first minute I was completely enthralled. Jennifer, who sat beside me, soon gave up offering me chocolates and jubes, and when she slipped her sticky hand in mine halfway through, I scarcely noticed it. My fascination with what was unfolding in front of me was complete, whether it was hatred for the wicked Queen, terror during the storm in the forest, affection for the seven dwarfs, or sheer joy at the happy ending. It was only when Jimmy banged me to get up because they were leaving that I realized that Jennifer still had my hand clutched in hers. I tried to withdraw it, and she tickled my palm.

We dashed around the corner from the Coronet in Bell Street to the Ritz Milk Bar and Café in Lawson Street. Mum and Mrs Cutler were already seated at a booth. Mrs Cutler treated everybody to ice cream. Mr and Mrs Andronicos were making a fuss over the Italian POWs, who were arranging themselves on chairs at the back, between the piano and the swing door to the kitchen. There were seven POWs altogether, all in well-washed, faded-to-pink uniforms. Four of them were going to play the music and three were friends seated nearby. As they talked animatedly amongst themselves, I took note of all their gestures and resolved to try some of them on Mr Buchanan.

The café was almost empty, except for the employers of the POWs, whose presence was required by law. The flies buzzed and squabbled, the fans slowly turned beneath the greasy ceiling, and Eddie played cocktail music on the piano. The atmosphere was so quiet that the supervising officers from the Control Centre paid for their tea and cake and left.

'Eddie's no country peasant,' Mrs Cutler informed us, blowing cigarette smoke up into the air. 'He's a city gent. Before the war he was a cabaret artist in Milan.'

'We listen to Italian opera on the wireless,' said Jennifer, 'and he sings along.'

'God, he looks like an angel,' said Mrs Cutler of Eddie. 'In that pink.'

The cocktail music turned into Italian folk songs, and Mrs Cutler kept us informed about what they were singing. 'Calabrian love song,' she would say, or 'Venetian gondola song.'

'If only Mussolini could see him now.'

'Mussolini's finished,' I said. 'That's why they're letting the Italian POWs sing in public.'

'Really?' Mrs Cutler read the papers but professed to know nothing whatever about the war.

Everything went along very nicely until Mr Kelly and Joan slipped into the booth in front of us, obviously both rather drunk.

'Oh God, closing time at the William,' said Mrs Cutler.

There was the sound of a slap and Joan said, 'Get your hand outta there, Bruce.'

'Elsie,' Mum asked, looking around for Dad, 'how much longer are they going to play?'

'Eddie's got a surprise. Don't worry about Joan. She'll calm down.'

'No she won't,' I said. 'She's tiddley, and Betty's not here.'

Mrs Andronicos came to take Mr Kelly's order, and he told her
to bugger off. Joan yelled for eggs.

'Show some manners, Bruce,' Mrs Cutler called out. 'Eddie has
a song coming up you might enjoy.'

'My, my, it's Mrs Cutler, the Pommie sheila,' said Mr Kelly. He
shifted his bulk around and looked blearily over the top at her. 'I
will say one thing. Your silver-voiced gigolo's got guts. Mind they
don't get spilled on the floor.' He smiled and added, 'Some sunny
day.' He turned back to Joan and they both laughed.

There was another big influx from the Prince William. Most of
the men stood in the aisle or in the space in front of the musicians.
Brown squeezed in with us at our booth, and then Dad appeared
with Blue Chapman and Ernie Williams, another friend of Mr
Kelly's. They all sat down in Mr Kelly's booth.

'Has Jack joined the Bush Brigade?' queried Mrs Cutler.

'Of course not,' said Mum.

'Dad's not like that,' I said. I had heard about the Bush Brigade.
Mr Buchanan said they were Australia's answer to the Ku Klux
Klan.

'Sit down in front!' Mr Kelly threw one of Joan's fried eggs. It
missed its target and splattered against the wall behind the
mandolin player's head. 'Waltzing Matilda,' Mr Kelly shouted.

There was a roar of laughter, but Mrs Cutler said, 'This is
Eddie's surprise.'

'We sing Australian song,' said Eddie, 'for Mr and Mrs Andron-
icos.' Mrs Cutler clapped, the violinist scraped out a recognizable
introduction, and the Ritz settled down to listen.

'Once a jolly swagman camped by a billabong,' sang Eddie in
his ripe Italian accent, 'Under the shade of a coolibar tree . . .'

It was the highlight of the afternoon. Several people joined in,
and when it was finished there was applause and whistling. Joan
stepped out into the aisle and blew a kiss. Only Mr Kelly had not
enjoyed it.

'Thank you,' said Eddie politely. He and the others took
sweeping bows. 'We finish.' There were calls for an encore. The
accordion player moved forward to where Joan was standing and
smiled.

'Mr Luigi,' said Joan, 'that was terrific.' Luigi doffed his cap,
and then lifted her hand and gave it a kiss. Mr Kelly reached out

and pulled Joan back sideways to her seat. In the next instance, he half rose, shoved the accordion player backward, and sat down again with a squelch.

'Take it easy, Bruce,' said Brown.

'You tore my blouse,' said Joan.

'Fuck your blouse.'

'Luigi's a friend of mine.'

'I bet he is, sweetheart.' Mr Kelly stood up and shouted to the café, 'They'll be letting the Japs out next to do *The Mikado*.'

There was laughter.

'What are you staring at, my young slicko?' demanded Mr Kelly of Luigi, who still stood awkwardly by the booth. Eddie called out something to him in Italian, but Luigi did not move.

Mr Kelly stood up and swaggered forward until his big belly pushed into Luigi's accordion. Luigi backed away at once, raising both hands in a conciliatory gesture.

'That's better, wophead,' said Mr Kelly, and, reaching forward, chucked Luigi under the chin.

Luigi yelled, 'Va fungula,' and tried to get away, but Mr Kelly grabbed him by the back of the collar and shoved him into the wall. The accordion strap broke, and Luigi began shouting in Italian.

'Fucking fascist! Dirty, fucking bloody dago,' roared Mr Kelly.

'No fascist, no fascist!' shouted Luigi.

'My God,' said Mrs Cutler, 'there's going to be a fight.'

Mr Kelly was very large. Luigi was small. Mr Kelly began punching him about the body. Luigi doubled up against the wall and the other POWs moved to help him.

'Stay out of it, Eddie,' called Mrs Cutler.

'Please, Mr Kelly,' Mr Andronicos shouted from behind the counter.

Mrs Andronicos screamed, 'I am calling the police.'

'Luigi's OK, Bruce,' shouted Joan. She got up and thumped him on the back. 'Get the other ones.'

'Fair go, Bruce.' Brown was on his feet. He reached out and gripped Mr Kelly by the shoulder. Mr Kelly turned his head. His face was wet with perspiration and his mouth hung open. His eyes were popping with excitement.

'Fuck off, cripple,' he said, pushing Brown away roughly. 'And get that bloody shirt off.' He yanked at the open collar. 'You're no digger anymore.'

Brown punched Mr Kelly in the face. Mr Kelly punched back and they began fighting.

'Fight, fight!' Shouts rose from all over the café. We slid into the aisle and Mum began pushing us desperately towards the door, but with men rushing forward, eager to take a poke at the Italians, we were swept back into the thick of it.

'Get yer kids outta here, lady,' a man yelled in Mum's ear as he pushed past her.

'Dad!' shrieked Heather, but Dad had moved away, to a position by the cash register.

'Under the table,' Mum ordered, pushing Heather down.

'I want to help Brown,' I cried, but Mum reached out an arm and dragged me under. It was a tight squeeze. The Cutlers were down there too.

I didn't really see anything of the great brawl in the Ritz. I wanted to, but my view was only of legs. And it wasn't a very safe view at that. Two men staggered against the table and sent our teapot flying. It fell down beside us and smashed. I looked sideways at Mum, whose face was no more than a few inches from mine. She managed to get an arm free and squeezed me even closer to her. Something dropped from the wall above. Heather closed her eyes, put her hands over her ears, and let out one scream after another. There were terrible noises coming from all sides – yelling and swearing, breaking of wood and crockery, the thud of fists, shouts of men trying to prevent the fight, and shouts of those promoting it. Mrs Andronicos screamed for everyone to take it outside. She screamed that there were women and children in the café. She screamed when the mirror behind the big counter shattered.

The biggest crash of all was the cash register falling to the floor. A florin made its way somehow through the melee and rolled under our table. Jimmy Cutler reached out for it from under the next bench, but I beat him to it. I smirked. A florin was a lot of money.

Between a pair of legs appeared the face of a young recruit. He might have been searching for money, but he looked scared, much more than we were.

'Go away,' screamed Heather, 'we're here,' but he was so determined to get in that Mum had to push him away.

'Sorry,' he gasped. There was a beery hiccup, a focusing of his eyes, and then he crawled off in the direction of the door.

I felt a hand slip into mine. It was Jennifer. She seemed half scared, half thrilled, which was exactly how I felt. I squeezed back, and we held on to each other tightly.

The fight seemed to go on for a long time, but it was probably no more than a couple of minutes. It ended even more quickly than it began. Above all the oaths and the terrible din came Eddie Larguili's voice, shouting in Italian, causing the tumult to die away as though by a miracle. There was a silence, and into the silence dropped the voice of Mrs Andronicos.

'My God, my God, enough! You want to kill in my café? Everybody out! Out! out, out!'

At once there was a movement towards the street. As soon as there was room to do so, we crawled from under our table. Mr Kelly was swaying in the middle of the floor, bleeding from his nose. Mrs Cutler ran to Eddie, who was up against the wall brandishing a carving knife. Heather ran outside to look for Dad, and Mum rushed over to Brown. He was sitting in a chair with his head in his hands.

'Oh, Brown,' she cried, taking both his hands, 'let me see.'

'I'm OK, missus,' he said feeling his chin. Mum took a good look at his eye, which was half closed, and then picked up his crutches. The POWs were all bleeding. Two were comforting each other and sobbing. The violin was in pieces on the floor.

'Give me the knife, Eddie,' Mrs Cutler was saying.

'He go,' cried Eddie, who was sweating and white-faced, 'then I give.'

Mrs Andronicos seized a broom and pushed Mr Kelly backwards with it. 'Get out my café,' she shouted. Mrs Cutler got the knife from Eddie and pushed him through the kitchen door. Jennifer and Jimmy dashed after them.

'Please forgive me, Brown, mate.' Mr Kelly placed both his arms on Brown's shoulders. His face was puffy with bruises and he seemed to be crying. He kept wiping the blood coming from his nose with the back of his hand. 'My inebriated condition is no excuse, but I ask for forgiveness.'

'Forget it, Bruce.'

Mr Kelly's head fell on Brown's shoulder, and his heavy body shook. 'To think I should do that to you, of all people.'

'Get off him.' Mum elbowed Mr Kelly out of the way and finished cleaning up Brown's eye. Then she began wiping Brown's chest, which was covered with Mr Kelly's blood.

'Mr Brown,' said Mrs Andronicos kindly, 'please use my sink.' She gestured towards the back.

'Missus,' said Brown to Mum, 'I'll see you outside.' Mum was reluctant to leave him. Brown looked at her for a moment, gave a little backward tip of his head, and then turned for the kitchen.

'Let's find Jack.' Mum let her breath out with a quavering noise and put her hand to her breast. As she hurried me out, I looked back. Mr Andronicos was on his knees with the waitress, picking up money, his wife was sweeping up the broken glass, and two men were lifting the cash register back to the counter. Mr Kelly was sitting in a booth with his head back and a handkerchief to his nose.

Outside we found Dad, Heather, and Joan in the crowd. Joan wanted to know if Bruce was coming.

'He's asking for you,' said Mum sarcastically.

'I'm not going back in there.'

'Oh, get in with you,' said Mum angrily. 'End the mess you helped start.'

Two police officers and the representatives from the Control Centre appeared and followed Joan inside.

'Always around when you're needed,' came a shout.

'Send 'em back to the camp,' yelled someone else.

'Dirty dagos.'

'It wasn't their fault,' said Mum loudly.

'You dunno what you're talking about, lady.'

'Dagos are dagos. He had a knife.'

'Bruce Kelly started it,' Mum insisted.

'Bruce didn't pull no knife.'

'He hit Brown,' I said.

'Brown hit him,' said Blue Chapman.

'That's enough, Lindsay,' Mum said. Dad moved over to us.

'They don't see things straight,' I said.

'No, they don't,' said Mum. 'Oh, Jack . . .' she began to cry.

'Come on, Lillian, let's go to the truck.' Dad took her by the elbow and began pushing her through the crowd. He seemed anxious to get away.

'Don't shove me,' said Mum sharply through her tears.

'We should wait for Brown,' I cried.

'He can look after himself. He should not have got involved.'

'You managed to keep yourself well out of it, as usual,' said Mum, shaking her arm free. 'I don't understand why you are suddenly in a rush.'

Dad had the answer all ready.

'No headlights. We have to get home before dark.'

15

WE HEADED NORTH along the old river road with the sun going down in a clear blue sky. The wind that had stirred up the dust that morning had dropped. Dad drove as though he were on the run, making the corrugations in the road shake the old truck like a rattle. Mum's nerves had been badly hit by the fight, and she hung tightly on to the dashboard with both hands. The smell of stale whiskey on Dad's breath filled the cabin.

'Jack, slow down, you'll kill us all,' she pleaded.

As we went round Mulligan's Corner, Heather let out a scream. It was clear we were not going to make it. The truck skidded into the ditch and almost overturned. Dad's head banged into the top of the windscreen, and we wound up at a forty-five-degree angle.

'I knew it, I knew it,' Mum cried, beating at his shoulder with her hands. He took no notice of her and revved up the engine. The wheels spun in the dust; the truck didn't move an inch. We were definitely stuck, and Mum burst into tears. As we all climbed out, Dad began kicking the side of the truck.

'If you are going to go on like this,' she said, drying her eyes immediately, 'it's high time I learned to drive.'

We stood around looking back towards Wudgewunda, sure that someone from Billarooby would soon come by. There was Mrs Cutler, and Brown . . .

'Bruce will pull us out,' Dad said thickly.

'He'll be in jail,' Mum said, 'and after what he did this afternoon, I refuse to be beholden to him in any way.'

The minutes went by. Shadows from the gums along the Lachlan stretched towards us and there came the sound of kookaburras. Two galahs perched together in the very top of an old dead tree, which glowed white in the rays of the setting sun.

Heather sat on the edge of the ditch reading *Anna Karenina*. Above, the three-quarter moon grew brighter and the first stars appeared.

As darkness fell, Mum and Dad began to argue, and they moved slowly off down the road. 'Stay there,' Mum said, glancing back.

Heather turned a page. No wonder she had to wear glasses.

Where was Brown? Where was Mrs Cutler? I gazed out across the paddocks. I was hungry. The rabbits would be out looking for grass. Wallabies. I strained to see. In the twilight the stricken landscape was very beautiful. The limbs of the dead trees gleamed under the moon, the earth was a luminous grey, and I thought of night-time in the woods in *Snow White*. Our parents' voices, drifting back clearly on the warm night air, grew louder and louder, and it was clear that they were having a terrible argument. I could hear Mr Kelly being mentioned, and Joan. Heather told me not to listen and put her hands over her ears. That was Heather all over. Like a horse with blinders. I couldn't stand not knowing what was going on, and moved closer to hear better.

Mum was saying that the writing was on the wall for Billarooby and we should get out immediately. And if Dad absolutely insisted on staying, he should get a job with Mr MacAdams as a stockman before our money ran out completely. She couldn't understand him. At Emu Plains he had given up too soon, and again at Booti Booti, but now when it really was time to move on, he was refusing to budge.

'There's no drought,' Dad shouted.

'Has that little bump on your head lost you your senses? There hasn't been a drop of rain since we arrived here, not one drop. If it doesn't rain soon I'll go mad, quite mad.'

'I see the river rising, Lillian. I see water flooding across the land. I have redeemed myself. I have, I have.' Dad's fist crashed into his hand. 'God will reward me.'

'You're a fool, Jack Armstrong. The river's gone. A few weeks and the waterholes will be empty. We can't go on like this.'

Dad was silent. I knew it was no good, Mum telling Dad how to run the farm. You couldn't tell Dad anything.

'Let's get out of this accursed place!' They moved farther off down the road, out of earshot.

'Come back here,' Heather snapped at me. 'Have some respect.'

There was no rescue in sight. In the hour we had been on the road, nothing had come by, in either direction. Billarooby was on a back road to nowhere and the world was empty but for us.

Mum is giving as good as she gets, I thought. Whether I wanted to leave Billarooby or not was another matter. I thought of all the good things, like Jennifer's hand, and began on the bad, like Mr Kelly.

My churning mind turned the friendly night into eerie darkness.

'What?' asked Heather brusquely. I had been talking aloud.

'I'm going back to England.' Mum's voice came floating clearly on the night breeze. 'I want to see a green field. I'm sick of Billarooby. If your heart was still in the farm it would be different, but something else is keeping you here.'

'You're happy here. I've seen you.'

'How dare you. It's not like that. Please, Jack,' Mum pleaded, 'let's cut our losses and leave. It's not just the drought. It's that camp. If it is as dangerous as you say, all the more reason for us to get away. Think of the children.'

'We have to be on guard, Lillian. Billarooby is closer to the camp than any other community.'

'Did you hear what I said? Think of the children, think of me. What you are saying is that we should leave, not stay!'

'I'm not going to let a few Japs drive me from my livelihood.'

There was a silence for a while, and then Mum said, 'His spirit has haunted you far too long, Jack.'

Dad did not reply, and Mum's voice rose into a scream. 'The old fool is dead! Dead and gone! He treated you like dirt. Let him lie.'

I began to fear for Mum. The fears mingled with another dread that seemed to be coming out of the ghostly twisted trees. 'No, no, no,' I whispered, 'not again.' I waved my hands across my eyes. I turned away from the dead trees.

'A strong man would admit defeat here, and move on,' Mum shouted. 'You're even prepared to go to war to prove him wrong. He was right about you all along.'

There was the sound of a stick breaking, the sounds of a scuffle. The night was exploding.

'Push me, push me! If what I suspect about you and Mr Kelly is right, I'm going to leave you. There, I've said it.'

It was Granddad. His spectre swelled out of the darkness – the gun, the teeth, the same flashes of bloody red, the falling backwards . . .

'Mum,' I screamed, 'there's a ghost.'

'Lindsay, what's the matter?' Mum came running back towards us.

'Dad, I'm scared,' Heather called.

At that moment I saw the lights of a vehicle on the plain.

'There's a truck coming,' I cried.

We waved frantically. The truck roared past us thirty yards before it came to a stop. It was Mr Kelly. In the cabin with him were Joan and Betty. They were all drunk, even Betty, and there wasn't a sensible word to be had out of any of them.

'You don't have a rope either?' asked Mum angrily.

'Ravening redheads in the front with me,' said Mr Kelly.

Heather jumped up into the back of Mr Kelly's truck and Dad handed our supplies up to her. Then Dad climbed into the cabin. Joan wriggled about until she was on his knees. She put her arms around his neck. Her skirt was hiked way up, and I could see her garters. I looked at Mum. She had seen them too.

'If you ever go across the sea to Ireland,' Mr Kelly was singing, 'Maybe at the closing of the day . . .'

'Mrs Armstrong, I'll get in the back,' said Betty.

'Get out of that truck, Jack. We are not riding with Mr Kelly. I'd rather walk. Heather, get down.'

Mum and Dad stared at each other for a moment. I could feel Mum's anger rising. She shouted, 'You have been warned. I'll leave you.' She grabbed the door of Mr Kelly's truck and slammed it. I could just make out the faces of Joan and Dad through the glass, looking at us. Joan pulled a face. Then Mr Kelly revved the engine hard, the wheels churned the dust, and the truck shot off down the road.

'Go with him,' Mum shouted bitterly at Heather.

As the lights disappeared and the clouds of moonlit dust settled once more, Mum began to cry and cry. She drew me to her. Some of her tears found their way on to my forehead, and then they trickled all the way to my mouth. I could taste their faint saltiness.

Shortly, the lights of another vehicle appeared from the direction of Wudgewunda. It was Brown.

16

THE DAY that Eddie Larguili pulled the knife in the Ritz (that's what everyone remembered it as) had repercussions that went on for weeks, mostly bad, but for me something wonderful came out of it as well. Jennifer's sticky hand in *Snow White and the Seven Dwarfs* had started something, and being marooned under the table with her during the fight had confirmed it. Within twenty-four hours I was hopelessly in love. I didn't fully realize it until Mr Buchanan yelled at me in school one afternoon. Young love was a favourite target.

'Your head, my boy, seems to be on a perpetual swivel.' Mr Buchanan's tone was biting. I faced the front, blushing. I was so mortified, I didn't dare turn around again even once. Behind me in the back row, Jennifer poked me with her ruler and blew spitballs on to my neck, to no avail.

I was besotted all the next day, and by Wednesday Mr Buchanan was sick of it and moved me into the back row beside her. I don't know whether he was being kind or whether he thought that proximity might end the romance and I would once more be able to concentrate on my schoolwork. Whatever it was, there I was in the back row, months before it was my due. It quite turned my head.

That particular afternoon, the little kids were all up at the front on the floor with large rolls of butcher's paper and pots of paint and water, while we older pupils were at the back learning bookbinding. We used a special glue that came in a large jar, inside the lid of which was a heavy seal made of white paraffin wax.

The blow came at the end of the day when Mr Buchanan came to put away the glue in his cupboard.

'Who broke the wax?' he demanded. He had had a black eye since the weekend and was in a liverish mood. Arts and crafts was not his strong suit, and he needed more brandy than usual to get through that day. He had gone home at lunchtime and come back reeling.

Everyone looked at me.

'It was already broken.' The wax was in six pieces.

'Brand-new jar,' said Mr Buchanan.

'Lindsay did it, sir,' said Jimmy Cutler. 'He was poking it with his finger.'

'I didn't touch it.'

'Go stand by my table. I'll deal with you after school.'

After Mr Buchanan had dismissed everyone, they hung around outside, waiting to see what was going to happen to me, but he sent them all on their way. As I waited, a shutter went down in my brain to protect me. I had to be perfect for Jennifer. I wondered why the big deal.

'Why would they lie?'

'They don't like me.'

Mr Buchanan selected his favourite cane, and I fought against a rubber-legged faintness, brought on by the sense of injustice about to be done. One minute I was a king in love in the back seat, and the next I was the victim of some plot.

'I didn't do it, sir. I didn't.'

Mr Buchanan put down the cane, lit a cigarette, and uncapped a bottle of beer from the ice chest. He hiccupped, then swallowed. A gust of wind came through the screen door and blew papers from his desk. I looked out the window. The MacAdams house, up on the hill, was hidden in the brown haze. A willy willy spun in the back playground.

Mr Buchanan wiped his face and his mottled, balding head with a large dirty handkerchief. His skin looked like oily paper. I had heard Auntie Annabel saying that he was not looking after himself in the way he used to. His shorts were frayed at the seat, and Jennifer and I had been giggling together at his underpants all day long.

'It's no good running home to your mother all upset.'

'Why is it so important, sir?'

'Remember the horseshoe nail.'

I said nothing. I knew all about how the kingdom was lost.

'Everyone saw you.'

'Jennifer didn't.'

Mr Buchanan gave a long sigh. 'You're addled,' he said, and picked up his cane once more. I tightened with the anticipation of pain and humiliation. He looked at me, snapped it across his knee, and then laid the pieces carefully behind him on the table. This histrionic gesture only made my heart sink to a new low.

'I don't give a damn about the wax. It's the truth that matters.'

'But I am telling the truth, sir.'

'Hell you are. I'll tell you what happened, Lindsay. You were fooling about with it. What is wax to a boy in love? The second you realized I was upset, you made up your own truth. You believe it, but you haven't convinced anyone else. It's a truth that covers up an accident or a mistake. What is really happening is that you are too frightened to admit your mistake.'

Silent fury took the place of desperation.

'Once you have your own story going, you soon don't remember where facts end and your fantasies take over.' Mr Buchanan dropped his cigarette to the floor and ground it out. 'Tomorrow you sit back in your old seat.'

He gave his black eye a little rub.

'You want to know how I got this black eye?'

I was taken aback by the change in direction. 'Sir?'

'Your dad punched me. Because I grabbed him. There's some truth for you.' Mr Buchanan hiccupped again. 'Your dad and I have a friendship and I abused it. But he shouldn't have hit me.'

I stared at him uncomprehendingly, and he said, 'You don't understand, do you? Forget it, I'm sorry. Tell me, what did the police find when they came yesterday?'

It had been a terrible afternoon. When I got home from school, the police from Wudgie were waiting. Mum said they were asking about money that was missing from the Ritz Milk Bar and Café. I had gone silently to my room and got the florin from its hiding place and handed it over. I was sorry to see it go. I had been planning to spend it on a present for Jennifer. As it turned out, I needn't have handed the florin over at all. It was Dad they were waiting for, not me. They said they had information that Dad had taken a lot of money. After the brawl, it was found that over twenty pounds in notes and silver was missing from the till.

'The police didn't find anything, sir,' I told Mr Buchanan. 'When Dad came home with Mr Kelly, they searched the whole house. Dad denied that he had taken any money. It was just that he was near the till. Mr Kelly told the police to clear out or there would be trouble, and they left.'

'Not facing the truth like this. Do you think you might have picked up the habit from your dad?'

'Dad's a church warden,' I said desperately. 'He wouldn't steal.' Since old Mr Packman had died, Dad had been taking round the collection plate. I would not accept the fact that my father would do wrong things. Despite the memory of Dad wanting to rush away from the Ritz so hurriedly, despite – I shut off the thought, but Mr Buchanan somehow picked it up out of the air.

'It's like when your dear old granddad died, isn't it? You know deep down what happened but you're too terrified to really face it. You dropped the gun when you were a little boy and killed your granddad, didn't you? I know, because I've been talking to your father. He told me the true story. It was a terrible accident, but it would be better to face up to it and then you wouldn't have those nightmares. And you might have a better time with your dad. It's just like the wax, don't you see?'

I killed Granddad? I killed Granddad? I felt as though Mr Buchanan had punched me in the head. I closed my eyes to shut him out, the menace of his yellow teeth, the stab of his tobacco-stained fingers.

'What do you say about that? Is your dad telling the truth? Come on, out with it.'

'I didn't see, sir. I didn't do anything,' I cried. 'I was down by the river.'

Tears gushed out, hot on my cheeks. They were boiling out of a cauldron of hellish wickedness deep inside me. Mr Buchanan's voice came from far off. I opened my eyes to the misery of it all. He was weaving back and forth in front of me, talking to me in the way he talked to Dad when they were alone together out in the shed. It was a jolly kind of hectoring, and he did it to make Dad take things less seriously, to enjoy life, be more friendly. I became frightened. I wasn't ready to be treated as though I were a grown-up.

Mr Buchanan stumbled. He stopped. He bent his face to mine. He swayed even closer until his eyes were burning deep into mine. I couldn't stand it any longer and hid my face in my hands. I could smell him, all his smells.

Then he took me by the shoulders and shook me very gently. When he spoke, his voice was completely different.

'There's something going wrong with your dad, and I'm trying to get to the bottom of it. I want to help him. We can all help him. There's a good man behind that iron mask of his. Go home now and think carefully about this afternoon. Remember what you did. Start off with the cardboard you used. Which colour? Then the binding. The red or the green? How did you put on the glue? With the brush or your finger?' He paused. 'Face your fear. That's the secret. Then it will all come back to you.'

Mr Buchanan's voice was soft, but I continued to cry.

'I'm sorry for the way I have behaved. It is not like me at all. I realize I am a little drunk. I have burdened you with too much.'

He gave me a little push.

'That's enough. Away with you now. The truth is not so dreadful. Even if I changed my mind and gave you a whack. Even if you admit what you did to your granddad.'

I ran home through the hot afternoon.

Mum made me lie down and put a cold flannel to my forehead. She brought me a cup of tea, and while she finished up her sewing she got the story of the wax out of me, although I could not bring myself to talk about Granddad. It was too terrible to face.

The tea had been stewing on the stove and was bitter.

'I want a note saying I have been unjustly accused.'

'I'll come with you to school tomorrow and talk to him.'

'No. I just want a note so he will leave me alone.'

'All right. I'll write him a note.'

'What are you going to say?'

Mum left the couch and went to the stove. I followed her. There was a rabbit cut up and soaking in the pot for dinner. Mum didn't believe that Mr Buchanan was just picking on me. I decided to keep adding details until she was convinced.

'He is usually a very fair man.'

'He was drunk. He picks on me because of Granddad.'

'What's Granddad got to do with it?'

'Nothing,' I said, and looked away.

Mum lifted a piece of wood from the basket and put it in the range. 'Mrs Bridges' children wouldn't say you did it if you didn't.'

'They don't like me anymore. They think I'm Mr Buchanan's pet.'

Mum turned from the stove and looked sternly down at me. 'Lindsay, you are not telling the truth.'

I stared back at her and suddenly spat out, 'I saw Dad and Joan doing it in the thistles.'

I ran from the house. I ran all the way down to the acacia tree in the rocks by the dunney, and there I crouched and waited. After a while Mum walked out through the fence and called to me, but I did not move. She came down the slope.

'Nobody believes me,' I complained, weeping.

'That's true, because you do nothing but lie. About your school, about your father. I am getting sick and tired of it.'

'I'm telling the truth.' I stood up to meet Mum's anger and looked her straight in the eye with passion and determination. Determination to be believed.

Mum swept her hair back with a hand. 'Did you break the wax?'

There was silence there in the rocks. Into the silence came the ripple of the river going below my secret cave, the croak of the mopoke in the halfway tree, and the sound of Mrs Cutler relishing her laughter. I had a picture of Brown with his head resting against the flank of Mavis, his favourite Jersey cow, while he milked her.

'Yes.' I could no longer look at her.

'And were you telling the truth about Joan?'

'No.'

She gave me a slap across the head. 'Look at me.'

I looked up and saw in Mum something that I had never seen before. And she was prepared to hit me again.

'They were doing it in the thistles.'

'When?'

'The day Tadao came.'

'Who?'

'The Japs.'

'Did you see them since then?'

'No.'

Mum smoothed the hair back from her eyes again, and looked down towards the flats and the pump. Then she turned and walked back up the slope. I caught her up and walked beside her.

'I'm sorry, Mum. I didn't mean ever to tell.'

'No flowers this year. Only the geraniums.' She broke a piece from the dead hydrangea by the verandah step. Inside she began doing her hair and looking at herself in the full-length mirror. I knew she was off to Mrs Cutler's. Since the fight in the Ritz, Mum had spent almost more time at Mrs Cutler's than at home.

'Can I come?'

She did not reply. She began looking around.

'It's out by the hammock.' I ran for the parasol.

'I won't be long,' she said. I followed her out to the gate. 'Make yourself a jam sandwich. There's fresh butter in the meat safe.'

'Mum, you mustn't tell Dad I told you. He'll break me like a snake.'

She paused. 'I'll keep it a secret. Just between us.'

I watched her go along the path until she was all the way to my quarter-mile marker. Then I went back inside and made myself the jam sandwich.

Dad and Joan came in from the fields together. They weren't arm in arm, but it felt as if they were. Joan immediately began preparing the dinner. Betty flitted in and out of the room, chattering with Joan. Dad took his place at the head of the table, and I sat in Mum's chair, studying *Collins' World Atlas*. Mum's absence was heavy in the air.

The wireless had been left running in the Landgirls' room.

'You're wasting the battery,' I said to Betty.

'Oops,' she said. 'Run and turn it off, there's a good boy.'

'It's your wireless.' I had no intention of leaving Dad with Joan. Ever again. Betty went tum-te-tumming along the verandah, and that was when Mum came home.

She went straight to the stove. She smelled the stew and said, 'It looks good and ready.' I could see that she had been crying, but nobody else seemed to notice.

'I'm going to lie down,' Mum said after she had eaten, and she had eaten very little.

Dad raised his eyes from his reading and stared. It was the first time that night he had even looked at her. Mum never went to lie down after dinner.

Mum refused an offer of Aspros from Betty, who was as bright and helpful as ever and seemed completely unaware that there was a terrible tension in the room. As Mum went by me she paused and said, 'You've had a busy day. I want you to go to bed early and get a good sleep.'

I glanced up at her and caught a look of iron.

The light was fading fast. Heather went to her room to study. Dad put away the Bible and lit the Aladdin lamp. After settling himself at the table, he took a figurine out of his pouch and began to sandpaper it.

I couldn't believe how long Joan and Betty took to do the dishes. I sat at the table reading Ernest Thompson Seton's story about the timber wolves, determined to outwait them. I dozed off and was awakened by Betty's voice.

'Good night, Mr Armstrong.' She put her hands behind her head and gave a friendly sway. She had big elbows and they were always red. I felt a peculiar pang of guilt. Betty was nice. Telling on Joan meant that Betty would suffer too. But then again, she and Joan had been friends ever since kindergarten. Betty had to be in league.

'Good night, Jack,' said Joan. She was cooing. To me she said sharply, 'You heard your mum. Go to bed.'

I won't have to take orders from you anymore, I said to myself, casting a cold eye at her cleavage. I could tell from the way she looked at Dad that they were doing it in the thistles all the time.

'I'll water the beans first thing after breakfast, Jack.'

'What would I do without you, Joan.'

Dad even gave a smile.

I watched him through my fingers. We were alone with the ticking of the clocks. The mantelpiece clock struck the quarter-hour. It was nine-fifteen. Dad put the little figurine down on the table. There was no mistaking what it was. It was Heather in school uniform with her suitcase and Panama hat.

'What do you think?' Dad asked after a while.

I didn't say anything, but he waited. I waited in turn. Despite my secret treachery, I wanted a sign of love and affection.

'Well?'

'It's all right,' I said begrudgingly. 'She wears her plaits up now.' I had one of those sudden recollections from the days when Dad liked me. I was lying between his legs on the Stour. We were on cushions in a punt on a spring day, and we were watching Mum with the pole.

'Don't tell Heather,' he said. 'It's for her birthday.'

Despair replaced the memory. Oh, why had I told Mum about Joan?

The sound of the wireless started up in the Landgirls' room. Dad rose and headed for the front door. He's going to their room, I thought wildly. He's going to dance cheek-to-cheek with Joan.

When he got to the front door, however, he reached up for the shotgun. From the shoebox he took the Adler's Grease and a rag, and then settled down at the table once more.

I knew the gun wasn't loaded, but I swear he had the barrels pointed right at me. I cowered, and my head suddenly filled with the sound of the explosion. I had dropped the gun. I remembered I had dropped the gun.

I got up from the table and backed away. I would go to bed and pull the sheet over my head.

I stood at the door to the corridor for a long time. Then I felt the question rushing out, and there was nothing I could do about it.

'Dad,' I said loudly. 'What did I do to Granddad?' He did not look up. His face was red in the lamplight and his hair was sticking up in untidy spikes. 'How did I kill Granddad?' My voice rose to a shriek.

'Lindsay?' came Mum's voice from the bedroom. 'Is that you?'

Dad's fingers flew with the rag over the fittings. His mind was far away. It wasn't even Dad. It was a stranger in the house. Or else he had gone deaf. Or none so deaf as those that don't want to listen, as Mr Buchanan always said.

'I told Mum about Joan,' I shouted, 'and I don't care.'

I ran from the room straight into Mum's arms. She was in her nightgown.

'What have you and your father been up to?'

'Dad told Mr Buchanan I killed Granddad.' I struggled to get away from her. 'Did I?'

Mum held me in a tight grip. She looked down the corridor towards the living room. 'How dare he,' she said in a low voice. 'Go to bed. And make sure you sleep.' She gave me a little push away and said, 'It was just like you remembered. And don't you forget it. Of course you didn't kill Granddad.'

17

I WOKE AT DAWN to the caroling of the magpies. I stretched under the sheet and gazed at the deep red streaks above the horizon. The clouds floated like fuzzy pillows all the way to the top of the sky.

'Red in the morning, sailor's warning, red at night, shepherd's delight,' I chanted.

There was a strong smell of carbolic and I turned to the door. It was Joan with a steaming cup of tea. I sat up in alarm.

'I'm your mum this morning.' She sat down heavily on the bed and the springs gave a creak. She sent me a cluck of a kiss and gave her crooked grin. Her hair was wrapped in a towel and she was wearing Dad's dressing gown over her pyjamas. A large glass pendant hung down between her tits.

'Present from Bruce,' she said, when she saw me staring, and gave me a quick flash of one of her nipples.

There was something fishy going on. I wasn't going to take a single sip of her tea. 'Put it there,' I said, indicating the chest of drawers. 'I have to get dressed.'

'Don't mind me,' said Joan, leaning forward to brush the hair out of my eyes. 'I got little brothers.' I shrank back and pulled the sheet up.

At that moment the wireless began to play very loudly.

'Blow!' Joan exclaimed, getting up. 'She'll wake the whole house.'

As she was leaving she turned and said invitingly, 'When you're ready, come and have breakfast.' She put one hand on her hip and reached up along the door frame with the other. The other nipple flashed. 'Scrambled eggs.'

My first wild thought was that Mum had run away to the dairy, but this was replaced by something more reasonable.

'He's got her tied up in the bedroom,' I muttered to myself. I pulled on my pants and ran into the corridor. Their door was shut. I listened but heard nothing. I desperately wanted to burst in, but I needed an excuse. I ran to my room and came back with the cup of tea. I was just about to knock when Heather came through her door.

'What are you up to?'

'I made Mum a cup of tea.'

'Liar. Anyway, can't you see they're sleeping in.'

She stared me down. I saw that she had an empty cup of Joan's tea in her hand, and I suddenly felt foolish.

'They're not sleeping in. They're fighting.'

'What about?'

'You're so busy reading Tolstoy you don't know anything about anything.'

Heather was all set to give me a slap, but Joan's voice calling us to breakfast came from the living room.

I had no intention of eating any breakfast cooked by Joan, but I was able to resist only the porridge. The scrambled eggs were delicious. I was still sitting alone at the table fifteen minutes later when Mum came in.

'I couldn't find the sugar,' I said, so glad to see her. 'Did we run out of coupons?'

'We eat too much sugar. Brown will bring us up a little honey. But you must remember there's a drought.'

'It's going to rain today, the clouds were red. So was the sun.'

She shook her head. 'Another false alarm. Did you wash?'

'No.'

'Use my water.'

Heather came rushing in. 'I'm late, I'm late!' she cried. She could not afford to miss the train. It was the only one and would not wait at the siding.

'Have you had breakfast?'

'Joan made breakfast, so there.' And she was off.

'Good luck with your exams,' Mum shouted after her, but the door banged and she did not answer. 'That girl!'

Mum went slowly to the mirror, smoothed her face, and then adjusted her skirt.

'Are you tired, Mum?' It looked as though she had been up all night.

'A little.' She came back to the table, sat down, and rested her head in her hands. I poured her a cup of tea. I wanted to help her deal with Dad and Joan.

'Is Joan – ' I began.

'Be quiet.' Suddenly coming to life, she reached into the big pocket in the front of her skirt and pulled out an envelope. 'I've written a note for Mr Buchanan.'

'I don't need a note,' I said firmly. Overnight I had grown up a bit. I had accepted the truth about the wax and got away with it. I had discovered the pleasure of virtue. 'I'm going to apologize and fix it.'

'That's a good boy, but give it to him anyway. You don't have to say anything.' She looked over at the grandfather clock. 'It's time you were off. Here's your stick.'

The stick was to ward off Gus the magpie. He had been more ferocious this summer than ever before.

'I'm going to write a story about the wax,' I said, trying to delay my departure.

'Don't forget that note.' Mum poured herself another cup of tea.

'Can I go to Jimmy's place after school?'

'I thought you and Jimmy didn't like each other any more?'

We didn't, but my passion for Jennifer was too much of an embarrassment to be open about.

'Your sandwiches are in your satchel.'

I sat obstinately at the table.

'Why did Dad lie about – '

'Oh, get off with you!' she shouted. 'You'll be late. I have to deal with those Landgirls.' I found myself leaving for school fifteen minutes early.

As I went down the back corridor I saw that Dad was still in bed. His knees were drawn up and he had the sheet pulled over his head. I stood and stared at this unusual sight.

He's had to hide, I said to myself. He's scared to come out and deal with life. For a moment I felt like rushing in with my stick and rousting him from his cover. The sound of the wireless came from the Landgirls' room.

If Joan goes, more vegetables will die, I thought, and she'll take the wireless. It was a most unfortunate situation. I gave a deep sigh and went straight to my stones. I sat down, took off my shoes and socks, and put them in my satchel. Then, with a glance back at the farmhouse, I opened up the envelope.

Dear Mr Buchanan,

Lindsay has told me the story of what happened with the wax and he is very sorry for any damage caused. He did not realize the seriousness of what he was doing, and frankly, neither do I. His father has dealt with him and I think he has been punished enough. I was shocked at how upset Lindsay was. It seemed out of all proportion to what happened. Is something going wrong? I would like to talk to you about his progress. And please don't ever discuss his grandfather with him. We have put that all behind us.

Yours truly,
Mrs (Lillian) Armstrong

I was admiring the fluidity of Mum's handwriting when there was a familiar flap of wings, *clack*, and up went my stick, too late. My hat went flying, but Gus had mistimed his attack slightly and failed to draw blood. A brush with his wing was all I suffered. I placed the envelope under the centre stone, folded the letter, and put it back in my satchel. Gus kept circling and twice he almost got me, but I chased him off both times.

'Get away!' I shouted. 'Don't you know when you're beaten?' I thought for a second that he did, for he suddenly left me and went flying swiftly off across the field. But it wasn't knowledge, just easier prey. A lone bird – it looked like a kookaburra, straying from its river haunts – was crossing his territory and heading, like me, in the direction of the school. Gus's new Gertie joined him in the chase. They began forcing the kookaburra lower and lower.

'Stop it!' I yelled, sprinting as hard as I could. When it got right down to it, I preferred kookaburras to magpies. Never had my field seemed so vast. Long before I got there, the kookaburra was on its back, its wings flapping feebly. The magpies were pecking away so intently that I was right on top of them before they realized it. All three birds were silent. I yelled and kicked, I raised my stick and could have killed Gus with a single swipe, but I restrained myself. The magpies flew away.

The kookaburra lay on its back, quite still. I had come too late. Its breast was bloody and both its eyes were hanging from their sockets. I looked around. Gertie had flown back to the nest, but Gus was wiping his beak on a fence post. I ran at him with my stick. I thought of all I had done to protect him from everyone. 'Murderer!' I shouted in a rage, but Gus flew off. He didn't care.

I wanted to show Mr Buchanan the terrible thing that had happened to the kookaburra. I had to tell him how hard I tried to help. I was a saviour, not a killer. Gingerly I picked the dead bird up by its feet and put it in my satchel.

School had already started. Mr Buchanan was playing the piano from inside the open door while everyone sang 'Advance Australia Fair' under the acacia tree. I went quietly to my place in the line and sang away but was unable to think of anything but the dead bird. We did exercises on the spot and marched several times around the playground, and I completely forgot about Mum's note. When the first lesson began, I sat next to Jennifer and waited for a chance to show Mr Buchanan the bird. Almost at once he came and leaned over me.

'Come outside. The wax.'

'Oh, I've got a note.'

We went out on to the verandah. The note was smeared with blood. 'It's this kookaburra,' I said, pulling the bird out of my satchel.

'Just a minute,' he said absently.

'I know how to fix the wax.' I noticed that Mr Buchanan had cleaned himself up since the day before.

After he had finished reading he said, 'I expected a prolonged tantrum.' He stared at me in his quizzical way and I knew he was just bursting to know what had happened at home. He looked at the bird. 'What's this all about?'

'It's a little one. It had only just learned to fly.' I told Mr Buchanan the story.

'It was out of its territory,' he said, blowing smoke out of his nose. 'You know what birds are like. It's a savage world out there.'

'I'm going to bury it under my centre stone.'

'Good idea.' Noise was rising from inside the door. 'Let's get back in there.'

'Dad's going to kill me,' I said calmly, 'just like Gus killed the kookaburra.'

'Kill you?' queried Mr Buchanan. I could see that I had startled him. 'If you think about that for a while, you will realize it's a lot of nonsense.' He paused. 'It's a good story, the kookaburra. I want you to write about it for composition this morning. Try and get everything in.'

Mr Buchanan held the door open for me.

'And if you want to work your dad into it, that's OK. Say what ever you like. Look fear right in the eye. That's our new motto, right?'

I looked straight up at Mr Buchanan and said, 'I dropped the gun, sir, but I didn't kill Granddad. Mum said.'

Mr Buchanan's gaze slid over my head to the classroom. I turned. Everyone was staring at us, but my eyes met those of Jennifer, waiting there vibrantly.

'You didn't, eh?' Mr Buchanan gave his black eye a feel and grinned down at me. 'Well, perhaps what we all need is a little more love in our lives. You may remain with Jennifer in the back row for the time being.'

That afternoon, after school, Jennifer and I were galloping towards the river on Bones, her gelding, when we saw Dad's truck coming down the drive from the farmhouse. 'Don't stop,' I said, my arms tight around her wiry frame, but Jennifer pulled over to let it go by. Dad, grim-faced, was at the wheel, and beside him were the Landgirls, in uniform. Their kitbags and luggage were in the back. As the truck turned slowly into the road, I looked hard for the wireless.

Joan stuck her head out the window and yelled, 'You little snitch.' (When I got home, I found she had scrawled the same thing in lipstick across my wall.)

'Joan!' came Betty's remonstrating voice. 'Good-bye, Lindsay.'

I hated being called a snitch, even by Joan, and went a bit red. I buried my face in Jennifer's hair. 'I don't care, I don't,' I kept repeating to myself.

'Somebody had to snitch,' said Jennifer consolingly.

I watched the truck disappear into the dust, and that was the last I ever saw or heard of the Landgirls.

18

THE CHERRY PICKING was Brown's idea. His mother lived on a cherry orchard on the slopes of Mount Canobolas and badly needed pickers. Mum jumped at the opportunity of making a little money, and when Dad refused to come along, even though Slow George and Auntie Annabel offered to do the watering, she had no trouble persuading the Cutlers to accompany us.

'Anything to get out of Billarooby,' Mrs Cutler said. I'm beginning to think my days here are numbered.'

For his knife-pulling in the Ritz, Eddie Larguili had been carted off in the paddy wagon and sentenced to ninety days' detention back at the prisoner of war camp. He would not be allowed out to work again on a farm. Mrs Cutler had been outraged, but her protests were ignored. The replacement that she eventually obtained, Leonardo Bacci, lasted only a week. I heard that he and Mrs Cutler could not come to a satisfactory arrangement and he requested a transfer to a less emotionally demanding farm. Her third application was summarily turned down, and Mr Mac-Adams, when asked to use his influence on her behalf, refused.

'If she had put in an occasional appearance at MacAdams' woolshed,' I overhead Slow George saying, 'her luck might not have run out.'

'A respectable woman doesn't need that kind of luck,' Auntie Annabel had replied.

It was what happened the night before we left for the orchard that put me in such a bad mood, I suppose.

It had been my fault. December that year was one of the hottest on record, and we took all the beds outside for coolness' sake. Mum and Dad had the mosquito netting hooked up to the pepper tree in the front yard, and Heather and I were out on the side verandah.

I was awakened by what I thought at first was a row between Mum and Dad.

Things had not been easy since the Landgirls' departure. Dad blamed Mum for the withering of the beans and peas, although it was the heat wave that caused it, not the fact that we could not get water to them. It was so hot that even the dockweeds were dying. Dad had accused Mum of running about with Brown. She had said that that was nonsense, but that if Dad didn't end his association with Mr Kelly and the Bush Brigade, she didn't see how they had a future together.

Dad's voice was coming from the front yard, loud and fierce. I should have rolled over and gone back to sleep. I knew by now what they were up to, but it went on and on, and then Mum began shouting, 'No, Jack, no, it's too much. No!' Even Heather began stirring in her sleep. I could contain myself no longer. I convinced myself that Mum needed help, and I got out of bed and went along the verandah towards the pepper tree.

There was a haze over the sky, and the night was dark, but Mum, I was sure it was Mum, had left the bed and was running towards the house. Dad was following. 'Come back, Lillian. It has happened. It has been granted. I feel it, I know it. Let's kneel and thank the Lord. A miracle this night.'

Mum had no clothes on. Neither had Dad. I was so shocked I was unable to move. Mum was almost on top of me before she saw me. She almost died, and tried to cover herself up all ways with her hands. 'Get back to bed, how dare you.' She rushed at me, grabbed my shoulders and spun me around. A great shove sent me stumbling back towards the side verandah. I couldn't get away quickly enough. I didn't even stop at my bed. I ran into the back yard and climbed through the barbed wire and out into my paddock.

Mum had said that Dad did not know everything about these matters, and I knew I was now twelve years old going on thirteen, but the unexpected way it all happened set me off again.

I don't want Mum to have a baby, I thought to myself. It'll be just the excuse he needs to really get rid of me.

I moved across the bare earth, scarcely knowing what I was up to. I found myself headed for the evil Gus's yellow box tree and veered away. Maybe if I sat on my centre stone I would feel better. The haze was clearing and the sky was full of stars. My stones gleamed from a long way off. Sheep and lambs grazed in the paddock, and their whiteness gleamed just like the stones. I walked forward until I was quite close to the first ewe. She stopped and looked up at me, chewing slowly, and then looked over at the other sheep. The whole flock stopped, considered me, and then, as a single mind, moved away across the paddock. Every few seconds they paused to look back, and I had the strangest feeling that I was to follow them, these sheep. And in my blue striped pyjamas, I did. They moved more and more slowly until I was among them. They no longer retreated but were on all sides, protecting me, calming me. They gave off a beautiful smell. Then I found that I had been led to my circle of stones. I began both to cry and to sing.

> 'While shepherds watched their flocks by night
> All seated on the ground,
> An angel of the Lord came down,
> And glory shone around . . .'

I sang to the sheep while I looked at the Southern Cross and all the stars. The verse came out of nowhere and went back to nowhere. Then I remembered that Auntie Annabel had been rehearsing it with us for the carol service, and, bumpety-bump, I came back to earth. I dried my eyes.

'Shoo!' I picked up a small stone and threw it. Then another. The sheep scattered towards the road, their hooves thudding softly. The lambs bleated. Dust rose into the hot midnight air.

'Stupid sheep,' I said ungraciously. 'You're no help.'

I left my circle and walked slowly, unwillingly, back to the house.

'Don't forget to wind the clocks.' It was Mum's final reminder as we moved off down the hill. Dad had his arm around Heather and they were waving.

I had no intention of saying good-bye to Dad. I could not even look at him. At the last second, as the lorry went round the outcrop, I relented and called out a good-bye to both of them. I don't know whether they heard or not. As for Heather, I was more sorry than glad she had decided not to come.

'I don't know what's the matter with him,' I heard Mum say in response to Mrs Cutler's enquiry when we went by to pick her up. 'He's been excited for days about the trip and now it's here he's miserable.' I lay curled up in a ball in a corner on one of the mattresses in the back of the lorry, made even more miserable by Mum's lie.

'I feel exactly how he looks,' said Mrs Cutler as she took her seat in the front with Brown and Mum.

The hot wind rushed by the canvas canopy that Brown had constructed to protect us from the sun. Jennifer did not leave me to my depression for long. She offered boiled lollies, chewing gum, and orange crush cordial and tried to engage me in conversation.

'Mother says your dad will be the death of your mum.'

I said nothing.

'Mother told her to leave him before it's too late.'

'But they're married.'

'In a case like this, when he's drunk all the time, it doesn't matter.'

Jennifer made loud sucking noises on her lolly and pulled funny faces. I couldn't help smiling, and my mood began to change. I was running away for good. I would live with Jennifer on the cherry orchard in the mountains. Dad would go down the drain with Mr Kelly, and Mum would have to come and live in the mountains too, with Brown. I sat up and watched the landscape go by. It was flat and grey, coated with dust, just like Billarooby. By the time we reached Cudal, however, and stopped for something to eat, the sense of desolation had gone. The foothills of Mount Canobolas rose ahead of us, replacing the grey with green and a haze of blue.

'I'm quite cheerful now,' I announced. I made eyes at Jennifer, but with Jimmy looking on, she pouted. I tried touching her secretly with my foot, but she bit it, and instead, as we wound ever higher along the dirt road through the hills, she started us singing – songs that we had learned at school, and others that I had never heard before, like 'On Top of Old Smoky,' 'Good Night, Irene,' 'Philadelphia Lawyer,' and 'Charlotte the Harlot.'

'I can't believe you don't know "Mairzey Doates and Dozey Doates",' said Jennifer.

There was the broad summit of Mount Canobolas ahead, clad in snow gum and pine, there was Brown's arm reaching out of the cabin to feel the air, there was Mum laughing with Mrs Cutler in the front, and Jennifer was starting Jimmy and me up on another song. I felt for the first time that I had really escaped from Dad, that a terrible weight had been lifted.

> 'Ah poor bird,
> Take thy flight,
> Far above the sorrows,
> Of this sad night.'

We sat on the mattresses singing this round for ten minutes, like a dirge at first, and then faster and faster until we were giggling and all in a heap, wrestling as we sang.

The sign at the orchard gate read 'TOORAGA.' When we pulled up outside the house, an enormous woman came out on to the brick porch and called, 'Hey, Artie.'

Brown kissed her on the cheek and said, 'Hullo, Mum.'

It gave me a thrill to hear him say it. When Brown's mother left Slow George in the big drought of '27–'28, she had come here, and had lived with Norm Haygate ever since. She was known as Meg Haygate. Brown's real name was Arthur.

'Even looks like an Arthur,' said Mrs Cutler.

'I knew his name was Arthur,' said Mum tartly.

We were all sitting around in the kitchen, having a cup of tea and getting acquainted, when Mr Haygate came in.

Mr Haygate was compact and wiry, with a neat grey crewcut and an evenly lined face. Mrs Haygate had the large, comfortable, housewifely look that Mum always avoided and commented on critically in others. Both of them moved about very quickly. 'I can see why she left Slow George,' I said to Mum that night.

'How's your dad?' asked Mr Haygate.

'Gets around,' said Brown, and they both laughed.

'Gradually,' said Mrs Haygate, and they laughed again.

'Still no rain?'

'Roof's leaking pretty bad,' said Brown. He grinned. 'It's pretty crook. Dad's cut way back. At this rate, be back to droving.'

'How's your leg?' asked Mrs Haygate.

'Still there.'

'That's the style.'

'What about those Japs you wrote about?' Mr Haygate wanted to know.

Brown looked at Mum. 'We got a real problem there. If you believe what they're saying in the pub, they're going to escape and God knows what. Billarooby's bit too close for comfort.'

'Another reason to leave,' said Mrs Cutler.

'The Japs are going to capture the camp,' I said, 'and regain their pride. It's no reason to leave. They will use the camp as a base and then rejoin their Emperor.'

Mr Haygate wanted to know whose side I was on.

Mr Haygate took some time off to show us the house, which was very different from anything in Billarooby. It was made of dark red brick. The mortar was mauve and the roof was of orange tiles. There was a telephone, hot and cold running water, an electric iron, a refrigerator, and a toaster. Billarooby was two hundred miles away, and I felt I had entered a new world. We had come from 'way out there,' as Mr Haygate kept saying.

Out in the back gardens, Mr Haygate proudly showed us his raspberry canes, which he said were much more difficult to grow than cherries. Beyond the raspberries were chickens, turkeys, and geese, and beyond that a tennis court.

'Thinking of a swimming pool,' he went on, 'but we have water restrictions now. So little rain.'

'Our vegetables are all going to die. Except the lettuces.'

'That's what you get, way out there.'

We had cherry pie for tea that evening. Afterwards, we sat in the lounge room, which had a large three-piece lounge suite covered in cream-coloured plush into which Jennifer and I sank almost out of sight. There was a thick purple wall-to-wall carpet and a chandelier in the shape of pink seashells which hung from a fancy moulding that Mr Haygate had plastered himself. Everything about the house was new. 'I like to be modern and up-to-date,' said Mr Haygate. He played records by Beniamino Gigli and Duke Ellington for us on his gramophone.

'We could be happy here,' said Jennifer.

We began picking cherries right after breakfast the next morning. The mountain air was hot, but a clean, crisp wind blew from the east, and the cherry trees, stretching in every direction, looked fresh and brightly green, without a trace of dust.

You had to work hard to make it pay, said Brown, and I did, although never having been paid to work before, I was pleased with whatever I got. There were Black Margarets, which were a rich, dark red, and White Margarets, which were pink and yellow. The blacks were so sweet they were irresistible. We ate steadily the whole of the first day and had the runs all the next. Jennifer, Jimmy, and I shared a ladder and worked on trees together. At the end of that first morning Mr Haygate came round and was very angry. He had shown us at the beginning of the day how to pick the cherries, to twist with thumb and forefinger the stalks from the spurs. The spurs were the part of the tree, he said, from which the next year's crop would grow. The ploughed ground beneath our tree was littered with spurs as well as cherry stones. It was Jimmy who had been so careless, and when Mr Haygate moved on to another group of pickers, we let him have it.

'I don't have to pick cherries,' said Jimmy. 'We get our money from England.' He was on a branch above me and spat a mouthful of cherry stones into my face.

'If you're not going to be nice to Lindsay, I'm going to push you out of the tree,' said Jennifer.

It was up and down the ladder a thousand times a day. We learned how to pick like the professionals, tying billy cans to our waists and using both hands. My memories of that happy, hard-working time were of heads and hats and sunbrowned shoulders poking through the leaves, of men whistling and of conversations shouted from tree to tree, of ladders crooked and precarious in the rough ground, of cherry-filled kerosene tins in the shade, of sunlight glinting off them as they were carried to the packing sheds near the road.

'Halcyon days,' said Mum. I looked the word up in Mr Haygate's dictionary and found that it came from a legendary bird who nested on the ocean and calmed the waves.

Mum worked busily in a big straw hat and cotton gloves in the company of Mrs Cutler, who didn't bother with a hat and hardly worked at all. She took frequent rests and smoked lots of cigarettes in the shade. Mr Haygate wondered politely if she really needed her ladder. If her whole day was a smoko, he might have more use for it with someone else.

Brown worked in the packing sheds and as handyman for the carters. Twice I accompanied him in one of the lorries on the long, tortuous drive down the slopes. We stopped at other orchards on the way until the lorry was completely filled.

'Glad to get outta the place,' said Brown confidentially to me on the second of these occasions. We were sitting on the asphalt pavement outside of the Railway Hotel with the carter. They were drinking beer and Brown had bought me a sarsaparilla. I felt very grown-up sitting there and pictured myself drinking beer with Brown back at the Prince William, until I remembered that I was never going back.

'Why?' I asked.

'Mum's giving me the bloody willies.'

Mrs Haygate's favourite time was after dinner, when everyone else was tired. Then she was at her merriest, keeping the tea and the beer flowing. She handed round fruitcake, cherry tart, and biscuits. I found her a very racy talker.

'These two here are spoken for,' Mrs Haygate said, waving her plump hand at Mum and Mrs Cutler, 'but don't let that cramp your style, make a move, Artie, make a move. Don't be so old-fashioned. Whisk them off to that property of yours down on the Nepean. I don't know what's come over you, Artie. You used to be fast on the draw. What happened to the Driscoll girl you were sweet on in Wudgie?'

'The Driscolls moved away, Mum,' said Brown sheepishly. He stroked his moustache and sat with his knees far apart on the sofa. Mum exchanged a look of sympathy with him. Mrs Cutler yawned.

'What about those MacAdams girls? They must be growing up by now. Get yourself a grazier's daughter. Lorraine must be quite a young lady by now.'

'Mum, Lorraine's only sixteen.'

'Sweet sixteen. Perfect age. Propose.'

Mr Haygate said, 'The saturation bombing in the Ruhr Valley means the end of Hitler.'

'You English types all stick together. You got a Pommie sheila socked away for young Artie here?' Mrs Haygate shook crumbs out of her orange housegown and her dark eyes twinkled as she waited for a reply. Brown put his bad leg up on a stool.

'Hitler's never been the same since Stalingrad. If the Russians . . .'

Mr Haygate kept his music going and never paid any attention to his wife's prattle. He interrupted her whenever he could and liked to talk about the war in Europe. He didn't like the Yanks or the policies of Mr Curtin, the Australian Prime Minister. He didn't think we needed Mr Dedman's austerities anymore, with everything going so well on all fronts. He listened with interest to all the advantages Brown outlined of Wudgie, with its access to cigarettes, petrol, liquor, sweets, and cheap labour. 'Sounds like Wudgewunda's making a mint out of the war.' I found Mr Haygate very urbane and would have liked to converse with him more.

'What have you done with your life, Artie? You going to milk cows for George for the rest of your days? Time you got out of Billarooby. Boy of your particular talents. What's wrong with Lillian here? She's got eyes for you.'

Mrs Haygate kicked her slippers into the air and laughed. The calves of her legs quivered like blancmanges. She gave Brown's muscles a squeeze, tickled his temples, ruffled his hair.

I heard Mum telling Mrs Cutler that Brown's mother was treating him like the boy he was when she left Billarooby fifteen years before, when Brown and his brother opted to stay with Slow George rather than follow her to the slopes of Mount Canobolas to live among the cherry trees.

'She seems to have made a very satisfactory new life for herself.'

'It can be done, my dear Lillian.'

It was at Tooraga that I first started to hear the word 'randy' used a lot. Mr and Mrs Haygate were a 'randy couple,' and when Jennifer complained to Mrs Cutler about Jimmy bothering us all the time, she said he was a 'randy little pest.'

'He's feeling left out,' Mrs Cutler went on. 'Try and include him in your activities. I don't want to have to wallop him.'

My first great moment with Jennifer came after work out by the raspberry bushes. We were alone, and I was aching to kiss her. Jennifer had blue eyes and large white teeth. Her lips were dusky red, and her skin had taken to the Australian sun in a way that the Armstrong family's had not. It was a golden brown. Her hair was slightly frizzled and untidy, like her mother's, and was tow-coloured, almost as white as mine.

My desire increased. I had never before found anyone so beautiful. I even saw how to do it. I took a step forward and went up on my toes, but something stopped me. My hands remained behind my back, and I trembled and sweated.

Jennifer's lips parted in anticipation. 'I know you didn't break the wax,' she said encouragingly. I swayed forward.

'Don't you want to kiss me?' she demanded, and lifted her smock. She had nothing on underneath, and I stared and stared. When I looked up again, she leaned down abruptly and kissed me hard on the lips. There was a click as our teeth touched. It was done, but it was her kiss. I had failed.

There was a shriek of laughter from behind the raspberry bushes and Jimmy rushed out with his pants around his knees and a hard-on. He turned and mooned us.

One evening, after Jimmy had fallen asleep, Jennifer suggested a naked run in the moonlight. We slipped off the back of the lorry, removed our pyjamas, and ran all the way to the packing sheds.

There was Mrs Cutler sitting in front of a tiny fire, just a twig or two, enough to keep the billy on the boil, drinking tea with some of the pickers. A bottle was circulating, and a game of dominoes in progress. Someone was playing a jew's-harp. Our giggles had us running away to the house, where we looked through every window that had a light. In the lounge room Mr and Mrs Haygate were dancing on the rug. 'Ramona, I hear the mission bells a-calling, Ramona . . .' sang Dolores del Rio. Mum sat close to Brown on the lounge. They were looking at a picture book together.

Jennifer slipped her hand in mine, and it frightened me because we had nothing on. 'Doesn't it make you want to live with me for ever and ever?' asked Jennifer. We walked decorously back to the truck and went to sleep with Jimmy between us.

One afternoon Brown drove us all in the lorry out to a limestone quarry off the Millthorpe Road. The water was deep and clear, turquoise in colour. I had never seen such beautiful water.

'Oh, Mum,' I lamented as I swam about with her, 'do we really have to go back? I want to stay at Mount Canobolas forever.'

'Stop worrying about your father. The holiday will have done us all good, him included.' Mum was treading water. She had her hair in a white rubber bathing cap.

'I'm not going back.'

'Suit yourself. Brown won't mind one less in the lorry.'

'I spoke to Mrs Cutler and she said it's all right if we run away and leave Dad to his own devices.'

'Don't take everything Elsie says so literally. She's a woman of the world.'

Mum splashed me with her feet and swam off towards Brown, before I had a chance to splash back. I gave an 'Oh dear' and floated on my back for a while, looking up at the blue sky. If Mum had met Brown before she'd met Dad, we would be living happily at the dairy and Dad would be the terrible neighbour up on the plateau that we wouldn't have to have anything to do with.

Brown was watching me from the edge with a big smile on his face. Mum climbed out and shook water all over him. Brown held one of the salad sandwiches in front of her mouth, and Mum took a bite.

'What are you going to give me?' Jennifer asked. We were together up a tree near the house – not to pick cherries, just to be up a tree. It was Sunday afternoon. Jimmy was asleep in the back of the lorry. The Margarets had all been picked, Christmas was almost upon us, and we were to leave the next day. Mr Haygate had arranged us all in our working clothes that morning and taken a picture with his box Brownie.

'Give you?' It was an impossible question. I remember looking at her cherry-stained lips. My courage came with a rush, but even as it did she said, 'I insist you seal it with a kiss.'

I hesitated, and saw below, coming from the direction of the house, Mum and Brown. He had left his crutches behind and was favouring his right leg.

'Look.'

'Shh,' said Jennifer. She was right. Ours was a secret love.

'He looks like an abo,' she whispered. Brown's skin had got even darker in the week we had been on the mountain.

'Don't say things like that,' I whispered back, putting my mouth very close to her ear and almost falling out of the tree with the pleasure of it. We looked down. Mum and Brown had stopped at the lone pear tree in the next row. They were considering whether the pears were ripe.

'That one might be,' said Brown, pointing.

'I'll get the ladder,' said Mum. She climbed up. Her skirt billowed in the breeze, and she held it down with one hand while she tested the pear.

'It might be.'

'Pick it anyway,' called up Brown.

'Catch.'

'You too,' he said as she started to descend.

'You'll miss.'

'Trust me.'

Halfway down the ladder Mum jumped, and Brown caught her. Her hat went flying; he staggered and then fell over backwards with her. I gasped, for I thought they must be hurt, but they both began to laugh. Brown lay on the ploughed ground with Mum on top of him. His arms were around her body, and she rested with her face next to his. Neither of them could stop laughing. Then Brown rolled over so that he was on top of Mum. Jennifer began to snigger and then stopped as they sent each other rolling over and over on the ground in each other's arms, until they were almost under our tree. I couldn't believe Mum was letting herself get so dirty. Neither of them seemed to care at all. Mum helped Brown to his feet. Then she put her arms around his neck and gave him a kiss on the lips.

'Oh,' she said once she had done it, 'I take that back. I'm sorry. You're not to take that seriously. I got carried away. Let me go.' She said all these things at once.

'Your kiss is safe with me,' said Brown, looking around.

'Stop it, Brown, someone will see us.'

Mum struggled a bit, and then Brown kissed her right back. That kiss lasted for quite a while.

'Mrs Armstrong,' he said.

'Mr Douglass,' she replied.

Brown let her go, and they dusted off their clothes. Mum shook out her hair and collected her hat. Then they walked off together towards the packing sheds. The pear was left lying on the ground.

'They're in love, just like Mother said.'

'No, they're not, they're just friends. Mum's happy because she's on holiday.'

'They're like us,' said Jennifer.

Our eyes met. I realized that I agreed and the moment came. My heart swelled. I closed my eyes, leaned forward, and planted a big kiss on Jennifer's cherry-stained lips before she had a chance to command me to.

19

No one greeted us as the lorry pulled up in front of the farmhouse late on Wednesday afternoon. Brown tooted the horn. Mum and Dad's big bed still stood outside in the front yard. The hot wind was blowing dust, thistledown, and wood shavings about the yard. Trillions of seeds were on the wing. Planking lay scattered everywhere.

'What's been going on here?' asked Mum, hurrying to get inside.

I took a look at the bed. The sheets trailed in the dirt, and there was a big tear in the netting.

'Heather?' Mum called as she opened the screen door. 'Oh!'

Mum's gasp was so loud, I came running up in alarm. Mum was staring down.

The living room had a floor. Unvarnished and with gaps between the boards, but certainly a floor.

'I can't believe it. Why, after all this time . . .' Mum suddenly turned her head away and closed her eyes.

I didn't understand then why a rich red flush was spreading all over Mum's face and neck. I realize now, of course, that Dad hadn't just put that floor in out of the blue. He was making amends for having had his way with Joan in the thistles.

Mum made a quick recovery. 'Well, about time. What a difference it makes! How nicely the furniture sits.'

'Something's missing,' I said.

'The ceiling's lower,' said Brown.

Mum called for Heather again as she put down her hat and bag. She continued to scan the room. Heather came in from her room yawning and rubbing her eyes.

'The clock!' Mum exclaimed. 'Where's the grandfather clock?'

Heather looked away.

'Where's the animal carpet?' I asked. That was my favourite. It was red and gold, and lions chased lizards across the design.

'Dad had to sell them.'

'They're not his to sell.'

Heather sat there glumly.

'Where's your father?'

Heather did not reply, and Mum gave her a little shake.

'What's the matter? Aren't you glad to see us?'

'Look at all the cherries we brought back,' I said.

'He went down to Mr Kelly's.' Heather began to cry.

I looked at the place where the grandfather clock had stood. I remembered the whirr as it gathered itself for its melodious clang. The pretty pictures in the corners of the face.

Mum put her arms around Heather and gave her a comforting kiss.

'Oh, Mum, why didn't you come back?'

'Didn't you get the telegram?'

We had stayed an extra two days at Mount Canobolas. We had dined in a restaurant in Orange and swum in the quarry again. Jennifer and I had played tennis with Mr Haygate and sworn eternal love. Brown had given Mum a couple of lessons on how to drive the lorry. We hadn't picked any cherries, and it had been a blissful time. Mum said it was the first telegram she had ever sent.

'Mr Kelly was sleeping here. He kept bothering me.' Heather hung her head, and Mum glanced at me.

'Was he helping your father with the floor?'

'That's where Dad got the lumber from. But he didn't have to stay here at night.' Heather began to cry again. 'They played cribbage for money. That man Blue was here too. And old Ernie Williams.'

'Your father playing cards?'

Mum was suddenly alarmed. She sniffed the air. She looked at all the flies around the sink.

'I couldn't do the dishes because there's no water.'

'Of course there's water. The back tank had water.'

'It sprang a leak and we didn't notice.'

'How could you not notice?'

Mum became angry. She went outside and searched the flats for signs of Dad. I pulled a face at Heather and ran out to join Mum. With Brown we checked the tanks and found that they all still had a little water. 'There's no leak,' said Mum. Heather was trailing behind us.

The chooks were standing around their trough with their beaks open, and Rita the Rhode Island Red was lying in a heap behind the henhouse.

'You killed Rita,' I said.

Heather shook her head. 'She died of old age.'

'She died of thirst. All the chooks are thirsty.'

'Dad said not to give them so much,' said Heather, 'and from now on we have to scrub with sand. It's better for the grease.'

Back inside, Mum lifted up Heather's plait and smelled it. 'Your hair hasn't been washed since we left.'

'Dad says we can wash only once a fortnight.'

'Oh, he does, does he?' Mum collapsed into a chair. 'What on earth are we going to do?' She looked at me.

'Let's make a quick cup of tea,' I suggested.

'Always ready with a solution.' It wasn't like Mum to be caustic.

'The Primus blew up,' said Heather, 'when Mr Kelly was . . .'

'My God!' Mum rose out of her chair in a fury. She gave Heather a push. 'I'll talk to you in your room about Mr Kelly later. Get yourself outside and bring in some sticks.' She shook the kettle. 'Sand, too, I suppose. Lindsay, go and fill this up at the back tank. I'm not going to put up with this nonsense a second longer.'

Dad returned just before dark. By then we had swept the new floor, washed the dishes, and got rid of the flies and the red-back spiders under the table and chairs. Mum had changed the sheets on the bed and repaired the netting.

I kept my distance from Dad but found it hard to take my eyes off him. His dark hair was greasy, like Heather's, and plastered across his forehead. His clothes were a dirty mess, and he stank of sweat and worse. He looked shifty in the way that Mr Kelly often did. His brow seemed permanently knitted, and his eyes would not rest on us. He kept shooting suspicious glances about the room. A blood vessel had burst on the side of his nose, and little veins had spread on his cheek. I wondered if he was ill, and then realized he was very drunk.

Mum made one remark about how he had not shaved since we had left, and then kept busy at the stove. She was preparing a treat – toad in the hole, made with a beef sausage from a butcher in Parkes that we had bought on the way home, and a freshly baked cherry pie with custard. There was a beer, from a brewery in Orange, that Mum had chosen especially for Dad. Mum brought out her best dinner service and the silver candleholders. The linen tablecloth had knife edges from the starch and storage. It was a home-coming celebration.

Dad slurred his way through the Bible-reading, and it wasn't long before he knocked over his beer. The subject of the clock and the carpet was not brought up. I was in suspense the whole time. Mum said how pleased she was that Dad had put in the floor. 'Jack, I'm very touched.'

Dad kept running a finger around a hole in the tablecloth and had nothing to say. He looked up darkly a couple of times from under his eyebrows.

'Well,' said Mum as she cleared away the plates, 'you were half starved. The both of you.'

'I bet you didn't cook once,' I said to Heather.

'You were supposed to go down to Auntie Annabel's now and then.' Mum set the teapot down.

'We went on Thursday,' said Heather.

'It's dangerous out there,' Dad blurted out suddenly.

We stared at him.

'At Auntie Annabel's?'

'Outside.'

I knew what he meant. My heart gave a thud.

'One of the Colonel's men was murdered.'

Mum gasped.

'A Japanese officer escaped while you were away. He ambushed a patrol in the hills between here and Glen Hogan. Rolled a boulder right on top of him. The man had a wife and three children.'

'Heather and Gordon ride through there every day.'

'Lieutenant Jenkins shot the Jap. He had been reconnoitring.

There were six different accounts of him staring through windows. It took them three days to catch up with him. The Japs are plotting to take over the whole area. They'll come through here first. Bruce and I intend to take measures to protect us all.'

Dad shouted it all out in a rush, and then seemed to be out of breath. Mum stared at him in disbelief.

'Jack, surely the army has everything under control. Colonel Smith said – '

'Does this sound like control? There are so many, the army doesn't know what to do with them. Ask Bruce. We have information from inside the camp.'

'What does Mr Buchanan say?' Mum always relied on his judgement.

'We drove him away.' Dad gave a kind of laugh that ended in a hiccup.

'What do you mean?'

'Dad and Mr Kelly were teasing him,' said Heather. 'About not being married.'

'What does he say about the Japs?' Mum insisted.

'He's gone away to Sydney until the end of the Christmas holidays.'

'Oh dear God.'

Dad rushed on. He had no interest in what sort of time we had had cherry picking. 'There was an uprising in New Zealand at a Japanese camp. There were more than thirty people killed. We heard it from Buchanan's friend Duffy.'

'There was nothing in the papers. Or on the wireless. Mr Haygate would have known.'

'It was suppressed. It's war. The military is keeping us in the dark.'

Dad was up from his chair, pacing the room. Up and down he went, his boots loud on the new floorboards. He refused tea and went to the china cabinet. He took out the whiskey and poured some into a cup.

'I'm not sleeping well,' he said, almost by way of apology, as it went down in a gulp. He poured some more.

We watched him pick up the Bible and turn around a couple of times in confusion. He didn't seem to know where he was for a moment. Then he headed for the couch.

'My clock . . .' Mum began.

'It's done,' he shouted as he flung himself down. 'There's nothing more to be said.'

'Your father gave – '

'Shut up! I'll not have the name of my father mentioned in this house. How else do you think I paid for the floor? You might as well get used to it,' he went on. 'There's more to go. I have a buyer for the other carpet. And the writing desk. I'm telling you now. The bureau.'

'You put in a floor and leave me with nothing to cover it.' Mum's voice rose to a shout. 'I demand to know who is buying my things! Is it Bruce Kelly?'

'I knew they would come in useful one day,' Dad shouted in reply. He got up from the couch and started his pacing again. He left the Bible lying on the floor, something he never did.

Mum darted in front of him, barring his way. 'Jack, who is buying my furniture? I have a right to know.'

'Helen MacAdams.'

'Oh my God!' Mum looked down at the floor. 'However will I face her on Sunday?'

'You don't seem to realize what is going on,' shouted Dad. 'We're going to have to make sacrifices. Sell things. There's a drought.'

'Now you admit there's a drought.'

Suddenly Dad made a dive for the window and climbed out. Even Heather was startled. Dad's boots could be heard stamping heavily along the verandah.

'Stay here,' said Mum, 'I'll deal with this. You've heard enough.'

'We're old enough now,' said Heather. 'You should have heard what Dad and Mr Kelly talked about. Killing.'

Mum went outside. Dad was still on the move. Up and down the verandah he went, almost running.

'Why don't you take that job with MacAdams instead of selling our furniture to his wife?'

'I have a business going with Bruce Kelly.'

'What business? The rest of my furniture for scrap?'

'Rabbits. There's millions of them.'

'And you'll have to catch millions to make any money.'

'Aren't you pleased I put in the floor? I did it for you.'

'Jack, I said I was pleased. Thank you.' Mum's voice grew softer, and she managed to make Dad sit down on the settee.

'You were supposed to come back on Monday. I've been missing you.'

There was a silence for a few moments, and then Mum said, 'Jack, you're a farmer. It would be better to work for MacAdams. It's more dignified.'

'He's laying off men. Henry Bridges is leaving.'

'Oh, no! Not the Bridges! Everyone's leaving. Even Elsie is talking of it.'

'Good riddance.'

'Jack, please, she's my only friend here. I don't know what I'll do if she leaves.'

'That Iti of hers started that fight,' Dad shouted.

'It was no such thing. It was Bruce Kelly and you know it. If he didn't have a few friends in the police force, he would have gone to jail. I will never forgive him for saying that to Brown.'

I heard the settee creak as Mum moved closer to Dad.

'Jack, let me wipe your forehead. You're in a lather.' Mum's voice began again, even more softly. 'I'm angry about the furniture, but I'm sure you did it for the best. I know we have to make sacrifices, but next time I want to be consulted. Be fair.'

I was getting angry myself. It sounded as if Mum was scared of Dad and just saying those things to keep him from flying off the handle again. I was going to get the Cutler twins, break into the MacAdamses' house one night, and steal the clock and the carpet back. If I couldn't bring them here I would take them to my cave . . .

There was the sound of a kiss.

'We brought home a goose for Christmas. It's in with the hens right now. I thought it would be lovely to have a traditional . . .'

Mum had done it again. The crisis was over. Heather went out into the warm night air to join them, and with some reluctance I followed. Mum's hand rested on Dad's brow. Her fingers moved into his thick, dark hair and began to massage his head, something Dad never minded her doing. He had a tight scalp.

'I know where there is just the right tree,' I said. 'I'll take the axe.'

'A Christmas tree?' Mum was doubtful there was such a thing in Billarooby.

'A casuarina. They're like a Christmas tree.'

'I'll cut the paper streamers,' said Heather.

'Lindsay and I made good money at the orchard. We'll have a feast.'

For a few minutes peace was restored on that evening of our return from Mount Canobolas. Heather even asked Dad why he used the window to leave the room.

'We might lose control of the door.'

'Oh,' said Heather.

Dad's reply sounded almost reasonable, but then without warning he threw up his dinner, all over the settee. Twice. The third time, Mum managed to get him to the edge of the verandah.

It wasn't any big deal, Dad vomiting like that, I told myself. It was just Mum's good food after a week of neglect and hard drinking with Mr Kelly. What could you expect? But later, in my room, I began to brood. I decided that Dad's vomiting was a bad omen.

'Why did we ever come back?' I wrote in my exercise book just before I fell asleep. 'The fact that Dad got off to a bad start in life is not the point. We should have run away while we had the chance.'

FOUR
Rabbits

20

THE FIRST THREE WEEKS of the new year were the worst we had ever experienced in Australia. Slow George conceded that he had never been through such a bad spell either, and that included the great drought of '27–'28. The temperature did not drop below ninety, and on eight consecutive days it was over a hundred. Sparrows and willy wagtails dropped dead from the trees. Mr Morrison lost over two hundred of his chooks, and even the Moorellen wheat crop shrivelled up and died.

Mr MacAdams ran scared and gave out the word that he had prevailed upon his old school friend the Bishop of Bathurst to come to Billarooby and lend his considerable weight to the prayers for rain.

It was the end of Dad's vegetables, except for the lettuces. Dad had some special thing about the lettuces, and he saved them by superhuman effort. He pumped by moonlight every night from the only waterhole left from which it was possible to pump, and by dawn had the lettuces all covered up with wet hessian bags.

'Can I help you, Dad?' I asked in the early hours one time as he set off in the dark down the hill. I had been wide awake and sweating for most of the night. He seemed to shy away from my voice, and I followed him as I might have followed some sick animal I had frightened in the bush.

To say he was glad for some company is probably putting it too strongly. The whole time we were pumping and squeezing out the bags he didn't say a word to me, although he muttered a lot under his breath and from time to time would jerk up his head and shout something into the dawn sky. At first I started looking around just in case there was anyone to see Dad acting crazy. Then I started feeling superior because he was mad and I wasn't.

Looking back now, I can see that he was exhorting himself to persevere, and was involved in some kind of desperate dialogue with Granddad.

When we were renewing the bags at noon, he began talking to the lettuces.

'Babes of Christ, oh, my little babes of Christ.'

At one point he knelt in front of the seedling bed with his eyes closed and his hands clasped. He must also have gone on to Mum about them, for I heard her saying in exasperation, 'All right, all right, babes of Christ. Don't let the Bishop hear you talking like that.'

Those hazy, heat-wave days, Mum and Heather could scarcely do any more than lie around gasping for air. It wasn't like Heather to break down, but she was in tears from the way the heat weakened her. When it was too hot to read, Heather was really in trouble. I almost got her down to the Lachlan one day for a wallow in the mud. She set off under Mum's parasol but got only halfway down the hill before she turned back.

Mum was sure this was the big fry and we were already on our way to hell. She threw propriety to the wind and stopped wearing her petticoat, saying, 'I don't care, I'm going to die in comfort.' Mum was almost as shapely up there as Joan and Mrs Cutler, and I couldn't help staring the same way I stared at them.

The scary thing really was that we had hardly any water in the house. What kept us alive was a single tub drawn from the back tank. By the time the heat wave was over, the water was pretty filthy.

'This is ridiculous. We're taking up Elsie's offer,' Mum shouted as she knelt by the tub, giving herself a last sponge before tipping the water into the copper for reboiling.

The Cutlers had offered us water from the old covered stone well behind their house, a well so deep it never ran dry.

'God gave us a river, and I'll take water from nowhere else. I'm not accepting charity from that woman.'

'I'm tired of your high moral tone. It's nothing but stupid pride.'

But the days passed and Dad did nothing. We were getting by on teaspoonfuls. Then one afternoon there was a scuffle out by the sulky. It was Mum refusing Dad's offer to take her to the mudhole below the ford to bathe. As far as she was concerned, that was the last straw, and she stormed down to the dairy under her parasol and arranged with Brown to harness up the dray the very next day.

'I'll do the dray,' said Dad when he found out about Brown.

'Do you swear by Almighty God?'

'I swear on the body of my father, so help me God.'

When we awoke the next morning, there was an unexpected accumulation of heavy clouds in the southern sky. Dad said that his prayers had been answered, it was going to rain, and that he intended to wait. Mum said she had seen those clouds before and there was no point in delaying another second.

By midafternoon the clouds had become low and black, covering the sky from horizon to horizon. The expectant twitter of the finches in the acacias and box-thorn hedge at school could be heard note by note in the oppressive stillness. Dust clung to us like soft gauze as we walked around the playground, and the bull-joe holes and the meat-ant nests were built up in readiness. The excitement was almost too much to bear, and Mr Buchanan let school out early so we could all get home before the downpour.

Jimmy galloped Lasseter, his rig, along the track to the Cutlers', and Jennifer and I followed closely on Bones. It was a race and Jimmy won, but I didn't care. I just wanted to be there for the water transfer from the Black Hole of Calcutta. That's what the Cutlers called the disused well.

The barbed wire and palings had been removed on one side, and our dray had been backed up to the very edge. On the dray were four 55-gallon drums, and Brown was drawing water up with the hand pump. Dad was up on the dray with Mr Kelly, and Mum was standing with Mrs Cutler. I could tell by their folded arms that they were both annoyed Dad had brought Mr Kelly along. Mr Kelly's trousers were almost falling off under his potbelly, his shirt flapping open, showing off all his hair, as usual.

The southwestern sun shone for a moment through a gap in the clouds and cast an ominous glow over the water. I looked in, remembering the baby mice that Jimmy had thrown in there. Goldfish swam through the scum and the lilypads, and floating amid the old tyres, bottles, and cans was something that looked like a dead possum or cat. The skin had rotted away from the mouth, exposing a row of sharp little teeth.

'You mustn't ever, ever, drink this water,' said Mum. 'Everything has to be boiled and boiled again before we use it for anything.'

There was a distant roll of thunder. We all stopped to make sure we had heard it. Then there was a dance of lightning. A bright yellow crevasse opened up beneath the clouds, and a blue electric claw went down into the Glen Hogan hills. It was followed by more thunder.

'It is going to rain, Elsie,' cried Mum, finally convinced. 'Billarooby will be beautiful again. You may change your mind.'

The Cutlers were leaving for the coast at the end of the month to look for a house. Jennifer said if I loved her, I would find a way to be with her.

Dad fell as he climbed up on to the dray. Mr Kelly hoisted him to his feet and got him going again with a little kick in the backside. It was almost as though Dad welcomed such treatment as his due.

'Give me that bottle,' Mum demanded of Mr Kelly.

'Mother's milk,' he said, slapping her hand away as he passed the bottle to Dad up on the dray. Dad took a swig, stared at the ground for a second or two, and then took another.

'Oh, put it down, Jack, and let's get moving,' cried Mum. 'Look how close it's getting.'

I climbed up on to Belinda's neck and hung on to her heavy work collar. Dad brought the whip down to Belinda's rump with a crack that made me flinch. The dray creaked forward. I waved to the Cutlers.

Our progress over the paddock was slow. The dray ploughed through the ant mounds, and Mr Kelly kicked aside my marker stones if they were in the way. By the time we reached our back fence, the storm was upon us. I was counting fewer and fewer seconds between the flashes and the thunder. As I slid down Belinda's neck, I noticed Mum was trembling. Brown told her not to reckon on too much rain, but she insisted that it was a godsend. 'Those clouds are full of water. I can feel it in the air.'

I caught a chook that was frantically trying to get back into the pen. The others had gone to roost, so dark was the sky. Dipper lay deep in the shadows beneath the Landgirls' old room, terrified of the thunder. I crouched near her and listened. It would start with a distant roll, gather power until a crescendo was reached, then climax with a tremendous, earsplitting bang. The lightning stabbed the ground against a background of fading flashes, like great golden-pink sighs.

'It's the beauty and the terror,' I said to Dipper. We all knew Dorothea McKellar's poem by heart. It was one of Mr Buchanan's favourites.

I raced around to the front of the house.

'Heather will have to take shelter,' said Mum. 'I hope she and Gordon have the sense to do that.'

I pictured Heather coming from Wudgewunda – the engine steaming its way through the downpour, the lightning illuminating her face in the rain-washed window of her carriage. I imagined her getting off the train and crawling under the siding, the rain wrecking her straw hat. She'll be soaked, I thought, laughing to myself, and then more soberly I remembered a cold rain one winter afternoon in England a long time ago. I gave a shiver.

Dad did not respond when Mum put an arm around him. 'It's going to be all right, Jack. Rain at last. Can't you smell it?' She shook him. 'Oh, what's the matter with you?'

We watched the clouds of dust billowing over the darkened flats and waited. The storm always seemed to be just there somewhere, rather than here.

Eventually Brown said, 'I've seen buggers like this before. It's a dry.'

As though he had uttered the most terrible blasphemy, there flashed upon us a lightning glare so bright I screamed. My scream was lost in a thunderclap that shook the verandah and rattled my teeth. Suddenly we were in the middle of a vast field of electricity. Heaven and earth were colliding.

'Lillian, we have to go inside,' said Brown from the verandah.

'It's raining,' Mum shouted. 'A drop. Right on my forehead.'

We looked. Water was streaming down her face. The drop must have been the size of a hen's egg. She began to laugh.

'I told you, Brown. It's raining. It's raining!'

But that drop was all there was.

'There will be no inundation today, Mrs Armstrong,' began Mr

Kelly in his flowery tones. 'Forgive me, but in my sad experience of Australian – '

'Shut up with your horrible jargon. It's raining, I tell you.'

Mr Kelly raised his hands, backed away, and went inside. He pushed Dad ahead of him. I sent my fingers in a quick stab of hate at Mr Kelly.

'Quickly, Lillian.' Brown reached for her. I jumped off the verandah and took her hand, but there was something wrong with her. She wanted to stay out in the rain, but there wasn't any. Even the smell of it had gone.

Twin forks skidded across the ground by the orchard. The thunder came in another tremendous explosion. From that moment it was nothing but continuous flashing, roiling, and rumbling. We were surrounded on all sides. Billarooby was under siege.

And then Mum broke away and ran out into the open. I couldn't believe she could be so foolish.

Brown and I both called for her to come back. She ran along the level as far as the shed, and then down the slope to my halfway tree, the pale, stark, splintered shaft going high into the sky, where the lovebirding galahs sat pink and grey in the rays of the setting sun, where the mopoke waited in the night for rodents. She threw herself sideways against the trunk and leaned back, looking up at the storm.

'She's safe. Lightning never strikes the same place twice,' I said. It was true that the tree had been struck before. Its top had been blasted out in a storm long ago, and a charred black scar ran all the way down the trunk to the ground.

'Bullshit,' said Brown. 'Someone's gotta grab her.'

At that moment Dad came out on to the verandah once more.

'She's gonna get herself killed,' called Brown. He and Dad stared at each other. Neither moved, and I saw some terrible thing pass between them. In those days I had no comprehension of such things as adult jealousy. And somehow I never even thought to question Mum's behaviour in the way I was always questioning Dad's. Years later, embellishing the story, I described the terrible thing as some elemental exchange, like the drama between earth and sky all around us.

What I did know was that Dad was frightened to go out into the storm.

'For Christ's sake,' said Brown. He swung off the verandah with his crutches and set off for the front gate.

'I'll go, Brown,' I shouted. 'I'm quicker.'

I passed him in an instant, but then Dad caught up with both of us. He pushed Brown aside, and then me, just outside the gate.

Dad ran. He was not a runner; in fact, I had seen him run only once before – the day Granddad died. Running away! My mind reached for a picture and lost it.

Mum twisted from Dad's first grasp and stumbled farther down the hill. He got her the second time but had to shake her by the shoulders before her resistance collapsed. They both came running back towards the house. Mum's head was down, her hair loose and streaming in the wind, which suddenly caught her dress and blew it up around her face. I saw the bloomers that she wore, white and fastened with elastic just above the knee. By the time they ran through the front gate, they were both choking on the flying dust.

'You saved her, Dad,' I cried.

'Inside,' shouted Brown, and even as the screen door was latched and the wooden one slammed, there was the most dreadful explosion, and then another and another. Some force threw me to the floor and I was sure I had been blown up and had gone to Hades. There was nothing but the harshest crackling noises both inside and outside my head. The room was filled with a most horrible incandescent brown light, and there was the smell of burning metal. The house shook again and again.

'We're hit, we're hit,' Dad kept repeating from under the table, and I think all of us were either shouting or screaming.

The shaking and the rumbling stopped. The smell remained. Mr Kelly remained stretched out on his stomach on the couch. Almost half the crack of his gross bottom showed above his trousers.

Brown called out from the window, 'It's the tree.'

I rose from the floor and ran to join him. The halfway tree was a pillar of fire, a torch held to the dark sky. The sparse dry grass around the base was a bed of flames.

Mum sat at the big table, her shoulders heaving. There were leaves in her hair and her tears made mud of the dust that caked her face. Brown went to sit beside her.

The next flash of lightning was not so bright, the accompanying roll of thunder delayed. The storm was beating a slow retreat, moving off in the direction of Wudgewunda.

Dad and Mr Kelly went outside to deal with the fire. I followed, spitting dirt. We soaked hessian bags in one of the drums and beat at the shreds of burning grass. The wind was in the west and blew the fire away from the shed and house. It wasn't even much of a fire until it reached the thistles.

Then it was a fire, and from that point on, there was nothing much we could do but watch it burn. The fire crackled through the dry thistles with glee, sending a thick blue smoke up into the clearing sky and turning them into a fine black ash in minutes. It galloped through the orchard, scorching the fruit trees, and continued to burn fiercely until it reached the paddy melons, the Patterson's Curse, and the ploughed irrigation area.

A line of trucks turned into our driveway. I could see the Morrisons, the Packmans, and the McCaddies. Mr Buchanan's Morris puttered up behind them. Jimmy and Jennifer came climbing through the back fence, and Mum emerged from the house with Brown. Everyone was gathering to help fight the fire.

It was a fire that Dad did not want fought.

The incineration of the thistles that day meant more to him than the water gathering. The fireball that hit the tree was a miracle. The swift inferno on the hillside and the flats was yet another visitation upon him at the hands of Almighty God, but this time God had smiled upon him. It was a purification by fire.

'Let it burn.' Dad threw his hat into the air, and for the first time that day he emerged from his alcoholic befuddlement and really came alive. He grinned a crazy grin, and his teeth showed white through a mask of soot and dust.

Everyone looked at each other and wondered about Dad.

'Fire,' he shouted, holding out his arms to the blackened hillside. 'Next time it will be flood. A blessing upon me. Thank you, Lord.'

Dad was not in the habit of ever thanking anyone.

'Look out, mate!' shouted Brown.

Mum screamed.

A branch fell from the burning tree and landed in an explosion of fire and sparks no more than a yard from Dad. Smoke and flames shot up all about him, but he didn't even move.

21

IT WAS TOWARDS the end of summer, creeping into autumn, when I found out Mum was going to have a baby.

I remember the occasion only too well. Dad was down on the flats, waiting for the flood, talking to the lettuces, and parading about in his crazy uniform. Shortly after the burning of the thistles, Dad had got himself an old slouch hat with a badge and an emu plume, and a pair of khakis over which he wore a cartridge belt. I was swinging on the knotted rope beneath the pepper tree. Mum came out on to the verandah in her fly veil, carrying some skeins of wool. She sat down on the settee. From the living room came the sound of the wireless, which Dad had bought from Joan the day she left. 'I don't know where he got the money from,' Mum had said, looking me straight in the eye. Mum kept the wireless going all day long. It made her feel safer. When Mr Buchanan had come back from Sydney, he spoke with Sergeant Duffy and then confirmed everything Dad had found out about the camp. The Colonel's dislike of the Japs had escalated, and, said Sergeant Duffy, he was becoming a bit of a Nero. By midday he was intoxicated, and in the afternoons he had taken to riding around inside the camp brandishing his revolver. Occasionally he would fire a shot into the ground near the prisoners' feet. He had requisitioned HQ in Sydney for cattle prods. Sergeant Duffy said that Tadao and the other prisoner who had been at our farmhouse were still in solitary confinement.

'You're not doing anything, Lindsay. Come hold the wool.'

'Get Heather. It's girl's work.'

'If you won't, then I might just have to get another boy to do it.'

'Who?' I knew Jimmy Cutler never would, and the Bridges had

left Billarooby the week before. There had been a party with a
fiddler, and Auntie Annabel had sung 'By the Waters of Minne-
tonka' and 'Gypsy Moon' at the piano. Dave Bridges' father was
going to cut timber up near Dorrigo. There had been rain on the
north coast.

'I might be going to get you a little brother.'

I let go of the rope and walked slowly towards the verandah.
Mum handed me the skein without a word or a smile. I silently
manoeuvred it as she rolled the wool into a ball.

'It made your father so happy when I told him,' Mum went on
calmly. Too calmly.

I looked away down to the flats. She must have told him that
week when Dad started shaving again and singing each morning
out by the water drums. I had thought it was because he was
catching lots of rabbits with Mr Kelly, or because Mrs MacAdams
had asked him to supply lettuces for the big reception she was
planning to hold up at Moorellen after the Bishop of Bathurst
said his prayers for rain.

I looked back at Mum. Dad's good mood hadn't lasted long.
The last few mornings he had been back to his unkempt ways and
his general lurking-in-the-shadows attitude. He was still using the
windows to get in and out of the house, and one day he carried
the full-length mirror into the washroom and bolted himself in
there for a whole afternoon. In my opinion, he had been as mad
as a meat axe ever since the burning of the thistles.

Resentment boiled up inside me.

'When?' I asked finally.

'In the spring.'

'Where is he?'

I wanted to be told. I knew that pups squeezed out of Dipper,
and I had seen the ewes licking the yellow afterbirth from the
lambs. I had seen a calf being born. The question I asked was one
I already knew the answer to. Sort of. I looked at Mum, could see
no signs of it there, and clung to disbelief.

As for the connection with Dad, I did not understand that very
well at all, except that I knew for certain that Mum was having a
baby because of that time when they had no clothes on, under the
pepper tree, the night before we left for the cherry orchard.

I pieced together mysterious snatches of conversation and

events. 'This is no time to have one, my dear,' Mrs Cutler had been saying when I surprised them in the living room. 'One what?' I had asked. I had heard Mum call Dr Abercrombie a quack, and there had been a strange and sudden trip to Dubbo with Mrs Cutler in the Vauxhall Cabriolet, a trip that had not been successful, for some reason. I know now, of course, what it must have been about, but then I was aware only of Mum's distraught state when she got back, which she took great pains to conceal from Dad.

'He's well hidden,' was all she said, handing me another skein. 'It's a secret for now. I don't want you telling anyone. Do you understand?'

'You're so sure it's a boy, aren't you,' I said angrily. 'Even the wool's blue.'

Mum took no notice of me. 'I want you to go down and remind your father that he is taking me to Nurse McCaddie's this afternoon.' Mum changed the tone of her voice and continued, 'When he does his rounds.'

For over a month, Dad had been going round the district on a regular schedule, warning everyone to lock their doors and windows, maintain their booby traps, and generally keep alert in case the Japanese made a move.

'Mr Kelly's bright idea, I presume,' Mum had said.

'Mine!' Dad shouted with a vehemence that put an immediate end to Mum's sarcasm.

'Crackpot,' said Mum, refusing to give in completely.

Billarooby knew from past experience that drought could cause strange turns in a man's life. Mum came in for some chaff over Dad's uniform and the Australian flag he had taken to flying from the back of the sulky, but round and about, Dad was becoming something of a hero. The district rather liked the idea of a crazy Pommie looking out for their welfare, particularly when Dad started using his rounds as a way of selling lettuces. Mr Buchanan said he was tickled pink about what was happening. To him, Dad was an example of someone who had had the wisdom to settle for less, and had been rewarded with more. He said the Southern Cross on Dad's flag should have lettuces substituted for stars.

Day by day, all those brave plans of Mum's that she talked about with Mrs Cutler at Mount Canobolas – about getting out

of Billarooby, about leaving Dad if he didn't mend his ways –
turned to dust, like the farm. She swallowed her pride about
Dad's working for Mr Kelly with the rabbits rather than for Mr
MacAdams with the sheep. There had been a fierce argument
when Mum found out that Ernie Williams, one of Mr Kelly's
gang, was an explosives expert and had been a gunner in the First
World War.

'He's a drover, not a gunner,' Dad had said.

'You'll be killed. What does Kelly care?'

'I do the rounds, Lillian. I just do the rounds.'

As far as I know, that's all Mum ever got out of Dad about the
Bush Brigade and what it meant to him. 'Let him lie, Jack, you
don't have to prove anything – ' but Dad was out the window.
Gradually Mum turned a blind eye to the Brigade.

'We have to dig in. Your father's managing quite well, consid-
ering how bad the drought is. Asserting himself. Your granddad's
spirit seems to be appeased. And *you* haven't been bothered, have
you?' I had to admit that I hadn't been bothered since the trip to
Mount Canobolas. 'I told you a little holiday would work
wonders.'

The end of her dreams had also meant, of course, the dashing
of mine.

'I'm married to your father and that's all there is to it,' she
shouted at me one morning. Her anger made me wish I was much
older, old enough to leave home. The revelation about the baby
explained to me Mum's change of attitude, but I have to confess
that my very first period of disillusionment with my mother began
right then and there.

Out of all my resentments came a demand.

'I'll take the message if I can drive the sulky.'

Mum thought for a moment. 'All right. But only if you can get
Heather to go with you.'

Mum waved gaily from the settee as we set off down the blackened
hillside. There she went again. I couldn't believe what a show she
was putting up. The worse things got, the more she seemed
determined to smile.

When we reached the flats, Heather opened up *Pride and
Prejudice*, her latest discovery, and began to read to me. I was

admiring of her ability to get through book after book, but that day I was in no mood for listening.

'Mum's going to have a baby,' I said.

'I know. You're not to tell Mr Buchanan.'

I hit Belinda hard with the whip, arousing her from her doldrums.

'How can I read if you make her jolt?'

In the distance, through the grey of the heat haze, I could see the shimmering oasis of the lettuces. There were four different varieties — Curly Green, Romaine, Red Oak, and Butter — and they were all doing well. With his successive plantings, Dad managed to keep the prisoner of war camp, and everyone else who wanted them, in continuous supply.

The lettuces were the only green on the flats.

The rabbits laid nightly siege. All around the patch were holes where they were attempting to dig under the netting. There were signs that they were even chewing at the wire itself. One evening when I was returning from a walk, I found the lettuce patch completely surrounded. The rabbits were six deep, pressed up against the wire netting. I raced at them with a stick and they went lolloping back to their burrows. Emboldened by lack of vegetation, they were straying farther and farther from their river haunts and not even waiting for dark.

'Remember last summer,' said Heather, 'how nice everything was?'

My head was filled with black thoughts. I could go down there tonight and cut the wire netting. It would serve Dad right if they got the lettuces. I itched to vent my bad mood on Belinda once more.

Her broad back glistened in the sun. Flies and wasps drank her sweat undisturbed. Her hooves clacked on the iron ground, so hard that Dad couldn't have got a plough into it even if he had wanted to. She plodded past the dried-up ditches, the dead thistles, the dandelions, and came to the paddy melons. The melons were yellow and soft, about the size of cricket balls. They were poisonous and unattractive, even to the rabbits. They were the only vegetation left, unless you counted the salt bush, but Slow George was cutting that all down for his cows.

Heather's voice went on and on. She started another chapter. I could see Dad sitting hunched up inside the wire netting, clutching his shotgun. I had overheard Mrs MacAdams outside the woolshed the previous Sunday, talking about the drought. 'Another one gone,' she said, and she was looking at Dad.

'No one else has any lettuces,' said Heather. 'Dad's done it again.'

A flock of crows crowded into the dead branches of the old apple gum on the far side of what was once the pumpkin field. Suddenly one of them swooped from a branch and descended upon a crow that was picking amid the rotting melons. There was a croak or two, and then they flapped upward and began an aerial fight, right in front of us. Feathers fell. It wasn't much of a racket, but Belinda reared up in fright, gave a high-pitched neigh of terror, and bolted.

I was taken by surprise. 'Whoa!' I shouted, pulling the reins hard. The crows all flew away towards the river, uttering harsh, callous cries.

'Pull harder, stupid,' cried Heather. Nothing I did made the slightest difference. Belinda was well away.

She left the track and careered amid the melons. She came to a ditch and leapt over it. The sulky lurched across, giving an ominous crack. We were thrown sideways and saved ourselves by clinging to the mudguards. Heather began to scream. Belinda's head was held high, and so was her tail. She had to be possessed by a demon. Another ditch. This time we were hurled the other way.

I saw that Belinda was headed for the main irrigation ditch and hauled desperately on the left rein with both hands. There was no way we could survive the big ditch – it was too deep, too wide. Dad must have heard the commotion, for he came out of the lettuce patch and began to run towards us. He was yelling.

'Jump!' I called to Heather as the big ditch loomed.

'We'll be killed!' she screamed.

At that moment, from out of the gum trees by the ford, appeared a rider and horse at full gallop. It was the Colonel. He charged towards us, leapt the stallion over the big ditch, and suddenly was right there, galloping along beside the shafts. He leaned from his saddle, caught Belinda's bridle in his left hand, and began to turn her away from danger and towards the lettuce patch. The sulky veered so sharply it rose on its left side and almost overturned. Belinda, even as we slowed, leapt over one of the smaller ditches. I lost my grip, went hurtling over the top of the huge wheel, and landed smack in the melons. There was a stab of pain, a flash of yellow light, and then nothing.

Brown's moustache appeared in the air, close before my eyes. Then came the rest of him. He was removing pieces of melon from my face. 'Lie still,' he said.

I saw the Colonel high above me on his stallion. Nearby, Dad was holding Belinda. She was sweating and trembling, her head hanging low to the ground. Heather was watching me, *Pride and Prejudice* open in her hand.

'You got concussed,' said Brown.

'Where did you come from?' I asked.

'Does it hurt anywhere?'

I told him about my ear, and my hands, which were rubbed raw from pulling on the reins, and Brown checked me for broken bones.

'Close thing, Mr Armstrong,' said the Colonel. 'She's burst a blood vessel.' Blood was flowing from Belinda's nostrils.

Dad hardly seemed concerned about Belinda's condition. Or mine. He was up to something with the Colonel.

'That was an extraordinary performance,' said Dad, mustering his best English voice.

'Not a bad bit of riding,' said Brown.

'It was nothing,' said the Colonel modestly. 'An old polo player like me.'

Dad was agitated, stroking the neck of the stallion rapidly, as if he had a fever. The Colonel was giving Dad's outfit the once-over.

'Your arrival, Colonel, was little short of a miracle. I feel the good Lord had a hand in it.'

The Colonel, anxious to depart, wheeled his horse around. 'So these are your lettuces. Quite a spread. Wouldn't know we were in the middle of a drought.'

'Here, take one.' Dad had a wet hessian bag full of them to take on his rounds, and threw a huge Romaine to the Colonel, who made a good catch but then did not know what to do with it. He said he wasn't used to carrying vegetables around; he left all that to his staff. Finally he pushed it into his saddlebag.

'The Japs are planning an insurrection,' said Dad.

'My Japs?' The Colonel was taken aback. He wanted to know where Dad had got his information. Dad just said there was talk in the pubs, and he wanted to know what the Colonel was doing about it.

'Is that what this uniform of yours is all about?' the Colonel said, sneering. 'You're one of Kelly's mob, aren't you? Think we can't handle a few Japs. Let me tell you, those yellow devils make a move, we'll cut them down so fast they'll regret the day they were born. I'll see to that. There's no Japs leaving my camp. Except in a box. We've got more barbed wire than sense around the place. You fellows are wasting your time.'

'Desecrate our churches, install heathen ways into our children.' Dad's voice rose. 'Rape our women. My wife was attacked. You know that. They've been out and they'll be out again.'

'Not those two.' The Colonel gave a laugh.

'You'll drive them to it.'

I sat up. 'You've killed them, haven't you?'

'Jack's not all wrong,' said Brown. 'You'd be surprised what people around here know about your camp, Colonel. We've heard stories of weapons. Baseball bats with nails, kitchen knives, razor blades, things like that.'

'We find a few things when we search. We beat the hell out of the whole hut. They don't do it again, believe me. What do you think we are running there? A kindergarten?'

'You're not prepared for war.' Dad had really begun to shout. 'You've got only two old machine guns and half your garrison doesn't have rifles.'

The Colonel shouted right back. About the new rifles he had requisitioned. About how four new Vickers machine guns were arriving at the end of the month. About how starvation rations did wonders for keeping the Japs quiet. They were a bit thick on the ground, but he'd broken their spirit, and he intended to keep them that way.

The Colonel pulled out his flask and took a drink. Dad pulled his out and did the same.

Dad and the Colonel must have yelled at each other for ten

minutes, both so red in the face they seemed about to have apoplexy. The Colonel finally decided he had had enough of it, particularly when it began to look as though Dad was going to get the whip and drive him off his land. As the Colonel backed his stallion away, he told Dad that he was a typical Englishman. Ran away from the war and then wouldn't give the Australian army any credit.

'I don't have to have Japs eating my lettuces,' Dad shouted. 'I can sell my lettuces anywhere.'

'To hell with your lettuces.' The Colonel took the Romaine out of his saddlebag, held it for a second, then dropped it disdainfully on the ground. 'Throw it to the rabbits.'

We watched the Colonel gallop off in the direction of the camp. Brown rolled a cigarette. I could tell Dad was really upset about the Colonel's affront to his lettuce. He picked it up, rinsed off the dust in his tub of water, then carefully put it back in the bag. He took out a plug of tobacco and peeled some off. His hands were shaking so much he almost cut himself with the knife. Chewing was a habit he had picked up from Mr Kelly. Our house now had spittoons, much to Mum's disgust.

'You bent his ear good and proper,' said Brown.

'He's lying.'

'Maybe. But those blokes in the William are pulling your leg, Jack.'

'Nobody pulls my leg.' Dad spat a stream of tobacco juice on to the ground.

'You can't be too careful, Jack. I'm with you there. Keep at the ready. But leave it to the army. The Colonel's a ratbag. He don't really run the place anymore. Brent, the second in command, runs it. Everyone knows that. Brent's a fair dinkum soldier.' Brown looked at Heather and me and changed the subject. 'Belinda's jittery. I'd get that blood cleaned up and give her a good rubdown.'

'We're off,' said Dad.

'Don't drive that sulky, Jack. Axle's cracked, wheel's all skew whiff.'

'Come on, you two, seeing you're down here. It's the Morrisons today, the Packmans, the McCaddies.'

'They should take it easy, mate. Young buggers almost got killed.'

Dad loaded up the lettuces, then climbed into the sulky. 'Watch your language.'

Heather climbed up beside him. I decided to stay with Brown and go with him to the dairy for a glass of cold buttermilk with Auntie Annabel, as he suggested. There would probably be cake.

'I'm not coming on the rounds ever again. I'm hurt and you don't even care. You've made Mum have a baby.'

'Get up here!' Dad roared. Brown motioned me to do as I was told and I climbed up without another word. Just as well. Dad stood up and brought the whip down on Belinda's back with such force that she really got the message about who was in charge, and set off at an unusually brisk pace. The sulky, amazingly, rode pretty well. I kept an eye on the wobbling wheel.

Why aren't you getting along with Brown?' asked Heather.

Dad did not reply, and when I reminded him that he had to go by home and pick up Mum, he told me to mind my own business.

'Dad, you've got to,' said Heather. 'She's waiting.'

Dad took no notice, even of Heather. There was an empty whiskey bottle rolling about on the floor of the sulky that none of us bothered to deal with.

As we went by Mr Buchanan's house, he shouted, 'Not at your post, you old poufter.'

'Dad!' said Heather. It was a rude word that he had picked up from Mr Kelly. Mum had had a fit when he said it at home one time. At school, Mr Buchanan joked about how he was supposed to do guard duty every day. I had seen him salute Dad when he received his orders. It had to be mockery, for he gave me a kind of wink at the same time, but Dad took the salute as his due.

The McCaddie house was situated on the edge of a dry creek bed by a stand of gums, in one of Mr MacAdams' lower pastures. Mr McCaddie was his head stockman. He had four kelpies, tethered to iron stakes. They leapt vertically in frenzy to the very ends of their chains at the sight of us, and their barking was ferocious. Heather put her hands over her ears. 'Good watchdogs,' said Dad. 'Good, good, good.' Dad had scared Heather and me by saying he would get rid of Dipper, who did nothing but snooze.

The sun was getting low, and Nurse McCaddie shaded her eyes as she came down from the top of the high steps. The honeysuckle, growing on the latticework beneath the verandah, was still doing well, despite the drought.

'Hullo there, lettuce man.'

Dad raised his hat.

'I'll take three, Jack.'

'Calling by to check.'

'All's quiet on the western front.'

Dad started his usual stuff about windows and doors and guard dogs, and Nurse McCaddie nodded and smiled and reassured him over and again. Nurse McCaddie beamed over at Heather and me as she paid for her lettuces. 'Oh, how lovely and fresh they are.'

She was the kindest lady in all of Billarooby.

'How's Lillian? I was expecting to see her this afternoon.'

'She's doing very well. She decided not to come today.'

'If she continues to have that same trouble, I'm always here.'

'The Japs threw stones at the guards yesterday.'

'Oh, my goodness.'

'Shots were fired over their heads to keep order.'

'I read nothing in the *Star* this morning, Jack.'

'You won't. We are the ones who are going to suffer.'

Nurse McCaddie walked back up a couple of steps and stood on the same level as our heads.

'Army's a bad, bloody joke.'

'Yes, Jack. I want you to be very careful with yourself. And these precious children. I hope that gun you have there is not loaded. You go over a rock, it might – '

'I have taken all precautions, Jean,' said Dad huffily. 'I am familiar with the safety measures to be taken with shotguns.'

'Well, of course.' Nurse McCaddie seemed uneasy about how overexcited Dad was. 'I have a very nice jacket that Angus doesn't need,' she went on. 'You could wear it Sunday for the Bishop. Let me get it for you, Jack.'

Dad shook his head vehemently.

'Dad has a nice suit,' said Heather.

'That uniform, Jack.' Nurse McCaddie paused. 'You should think about it. The Japs might mistake you for a soldier.'

Dad gave such a peculiar grin, as if his jaw were wired or something, that Nurse McCaddie turned away quickly.

'Well, I can smell my bread.' She mounted another step or two and then turned back. 'Lillian should really come and see me very soon. With it keeping like this, we mustn't take any chances.'

Nurse McCaddie gave a look up at the hot, murky sky and shook her head.

As we headed back to the road we could see the sheep moving rapidly through the bare paddocks. The mounds of wool in the distance, half-scattered by the winds, were sheep that had died and been left to rot. Cawing filled the air, and flocks of crows were feasting. The smell of carrion came on every breath of wind.

I opened the McCaddies' gate and the sulky rolled its way into the road.

'Here comes Brown,' I called. The Douglasses' lorry was approaching fast along the plateau. We waited for it to come by.

'It's Mum driving,' cried Heather as the lorry pulled up. Brown got down and opened the gate I had just closed.

'You can't drive!' Dad shouted, suddenly in a temper. Only then did I realize that he didn't know. Brown had given Mum quite a few lessons since Mount Canobolas, but she had kept quiet about it. And Heather did not know either, for if she had, she would have told Dad.

'Teaching her, mate. Part of me war effort.'

'Get out of that lorry.'

'Jack, I have to see Jean. What's happened to your memory? Didn't Lindsay remind you?'

'I'll take you now.' Dad began to wheel the sulky around.

'Jack, mate, Belinda looks dead on her feet.'

'She bolted,' Heather called out. 'Lindsay got thrown out.'

'The sulky's damaged,' I put in.

'I know, dear. Brown told me. Your father should have brought you both straight home.'

'Jack, take Lillian in the lorry,' Brown offered. 'I'll drive the mare home with the kids.'

'I'll take you to see Jean tomorrow.'

'You don't understand, I have to see her now.'

'You're getting out of there.'

Dad began to get out of the sulky, and Mum, in response, put her foot down hard on the accelerator. The truck shot through the gate, narrowly missing the left post. She jammed on the brakes. Brown quickly closed the gate and gestured to Dad with both hands.

'Sorry, mate. She's got a mind of her own these days.'

He climbed back into the cabin. The tyres burned on the gravel and the lorry rattled off in the direction of the McCaddies'.

I stood in the road watching it go.

Before I even realized it, Dad had loaded the shotgun and fired a shot at the departing lorry. Belinda was startled and caused Dad to overbalance slightly. A flock of crows in the dead trees north of the gate all rose in the air, and Dad fired a second shot into their midst. He hit one; it fluttered to the ground.

The lorry stopped. Brown stood out on the running board and looked back. The acrid smell of the shots was all around us. Dad reloaded.

'Look out, he's shooting at you!' I screamed at the top of my lungs. Dad reached down and clouted me over the head.

I don't know whether Brown heard me or not, but he got back into the lorry and it backed up rapidly. Brown climbed out and limped over.

'What the hell do you think you're doing, mate?' Brown leaned forward and rested his elbows on the top of the gate. Dad was still standing up in the sulky with the gun. He made no reply. He and Brown stared at each other. I could see Mum's frightened face looking through the back window of the lorry.

'He was shooting at the crows,' cried Heather. 'He got one.' She pointed to the fallen crow. Brown looked.

'That first shot was pretty wild,' he said.

'Belinda jerked,' said Dad, putting the gun back in the corner of the sulky. 'We had trouble with the crows earlier today, remember,'

'Scared the shit outta your missus.'

Dad and Brown continued to stare at each other.

'You want her to have that baby or not?' Brown asked, and then turned and headed back to the lorry.

We watched the lorry drive away until it was lost to sight behind a clump of black wattles.

There was silence but for the harsh rasp of Dad's breathing. He sat down and gathered in the reins. 'Giddyap!' he said, bringing down the whip.

'I suppose you're going to write this all up for your precious Mr Buchanan,' said Heather.

'You never see anything,' I said to her in a low voice, hoping Dad would not hear. I could see what a state he was in.

'You never tell what really happens. Just stories.'

I stared at her, full of anger. How could she see things so differently? I hated her as never before.

'Why don't you kiss him then, if you think he's so good?'

Heather glared at me for a moment and then looked up at Dad, who was staring grimly straight ahead. He gave no indication that he was listening to us, and I don't think he was. Heather steadied herself with a hand on the back of the seat and planted a big kiss right on Dad's unshaven cheek.

'There,' she said to me. 'You dumb cluck.'

Dad made no response to Heather's kiss. He did not even look at the Packmans' gate when we passed it, nor the Morrisons'.

Dad's not mad, I said to myself, he's bad.

By the time we reached home, the sun was setting. We found Mr Kelly playing quoits in the front yard. He had his gun and a bottle of whiskey with him.

'Been waiting for something to shoot at,' he said, and took aim at Belinda's head. I almost believed he was going to do it.

'Come on, Armstrong, you bloody longface. Let's go. Ernie's coming round. This might be the night.'

Dad went off with Mr Kelly immediately. It was terrible to have him yelling at the family like a maniac all the time, but I still hated to see him turn whippet with his tail between his legs whenever Mr Kelly showed up.

Heather put the lettuces in the charcoal safe, and I began to unharness Belinda. The blood around her nostrils had all dried and hardened, so I wet a rag and dealt with it.

22

I WAS AWAKENED the next morning by a loud clanging. I sat up and looked out my window. Dad was pounding an iron stake into the ground. He lifted the sledgehammer high each time, and brought it down with such unnecessary ferocity it was frightening just to watch him. One time he missed completely and went sprawling forward. He stared at the hard ground for a moment or two, then picked himself up and went right on swinging.

Mr Kelly appeared in my view, and I was out of bed in a second.

'Mr Kelly's in our back yard.'

'They're putting more barbed wire around the house.' Mum was at the stove. She had been crying.

'What time did he get home?'

'He didn't come home at all last night.' Mum's tears began to flow again. 'He won't even speak to me.'

'Because Brown is teaching you to drive?'

'Keep away from him. He has the shakes.'

When I got home from school that afternoon, the new ring of barbed wire completely surrounded the farmhouse. I walked all the way round to the front before I found an opening. It was as mad as Mr Morrison's maze. Mum was sound asleep in the big chair by the window, her slippers kicked off beside her, her fan fallen to the floor. I inspected her closely and was sure I could see the swelling where the baby was.

On the table was a card from the Cutlers, who were down at the coast. I read it eagerly. Mrs Cutler had found a very nice house by the water at Woy Woy and was seriously considering renting it. She said it was wonderful being away from the heat and the drought for a bit. 'It's been raining and it's cool, and it's absolute heaven.' I looked for a message from Jennifer but there was none.

Before the Cutlers left for Woy Woy, my affair with Jennifer had begun to go the way of that with Jimmy. The lovely swoony feeling I had had for her had disappeared. Romance had been replaced by crudity. As a very special favour I had taken her to my secret cave, intending to confide in her about Tadao, but from the start, all she could say was how dirty it was. If we were serious about settling down, she expected me to provide something better. Then she somehow manoeuvred me up against the back wall and wouldn't let me go until I touched her thing. It was years before I was ready for such pleasures, and at the time I regarded her demands as an abuse of my hospitality. I changed my mind about telling her anything at all about my noble friendship with Tadao.

Mum gave a groan and stirred in her sleep. I tiptoed out. I was going ferreting with Brown.

I had told him about how the rabbits had taken over my grove, and he was keen to go there.

'Haven't been to the big trees for ten years. Reckon I can make it now.'

'I want to show you my secret cave. I haven't shown it to a single soul,' I lied.

'I'll be in good company then,' said Brown.

'Let's keep away from Old Kelly Bag's place,' said Brown as he drove the Douglasses' red lorry towards the ford. I was only too glad to. Mr Kelly had said he would skin me alive if he ever caught me snooping around the dump. Mum had said much the same thing, although she did not mean it the same way. I had sneaked a few looks there anyway. The dump had turned into a slaughterhouse. There was constant movement among the crows, who sat in the branches above or perched all over the rusty old iron. Under the trees hundreds of rabbit skins were stretched out on wire frames to dry. Dad and Mr Kelly, both stripped to the waist, worked away steadily, scraping off fat from the skins and rubbing salt in. They tossed the carcasses into a pit dug amid the junk on the eroded bank. I saw Dad one time shovelling dirt over the rotting remains, and Mr Kelly walking over with a bucket of quicklime. The smell was horrible.

The ferrets, on the seat between us in a hessian sack, stank also, but not of death, and I didn't mind the ferrets anymore. Brown and I regularly killed rats with them down at the dairy.

'Stiff as a board,' said Brown after he had almost fallen on the steep bank. 'Gonna be an early winter. We shoulda gone to Simpsons Creek. Bunnies galore there too.'

'I'm sorry, Brown. It gets easier in a minute.'

'I coulda driven all the way. Back to the old crutches at this rate.'

Once we were through the silky oaks, it did become easier. The rabbits disappeared as we approached, but they seemed to do it reluctantly. The smell of them caused the ferrets to writhe and fizz with frustration.

'My cave is just through there.'

'I've walked enough, mate.'

Brown chose a small warren and showed me how to peg each hole with the nets. I already knew how to handle the ferrets from working them with the rats. I stroked Fanny, the female, while he slipped Filbert into an entrance. The more excited the ferrets became, the more they stank.

'Too excited,' said Brown. 'He'll kill. We'll be lucky to get him back.'

We returned Fanny to the bag. After a short wait, a squealing rabbit hurled itself into one of the nets, struggling wildly as it became entangled. Brown killed it with a single sharp blow, then extricated it. Suddenly all the nets were filled. Brown clubbed the terrified rabbits, every one, cut them open with his knife, and ripped out the innards. He skinned one for Jojo. I held my breath and forced myself to look closely. It was not as bad as when Dad chopped off the heads of the chooks. I knew the rabbits were a plague, and were part of the problem at a time when we needed all our resources because of the war and the drought, but I still felt sorry.

Brown did not want to peg out a warren for Fanny until Filbert finished eating his rabbit down there and chose to come out. It would be half an hour, at least.

'We can wait at my cave.'

*

'Crikey, I didn't know the big bloke was down.'

'It's been down ever since we arrived in Billarooby. It made my cave. Come and look.'

'Bonzer little place.'

'Home away from home,' I said, pleased.

'I'll sit here, unless you want to lift me down.'

Brown sat on the platform outside and put his bad leg up on a stone. He brought out a bag of Auntie Annabel's biscuits and opened a Thermos of tea. The tea was sweet and milky. Brown took a swallow of whiskey with his and then rolled a smoke.

One by one, I showed him the treasures that I kept on the ledge – the quartz stone, the kookaburra feathers, the galah wings, the lacquered box in which I stored my marbles. I handed up Tadao's cap, embroidered with chrysanthemums.

'I found it floating in the river. It's a talisman.'

Brown smelled the cap and returned it without a word. He flicked a look at me. 'Jap.'

Quickly, to divert attention from the cap, I handed up the lacquered box. I was fearful of censure. 'Here, this is for you.'

'No, no,' said Brown, opening it.

'I'll take the marbles out. It's a present.'

Brown took the box unwillingly. 'I'll put it in my room. If you ever want it back, you know where to find it.'

Finally, with some ceremony, I brought out *The Knights of Bushido*. Brown blew off the dust and thumbed through.

'Pretty pictures. Bit warlike. Didn't them samurai have any home life?'

'Listen to this,' I said, seizing the book from him. ' "The taking of one's life is an act of courage, not of cowardice. It is a virtue, not a sin." '

He looked at me, down in the cave. 'Sounds a bit morbid, mate. What are you up to, suicide?'

'Not me, the Japs.'

'Oh, the bloody Japs.' The wind caught the Red Ensign, which I had hanging from one of the roots high above. 'Nice flag. I got a little Jap one you could hang.'

'You never told me,' I cried.

He grinned. 'Sorry, mate. Forgot all about it. I'll get it out of

Auntie's room for you. Me one New Guinea souvenir. Besides me
legs.'

I was silent for a moment or two, on account of the legs, but I
was impatient to convince him of the importance of the book.

'Let me read to you from the story of Kublai Khan.'

'Fire away.' Brown rolled on to his back to make himself more
comfortable. Smoke curled up into the air from the cigarette stuck
to his bottom lip.

'. . . the Emperor called upon the Gods to destroy Kublai
Khan's armada, and the Gods sent a Divine Wind, the Kamikaze.
From the cliffs of their homeland, the Emperor and his noble
samurai watch the ships of the Khan sink beneath the waves . . .'

'Did you read in the *Herald* about the garrison of Attu?' asked
Brown when I had finished.

'Yes. When there was no hope, they all killed themselves rather
than be taken prisoner.'

'Well, our Japs are different. They already been taken prisoner.
These are the ones who don't want to die. We both been to that
camp. They sit around, play games. They're waiting for the war
to end just like everyone else, so they can go home to their mums
and dads.'

'They can't go home. They're disgraced. And they make them
wear red uniforms. It says in the book that red is the colour for
murderers and thieves in Japan.'

'If they try to get out, they get mowed down with machine
guns.'

'They don't care about machine guns. They're invincible,' I
cried. 'They believe it's better to die with honour than live with
shame. They are all going to get out. All of them.' I had it all
worked out. 'They can't live with shame, Brown. It says so in the
book.'

'People can live with shame. Yer mum makes me ashamed of
me bare feet.' Brown wiggled his toes and grinned.

'That's not the same. There's big shame and little shame.'

'And big ideas for a little boy. So what they gonna do when
they're all out?'

'Well, personally,' I began, 'I believe they will go north and try
to rejoin their Emperor. They are samurai. Once they have dealt
with the soldiers, they will leave. I don't agree with Dad or Mr

Kelly or any of them that we are in danger in Billarooby. We are innocent people of no concern to them. We just have to keep out of their way while they make their journey. They didn't hurt Mum. That was just Mr Sullivan's story.'

Brown was silent for a while. He blew a smoke ring and then said, 'If the Japs go for the wires, the Colonel will just machine-gun them. That means hundreds of them gonna die – '

I interrupted. 'They won't die. They're going to tunnel out. They're digging right now. The Colonel doesn't even know.'

'There's no tunnels, mate. If they go, they go for the wires. Samurai. Isn't that what you said? They will get mowed down in their hundreds. Maybe hundreds of soldiers at the camp will die trying to stop them. You met Peter Duffy, your teacher's friend. You want him to get killed? That's what war is. Friends getting killed for no good reason.'

Brown rolled over on to his stomach and looked down at me.

'Maimed and wounded, killed. Do you understand those words? Come on out of there, it's time to get Filbert.'

I put the book away, shocked to silence. As I began my climb out of the cave, Brown reached down and grabbed me by the elbows. He lifted me up until I was on a level with him and pulled me close so that our noses touched. He grinned and rubbed his nose back and forth over mine. His moustache tickled me and I could smell the cigarette on his breath and the brilliantine in his hair. 'That's how they say g'day in New Guinea,' he said, and shook me out like a bag of chaff. Then he rolled on to his back and dropped me, so that I went sprawling on top of him. We both began to laugh and then sat up and brushed off the dust.

'You're my dad now,' I said, overcome with a wild happiness.

Brown measured me with a look.

'If I'm yer dad now, listen to me. That book's put a lot of bullshit into yer head. Yer as bad as yer dad with his bloody Bible. It's just a book. Those Japs are real. Everybody in Billarooby is real. Let the Colonel and the army do the worrying about the Japs. That's their job. Colonel don't do his job, he gets the sack. He's got his pride too.'

'Mr Buchanan says he's a dingbat.'

'Dingbat he is, and an old boozer, doing the best he can under the circumstances. We hope.'

'But he doesn't believe they will all try to get out.'

'Neither do I. But maybe they will. Just to get away from the old bastard.' Brown chuckled. 'I just hope to God they don't. In the meantime, we just keep our doors locked, like yer dad says. I don't trust your bloody samurai. And I don't think you should either. War is war. It ain't *The Knights of Bushido*, and it never was. Even then.'

'Dad wants the Japs to escape.'

'No, he doesn't. But he wants to be the big hero in Billarooby if they do escape. Give him the benefit of the doubt.'

'Mr Kelly wants them to escape.'

'And so do you, mate.'

'No, I don't,' I cried desperately, suddenly caught at my own game and off guard. 'Well, it's different. Mr Kelly wants to go hunting. Man-hunting.'

'You let the Japs out they go man-hunting too. Maybe that's what you want.'

'No, no, no. It's only Mr Kelly who will do the terrible things.'

Brown gave a big sigh. 'Kelly's even fuller of crazy ideas than you and yer dad. I hope yer dad's not crazy enough to believe them. He goes to war with Kelly against those poor bloody Japs, he's likely to get his head blown off. By the Divine Wind. You tell yer dad I said that.'

Brown took another drink from the Thermos and handed it to me. I was silent, and then as we looked down to the muddy waterhole I began to unburden my other fears.

'Dad fired at you. Heather says he didn't, but he did.'

'Whatever he did, he missed.'

'And now he's not speaking to Mum.'

I had caught Brown by surprise for once. He let out a little *ah*.

'Brown, I don't like it when Dad's home.'

'I'll come by for a visit. Smooth things over. What do you think?'

'You're not scared?'

'I'll bring Auntie Annabel along to protect me.'

I searched Brown's face anxiously for clues. His green eyes danced like the gum leaves in the wind. His face was even more tanned than it had been at the cherry orchard. His moustache was trimmed and his sideburns freshly cut. His teeth were as white as the salt he cleaned them with. There were no clues. Was Heather right? Had I imagined it? My search caused him to grin broadly.

'I'm going to brush my teeth until they are as clean as yours.'

Brown laughed. 'Yer Dad got the rough end of the stick this summer. Drop of rain, you see what happens. Don't be so hard on him.'

I stared at him in puzzlement. Why did everyone keep saying that? 'It's Dad who is hard on me.'

I wanted to add what Dad was going to do to me when the baby came, but I knew that Brown would just laugh.

'You're the hard one. You don't understand what he goes through every day. Keeping you fed. Protecting you from the drought. You got no sympathy. And yer mum and me don't know why.'

I almost hated Brown at that moment. How could he be saying such horrible things? He was my friend. Didn't he understand that Dad had it in for him too?

I turned the discussion away to something else, it was too scary.

'Mum says if it wasn't for Mr Kelly, Dad wouldn't be a drunk.'

'Yer dad needs a drink. Keep his courage up. How else he gonna get them Japs?' Brown laughed.

'Mr Kelly hit you.'

'Gotta watch out for Bruce. The Kellys always taking a poke at the Douglasses.' Brown laughed again, but this time he didn't fool me. Brown took Mr Kelly seriously. He hadn't worn khakis once since the day of the brawl in the Ritz.

'Mum says we're getting out of Billarooby if it's the last thing we ever do. As soon as the baby's born.'

'She says that every day.'

'Mrs Cutler sent a card with a palm tree and a beach. She says there's koalas in all the trees.'

'Mrs Cutler,' said Brown, and laughed.

I could not pin him down to anything.

'I have to leave home when the baby is born!' I cried.

'Hey, come off it, mate. Gonna be the baby that brings the rain.'

'I'll have to come and live with you.'

'If it's OK with Auntie Annabel, it's OK with me.'

I looked into his eyes and he looked away suddenly. I had a

feeling of deep disappointment. Were all my fears so groundless? Was it just me, fantasizing and unable to see things straight because I was filled with fear and hatred of Dad?

'Are you kidding me, Brown?' I stared earnestly at him and then grabbed his hand, in an attempt to get him to return my gaze.

'Shhh. Look.'

While we were talking, the rabbits had begun reappearing, snuffling at the dust and burrs, edging closer to the water. Jojo raised his head and then went back to sleep. He didn't care about rabbits. He was a cattle dog. Soon, heads were popping out of burrows no more than ten yards away. The opposite bank was alive with them. I turned round and looked up the slope. We were surrounded. They were only rabbits, but my skin began to creep. They were taking over. Brown threw his cigarette butt down towards the water. Rabbits gathered round it. I broke up Auntie Annabel's biscuits and tossed them. They ate them in a flash.

'They're starving, Brown. We don't even need ferrets. I bet I could catch one with my bare hands.'

'You're on.'

I sped down the bank for the nearest ones. Several times I just missed. Once I actually felt the fur. But every single one, big or small, eluded me. Jojo finally got excited and joined me in the chase, and he didn't do any better. Within a few seconds the riverbank was deserted once more – except for some of the bolder rabbits on the other side of the muddy waterhole, who stared and did not even bother to run. The dust settled on the droppings. I managed a small smile.

'Jojo's getting old,' Brown said, and laughed.

Filbert's orange nose was twitching in the mouth of the burrow when we got back to him. Brown reached in and put him in the sack.

'That's enough for today. We'll give Fanny a run next time.'

At the ford, Brown was starting up the engine when we heard another truck, coming down from the flats. It was Mr Kelly. Beside him on the front seat were Blue Chapman and Ernie Williams. Dad knelt in the back seat with his shotgun, looking downriver. Mr Kelly was driving very fast. He gunned into the riverbed, and up the other side.

'Dad was supposed to be picking up Heather at the siding,' I told Brown. 'She'll have to walk home.' As more and more news came out about the camp, Mum had decided that it was not wise for Heather to be bicycling through the lonely hills to and from the siding.

'The bloody Bush Brigade,' said Brown, gazing after the truck. 'The rabbit kings.'

Brown put the lorry into gear and began to drive slowly up the bank. 'You know what you could do? You could find out what those blokes are up to.'

'They go to the lean-to in Mr Kelly's field.'

Brown stopped the truck at the top of the bank. 'Take a gander.'

I looked pleadingly at Brown. I didn't want to go anywhere near Dad or Mr Kelly. 'I'd rather stay with you.'

'Gotta take Auntie up to Moorellen. She's helping Helen MacAdams with this do for the Bishop tomorrer. You don't have to go close. They won't even see you. Twelve-year-old boy. Yer safe.'

'They just sit and drink.'

'Be a scout for me. They might be on their way to the camp. Up to no good.'

Ah! Brown knew more about what was going on than he admitted. Picturing myself with him and Mr Buchanan going into Wudgie with a story for Mr Sullivan at the *Star*, I experienced another wild moment of happiness.

My fears evaporated, and I opened the door. 'I'll wear my cloak of invisibility.'

'Here's yer sweater. Don't forget. We're in this together. Just the two of us.'

'Conspirators,' I said, hanging the sweater around my neck.

'Don't get caught.' The lorry began to move forward slowly. 'Skid.'

I leapt out, slammed the door, and then ran.

Whap! 'Eight,' said Mr Kelly.
Whap! 'Fifteen for two,' said Dad.

Whap! 'Twenty-five,' said Blue Chapman.

'Thirty-one for two,' said Ernie Williams.

'Shit.'

It was the Kelly gang, and they were playing cribbage. I could play cards. The Landgirls had left some, and Heather and I played secretly in my room. If Dad had known about it, he would have confiscated the pack.

I was crouching outside the window at the back of the lean-to amid castor oil plants and dead mustard. It was one time I wished I had shoes on. The ground was littered with broken glass and there was a strong smell of urine. A beer bottle came hurtling out and fell with a crash.

Someone left the shed and footsteps came round the side towards me. I was ready to run, but the footsteps stopped, and the person began to take a leak by the corner. The sunlit stream of liquid splashed on the ground no more than a yard away. I squeezed up against the wall, terrified that he might take another step and see me. I didn't know whether it was Dad or Blue Chapman. Whoever it was, he finished and went back in without noticing me.

The game, the joking, and the swearing continued. The sun began to lose its warmth, and I put my sweater on. Another bottle came flying out. I realized that in the middle of Mr Kelly's jokes was another conversation that I was missing.

'Hit those bastards. Shoot their tiny dicks off. Kill the cunts.' It was Mr Kelly's constant refrain.

'Before the cunts kill us,' said Blue Chapman.

'I'm sick of waiting for the cunts,' said Mr Kelly. 'Kill, kill, kill. They're the enemy, Armstrong. You don't kill them, they kill you. Right, Ernie?'

'Your deal,' said Ernie Williams.

'Our terribly heroic friend here seems to be backing out.'

'Deal up.'

'After all that hot air.' There was the sound of a whack upon the back. 'Stop your cringing.'

'Fair go, Bruce,' said Blue Chapman.

'Stay home with the lovely Lillian. Cowards die many deaths.'

My mind went back to those early days at the Cutlers', when I was unable to swing on their rope across the gully to Lizard Rock.

'Cowardy custard, cowardy custard, poop your pants, can't cut the mustard.' Jennifer's and Jimmy's derisive voices were still with me. So was Granddad's, raised in contempt against Dad on a wintry afternoon.

'Oh, how he suffers, does Jack,' said Mr Kelly. 'Fortunately for us, in silence.'

The game continued.

'We going to let those cunts see their mothers again? Armstrong, we're going to get those cunts.' His voice rose to a bellow. 'I'm ready to kill. You know what the camp is like. It's like a bloody boil. If we don't lance it, the yellow pus is going to explode all over us.'

Mr Kelly began laughing hideously at his own joke, and then he said something that made my scalp crawl.

'It's as easy as pie. They wouldn't know what hit 'em. All of us up there in the rocks, we could get twenty of them before they got to cover.'

Mr Kelly went on and on. He began outlining another plan. I listened, aghast. The Colonel didn't care, he said. If they didn't shoot the Japs, the Colonel would. That's why the old fart wanted them to go for the wires. What did Dad think the new machine guns were for? For a little fun, that's what they were for. The Colonel had been denied a front-line post overseas because he was too old. The Colonel had met T. E. Lawrence in Damascus. A man like the Colonel wasn't just going to be a babysitter. So he was creating a front line back here. Blood, that's what the Colonel wanted.

'And so do you, Ernie!' Mr Kelly roared. 'You can do it, Ernie. They don't even man them at night. We've got the rounds. You'd be away before they even knew.'

'My legs ain't up to it, Bruce.'

Ernie did not seem to have much enthusiasm for whatever it was Mr Kelly was suggesting, and Dad did not sound very convinced either. I was glad to hear that Mr Kelly was having trouble with his gang's morale.

The card game got going more seriously again, and I decided to leave. I crawled for the fence and then hared off up the hill.

*

I had to confirm what I suspected from Mr Kelly's conversation, and I was halfway there before I even had a doubt that it was the right thing to do. I stopped briefly and thought of Brown's warnings, Mum's warnings, Mr Buchanan's warnings, but the face of Tadao loomed up, the face of both ally and enemy. And it was too late to turn back.

The bare hillsides were crisscrossed with tracks that had not been there before. The rabbiters. The Bush Brigade on patrol. It was months since I had visited my outcrop, and the second I arrived I knew my suspicions were right. It no longer belonged just to me. It was an outpost for the Bush Brigade.

Dad has been here, was my first thought. There was a jam jar crawling with ants, and they had left empty beer and whiskey bottles, dozens of cigarette butts, and a newspaper stuffed in a crevice. Right by my favourite niche in the rocks was a curled pile of shit. It was black and a couple of days old, with green bottle flies desultorily buzzing around it. The paper used to wipe with was still there. I looked around uneasily and peered up into the kurrajongs. I remembered Brown's story of the Kokoda and half expected someone to be in the branches.

The Japanese were running around their exercise yard, shouting in rhythm as they ran. I almost wanted to see the Colonel galloping his horse about and firing his revolver. I shaded my eyes against the setting sun.

There, outside the barbed wire fences, were the Colonel's new machine guns, all trained upon the Japanese compound. One of the guns was almost directly below me, and I suddenly realized what it was that Mr Kelly was trying to convince Ernie Williams to do – go down to one of the machine guns one night, activate it, and fire into the Japanese compound while the prisoners were asleep.

I groaned and put my head in my hands. Instead of feeling like a god, an eagle up there, looking down from my eyrie, I felt trapped and powerless.

The smell of the shit began to bother me. With a stick I pushed it on to a wad of the newspaper and threw it away over the rocks.

As I once more positioned myself in my niche, the shouting from the Japanese slowed and then turned into a song.

It sounded like the mournful hymns that Dad liked to sing. The ones that made him stretch his voice to its richest, fullest extent, the ones that had dozens of verses. The Japanese stopped running and formed themselves into lines. Still they sang, and I wanted to climb down the rocks and run to the barbed wire fence so I could get a closer look at their faces, see if Tadao was back with his friends, shout out a warning that Mr Kelly and his gang were planning to shoot them as they slept. I wanted to, but I did not dare.

The sun hit the horizon, a whistle blew, and when the song finally ended, there was a lump in my throat. The samurai were going to go home.

'It's the saddest song I ever heard,' I said aloud. 'He's going to die.'

'Do you know what killing is?' Brown had asked. A blackness grew inside my head. Whether the samurai chose to die or not, I wanted them to deal with the Kelly gang. My mind went the next dreadful step, deal with Dad, but even as I had the wish, I felt a touch on my neck. I spun around, ducking as I did so, but there was no one there.

It was Granddad himself who had laid a warning hand on me. Suddenly I had the shivers. I climbed down the rocks and ran like the wind all the way to the house, but I could not get warm.

23

IT WAS DARK by the time I got home, and Dad was already there, getting the copper going for hot water. We all had to smell good for the prayers and the reception for the Bishop of Bathurst the following afternoon.

Dad was in a strange state. I was willing to bet it was Mr Kelly's taunts about cowardice that had him upset. He kept stirring the water, clutching the copper stick tightly with both hands, as though he were concocting some magic potion. When it began to bubble, he put his head down close to the surface of the water and held it there. The rest of the family stood in a semicircle behind him, wondering how long it would go on. It was Heather who finally stepped forward, touched him on the shoulder. 'Dad . . .' she began.

Water. His objections to the water from Mrs Cutler's well had long since been forgotten. Now that we had it, it was like holy water from Moses' rock in the wilderness. I had heard him talking to the Reverend Pitts about Mum's single drop in the dry electrical storm as though it was the harbinger of something approaching the Flood.

There was no formal dinner that night. In fact, with the disruptions and crises the ongoing drought brought on, our formal dinners had become a relic of our English past. Mum just put the potato hot-pot in front of me and I wolfed it down. She herself ate on the run while Dad ordered her about. The big galvanized tub had to be brought into the living room from the washroom, the silk screen placed around it for privacy, a fire lit in the main fireplace.

'I'm not washing in here,' I announced from the kitchen table.

'It's a very special occasion. Your father is going to give each of us a bath. Heather is first.'

'Wait in your room.' Dad barked at me, leading Heather in from the corridor by the hand. Heather had nothing on under Mum's dressing gown, and she wouldn't look at me.

'Away you go, Lindsay,' said Mum. Gently, to take the rough edge off Dad for me.

Half an hour went by.

'Leave her alone,' I heard Mum cry.

A few minutes later Heather came running down the corridor. Her door slammed.

'Lindsay!' Dad's shout was like a sergeant major's.

In the living room Mum was pouring jugs of boiling water into the tub. The fire burned high in the fireplace, the air was full of vapours, and the room was very hot.

I waited until Mum had finished pouring, then began to take off my clothes. As I stepped into the tub, Dad came round the side of the screen.

'You've got to be purified, inside and out, for the Bishop tomorrow.'

I dropped down into the water to hide myself, but he caught me by the hair and pulled me to my feet. He then took off his dressing gown. For the first time in my life, as far as I could remember, Dad and I stood alone together, naked. I was embarrassed and a little scared. I didn't know which way to look, but my eyes were drawn inevitably to the most forbidden part. Even in the candlelight I saw that Dad had a large mole on the side of his dick. He took the soap and flannel and began rubbing me up and down vigorously.

'Wash it away, wash it away . . . he it is whose shoe's latchet I am not worthy to unloose . . .'

A few minutes later he began to shout. 'The devil . . . !'

'Lindsay, are you all right?' Mum called out nervously.

'I can do it,' I protested, for Dad had become obsessive – over and over again, every part of my body, washing me as though I were a little boy. I tried to take the soap away but lost the struggle. He pushed me down in the water, hauled me up. Three times he did it. The water kept sloshing over the side of the tub.

'Lean over.' Dad picked up a switch of gum leaves and began swatting my back with it. It stung a bit but I quickly decided I didn't mind. Water was spraying everywhere and both candles went out. The smell of the wicks mixed with the eucalyptus, the soap, and Dad's nervous, sweaty smell. He should have had the first wash.

He gave me one last swipe with the gum leaves and then picked up the nail brush. There was a pause.

He looked at me with something I took for a smile, something affectionate. It was something so rare, unexpected, and wonderful that it made my heart jump. I remembered Brown's words that afternoon – 'You're the one that's hard' – and there came rushing over me waves of tenderness and sympathy for Dad. I have to confess that they were followed by feelings that could only be called lustful. I covered up my hard-on with my hands, but he took them away to scrub my nails. I looked up with half-closed eyes and sank farther down into the water, trying to draw him down.

'Daddy,' I said softly. I was an all-powerful seductress, luring him into the water to play. When he resisted, I got tougher.

'Dad, I know what Mr Kelly is up to. The Bush Brigade are all going to die.'

Dad looked down at me. His mind had been far away. 'I will die?'

'I heard him being horrible to you in the lean-to this afternoon. Playing cards.'

Brown had said not to get caught, but sometimes it was necessary to get caught. I tugged Dad's hand, still trying to get him down into the water. I would baptize Dad, three times, as he had me, make him a new man.

'I can help you,' I whispered urgently. 'But you have to stop wearing your uniform. And you have to keep away from the river. You have to keep away from Mr Kelly. He killed a man. He wants to kill the Japs.'

'Stop that!' Dad shouted, perhaps becoming aware of what I was up to. I had his hand right on my dick. He wrenched himself away and the spell was broken.

A sense of loss came over me. Loss, and then that resentment.

'Get out of there.'

'I'm dirty. I need to soak longer.'

'You're clean. Go.'

Reluctantly I took the towel and stood up. As I began to dry myself, he asked, 'What was that about Mr Kelly?'

I lost my temper. 'You're crazy. You didn't hear a thing I said. The Japs are going to get you and I'm going to the police. I'm going to tell them about Ernie Williams.'

'Lindsay, what's all that shouting?' came Mum's voice.

Dad and I were face to face in the steamy dark. I felt self-righteous, despairing, not the least bit afraid. Looking back now at that night, extraordinary for its many improprieties, I realize I was as distraught as he was, but much more in control.

'You let Mr Kelly treat you just like Granddad did,' I said.

Dad's fist came out of nowhere and crashed on the side of my face. I staggered but did not fall. Dad didn't have much strength in his arm, and he didn't do anything else to me. Instead, he backed into the screen, sending it rocking, then turned and ran naked out into the living room.

'Jack, go and put your trousers on. You're indecent.'

He left the room. I heard him knocking on Heather's door, and I cautiously came out from behind the screen.'

'Dad hit me.'

Mum was taking a slug from the whiskey bottle. She corked it hurriedly and thrust it away.

'It didn't hurt. Mum, it's more than just the drink with Dad.'

'Put the rest of your clothes on before you get a chill.'

'Dr Abercrombie is going to have to give him something to calm him down. Nurse McCaddie said.'

'He's very concerned that you be clean for the Bishop tomorrow. That's all. Here's your cocoa.'

I looked at her closely, but she turned away and began to take her hair down. She was behaving as though nothing were amiss, as usual. More water was ready in the cauldron on the stove. I looked in. It was simmering and seething, like Dad's brain.

I was sent off to bed before Mum took her bath, but I knew that there was a ritual bathing for her also that night.

When Mum woke me in the morning with a cup of tea, I saw that she had been crying for a long time.

'I couldn't get him to sleep. He went out in the middle of the night and hasn't come back.'

In the living room I noticed that the shotgun was missing from above the door.

'He probably went to Mr Kelly's again. That means he'll have a hangover for the Bishop.'

'Something made him go,' said Mum in a tremulous voice, holding her head forward and to one side, which is what happened when she was really tired and troubled. There was that question in her eyes I had seen many times before.

'Dad's off his rocker, isn't he?'

Mum didn't answer me. 'I couldn't keep him.' She sat briefly at her sewing machine, then switched on the wireless. She waited impatiently for it to warm up and then went to the stove, where she moved the pans back and forth. The sound came on in the middle of a Sunday morning commentary programme. Mum listened for a moment and then said, 'Find some soothing music for me, Lindsay, for God's sake.'

It was a leaden, overcast morning. Heather remained in her room, dutifully copying out her hour's worth of the Bible, our regular Sunday task, but I decided to take a chance and not do it. I sat at the dining table and watched Mum prepare a cake for the reception from her precious stock of flour.

At nine o'clock Dipper began barking, and I ran outside.

Dad was walking up the blackened hillside in his overcoat. Slung over one shoulder was the shotgun, and over the other was some sort of bundle. It looked as though it might be rabbits, but there was something peculiar about him, and I called Mum.

We went together to the gap in the barbed wire, and as Dad came close we both cried out. His face and hands were bloody, and so was his overcoat. We saw that the bundle did in fact consist of rabbits, but they had been ripped apart in the most horrifying manner and were a gory mess. In Dad's left hand was his skinning knife, dark with blood.

'Get back inside, Lindsay,' Mum said quickly, pushing me hard with both hands.

At that moment Dad said, 'We won't starve while there are rabbits.'

He was a frightening, wild-eyed sight. At first I found it difficult even to look at him, and I shrank away, but he made no move, merely standing in front of us, his head sunk forward, his shoulders hollow, not threatening, quite defeated and helpless. My terror drained away.

'They got the lettuces.' Dad let the knife slip from his fingers to the ground.

'Oh, Jack!' Mum cried, and went to him. 'Lindsay, get rid of those things,' she commanded.

I approached warily. It was hard to tell how many rabbits there were, so savagely had they been hacked, but there must have been at least a dozen. The heads hung down, attached to the bodies by a few threads of skin and sinew. The eyes had been stabbed through and through, and the entrails were spilled out and dragging in the dust. I reached up and pulled at the rope holding all the pieces together. The grisly bundle fell to the ground with a thud. Dipper began sniffing at the intestines.

'Put it down, Jack,' Mum said of the gun. He made no response. She took it gingerly and then didn't know what to do with it.

'Give it to me,' I said, and took it into the house. I checked to make sure it was unloaded, got the tall stool, and replaced the gun on its hooks. It was the first time I had touched that gun since the day Granddad shot himself. I looked up at it, and then at my hands. A sharp little thrill ran up my spine and caused a flower of light to open in my head. There was a bright molten glow and I had the feeling that Granddad was in heaven and about to reveal everything that had happened that afternoon in Suffolk. The glow faded without any revelation, and I was left staring at the gun, unsure of whether I was glad or sorry.

I leapt off the stool and ran outside. Mum had removed Dad's stained overcoat and was helping him up the steps to the verandah. I chased Dipper away from the intestines.

The Bishop's special service was at two. Mum said Dad was in no condition to go, and of course there was no question of our going without him. It was his God, his Church, and we endured it stoically to show family solidarity. Only the socializing afterwards under the acacia trees made it bearable.

She washed Dad's face and hands and fed him a big breakfast.

He was silent but ate everything Mum put in front of him. After breakfast she got him to bed, and he slept until almost one in the afternoon. Then he was suddenly awake, on his feet, excited and anxious about getting to see the Bishop.

'The Bishop will bring rain. Rain, Lillian.'

'Jack, you have suffered a terrible shock. I want you to rest. I insist.'

'Heather, you must wear your very best for the Bishop.' He took her hand and caressed it fiercely.

'Yes, Dad.' She had shown him her copperplate writing and Dad had wanted to know where mine was.

'I think he's all right. We will just have to watch him like a hawk.'

'Yes, Lindsay.' Mum gave me a very strange look.

Dad shaved without cutting himself, dressed carefully in his best suit, and was ready to go even before the rest of us. By the time we got rolling, the overcast sky had cleared and the sun was searing down. We were on tenterhooks, and every time that Dad hit Belinda, Mum and I flinched.

The presence of the Bishop attracted the largest congregation ever to the woolshed. There were over two hundred people in attendance, many of them from Wudgewunda and some from as far away as Condoblin and Cowra. Even confirmed non-churchgoers like Brown and Mr Kelly. Even the Colonel and several officers from the camp. Even Mr Sullivan from the *Star*, taking notes.

Nobody had been able to come up with any flowers, but Mrs MacAdams had snipped away at her oleanders, which were still hanging on, and the woolshed was decorated with those. Auntie Annabel pulled out all the stops on the organ.

The Bishop, well over six feet tall, was a very imposing figure indeed in his mitre and cope. His eyes were red-rimmed, and he had thick white hair that stuck out in wings over his ears. I had never before seen anyone quite so important and could not take my eyes off him throughout the service.

Dad's behaviour was erratic. He sang 'When I Survey the Wondrous Cross' so magnificently that the congregation lowered their voices a fraction to listen better, but he caused some awkwardness later by requesting permission from the Bishop, just as he was about to begin his special prayers, to do a short reading. Dad's request was polite, and the Bishop looked over to the Reverend Pitts for guidance. The Reverend Pitts shook his head violently, but the Bishop took a chance and graciously gave his consent, and off Dad went from his favourite part.

' ". . . the Lord shall make the rain of thy land powder and dust; from heaven it shall come down upon thee, until thou be destroyed. The Lord shall cause thee to be smitten before thine enemies; thou shalt go out one way against them, and flee seven ways before them; and shalt be removed into all the kingdoms of the earth.

' "And thy carcase shall be meat unto all the fowls of the air, and unto the beasts of the earth, and no man shall fray them away.

' "The Lord will smite thee with the botch of Egypt, and with the amerods, and with the scab, and with the itch, whereof thou canst not be healed.

' "The Lord shall smite thee with madness, and blindness, and astonishment of heart.

' "And thou shalt grope at noonday, as the blind gropeth in darkness, and thou shalt not prosper in thy ways: and thou shalt be only oppressed and spoiled evermore, and no man shall save thee.

' "Thou shalt betroth a wife and another man shall lie with her; thou shalt build a house and thou shalt not dwell therein; thou shalt plant a vineyard and shalt not gather the grapes thereof.

' "Thine ox shall be slain . . ." '

There wasn't a sound in the woolshed but Dad's voice. Louder and louder it grew. He began to sway. The Reverend Pitts consulted with the Bishop and Auntie Annabel and then came quickly down the aisle. Dad was so intent on his reading that he did not even see him approaching. The Reverend murmured something in his ear. Dad faltered but did not stop. Suddenly the Reverend snatched the Bible from his hands and pushed him down into his seat. Auntie Annabel struck up the organ, the Bishop announced Hymn Number 47, and in great relief the congregation rose as one body and sang out mightily 'What a Friend We Have in Jesus.' Nurse McCaddie came up the aisle from the back to see if Dad was all right. He was sitting rigid in his seat, breathing hard. Mum put her arm around him, and both

she and Nurse McCaddie asked if he wanted to go outside. He
shook his head, suddenly stood up and took hold of his hymn
book, and asked which page. In a moment he was singing along
as though nothing had happened.

After he had dropped the collection plate during the final hymn,
Mum whispered, 'You and Heather are going to have to help me
get him home.'

Dad had his teeth bared as he came down the steps after the
service and pumped first the Bishop's and then the Reverend
Pitts's hand.

'I'm happy to see that the drought is not getting you down,'
said the Reverend. 'The spirit, at least, is strong.'

A willy willy hit the departing worshippers at that very moment,
covering everyone with dust, dead leaves, and sheep droppings.

'Dear God,' exclaimed both the Bishop and the Reverend. They
held up their arms and waited for it to swirl away.

Dad took the chance to retrieve our Bible from the Reverend's
hand. The Reverend made an automatic grab for it back, then
stopped himself before he did anything unseemly in front of the
Bishop.

'I pray that the strength of Our Lord Jesus Christ will fortify
you in this time of trial, Mr Armstrong. You will prevail. We will
prevail.'

'Amen,' said Dad.

'And you with your precious burden, Mrs Armstrong. The good
Lord will care for you.' The Reverend played with his nose as his
eyes swept Mum up and down, looking for signs, causing her to
colour under his scrutiny.

'August,' she said.

'I will talk to you in private,' said the Reverend in a lower voice
to Dad as Mum moved away. Dad was standing stock still, staring
at the Bishop. 'Meet me inside before you leave.'

'Amen,' said Dad once more, throwing his eyes skyward. The
Reverend Pitts took him by the shoulders, turned him, and gave a
little shove so he could get on with the next person.

I found out later that one of the two ten-pound notes that Mr
and Mrs MacAdams had put in the collection plate was missing.
Dad was not actually accused of taking the money, because

someone else might have grabbed it when he dropped the plate, but the Reverend Pitts decided that because of his shaky hand, Dad was not to take the collection plate around in the future.

It was during the slow promenade up the gravelled track from the woolshed to the Moorellen residence that Mum and I let Dad slip through our fingers. One minute he was there shuffling along beside us, the next minute he was not.

The unexpected arrival of Mrs Cutler had distracted us. She came sailing up in her Vauxhall Cabriolet, back that very minute from the coast.

I caught Jennifer's eye, but I had more important things to do than greet her. I ran back to the woolshed to see if Dad was there, and searched through the shearers' quarters, then went around all the pens and looked into the concrete trough where they did the sheep dipping. Finally I went down to the trees where the horses were tethered and found that the sulky was missing.

'He's gone off somewhere with Belinda,' I reported to Mum as she and Nurse McCaddie were about to go through the MacAdamses' cast-iron garden gate.

Mum was aghast, but Nurse McCaddie soothed her. 'It might be best to let him be. A crowd like this is no place for him at the moment. He's gone off to be at peace somewhere.'

'He'll be OK, missus.' Brown squeezed Mum's arm. 'I'll drive you all home. If you ask me, that reading of Jack's was the best thing about the whole bloody shebang.'

'Brown!' said Nurse McCaddie reprovingly.

I had been up to the MacAdamses' mansion on many occasions. Mad dashes with Dave Bridges after the regular Sunday services had often taken me past their arbour with its pink rambler roses. But I had never before been inside.

The drawing room was enormous. It had a lofty ceiling with two chandeliers and was as splendid a drawing room as I had ever seen. One of its splendours was our lion-and-lizard carpet, and another was our grandfather clock. I remember that before things got out of hand, I stood proudly for some time in front of it. 'It's ours really,' I said to everyone who stopped to have a look. 'It has the four seasons around the face.' I pointed. 'Spring, summer, autumn, winter.'

The buffet – for which, had the rabbits not eaten them, Dad would have provided the best lettuces in the whole shire – was laid out on long trestle tables and was immediately set upon by the arriving guests, including me.

I was so busy eating, I forgot about everything except food for a while, even about Dad, even about my plan to tell Mr Sullivan about what Mr Kelly and the Bush Brigade were up to. I had decided to talk to Mr Sullivan directly rather than get Mr Buchanan to do it. I had not really confided much in Mr Buchanan since the terrible day I broke the wax.

'Are you hoping for a little brother or a little sister?' asked Auntie Annabel, in a hat decorated with rooster feathers, her mouth full of turkey.

'It's definitely a brother,' I said.

'That's the devil in you talking. You can hope, but you cannot know. The good Lord alone has the privilege until the time has come.'

'It is,' I said stubbornly. 'I know.'

'Dad wants a son,' said Heather.

'Well, if the poor man has been praying for a son, let us hope that his prayers will be answered.'

'Yes, my beauty,' said Mr Kelly, who came by at that moment, 'like the prayers for fucking rain.'

'The Bishop is a sincere and wonderful man,' snapped Auntie Annabel.

'I agree. The prayers for rain were irresistible.'

Mr Kelly did his belly push, then took her by the hips and moved her to one side.

'I am doing this, my powdered pretty, not because you are an object of desire, but because I want to get at that fowl.'

Auntie Annabel spat a tiny piece of turkey in Mr Kelly's face and then stamped on his foot. For once I warmed to Auntie Annabel.

Word about the loss of the lettuces flashed round, and sympathy was expressed on all sides. Nurse McCaddie came over to talk to Mum about her midwifery services. Dr Abercrombie said he would make a special trip out from Wudgie to see her any time, not to worry about the cost. Slow George said he was betting on rain – odds on it would come before the baby.

Then Mr Morrison said, 'Ah, Lillian, the drought bends the best of us,' and Mum burst into tears.

'Everyone is so kind.'

Mrs Cutler handed her a napkin and she began to dry her eyes.

'You're going to have that baby down at the coast, Lillian, my dear,' boomed Mrs Cutler. 'At my new abode.' She had leased the house at Woy Woy and was moving there at the end of the month. 'I can tell which way the wind is blowing.'

'Oh, Elsie,' said Mum, and burst into tears again.

Mrs MacAdams came up with Lorraine and Margaret, her two daughters, who were home for the holidays. She elbowed Mrs Cutler out of the way and steered Mum through the French doors into the sitting room. 'Don't let that dreadful woman upset you, Lillian. I told the Bishop about the lettuces. He said he was so sorry to hear and understood perfectly.'

Mrs MacAdams stood Mum in front of our rosewood desk.

'I know what a sacrifice it was, Lillian. I want to show you that it has found a good home.'

The money from our latest sale had meant, among other things, food on the table, repairs to the truck, and a winter school uniform for Heather.

Mum revealed to them the secret panel at the side.

'Better and better,' crowed Mrs MacAdams. 'A priest's hole. See that, girls?'

Lorraine and Margaret both leaned forward. 'Yes, Mum,' they said. They were both tall, with long faces like their father's, and snub noses like their mother's. They had excellent manners. Earlier, Heather had been admiring their vivacity and poise.

'The girls have acquired my taste for quality,' said Mrs Mac-Adams. 'Look at their frocks. Dowlings of Pitt Street. Very chic, for the war, don't you think?'

Mum's eyes flashed. She had been looking through the sitting room window, almost as though she feared to see Dad skulking out in the shrubbery somewhere. Her nerves were on edge, despite Mrs MacAdams' effort to be nice.

'No,' she said sharply. 'The cut is wrong, the finish is shoddy, and the girls don't know how to wear them yet.' Mum turned away. 'Excuse me, I am going to find my husband.'

'Let him find himself,' Mrs MacAdams called out. 'Lillian Armstrong, stop right there.'

Mum stopped.

'You obviously feel you can do better, so I am going to take you up on that. You're going to do a fitting for Lorrie and Maggie. Winter suits. Right, girls?'

'Yes, Mum.'

'Well, Lillian. That's settled. I'm a mean old stick, so you can't expect me to be exactly fair, but I'm sure we can come to some satisfactory arrangement about price.' Mrs MacAdams rubbed her thumb and forefinger together. 'You need a little independence from that burden of yours.'

Mrs MacAdams turned towards the drawing room, from which, above the roar of conversation, came the sound of Mr Buchanan at the grand piano playing 'California, Here I Come.'

'I suppose I had better say good-bye to Mrs Cutler. This no doubt will be her last public appearance. Thank God she's finally leaving.'

I couldn't understand how pleased everyone except Mum seemed to be about the departure of Mrs Cutler, although I knew it had something to do with her not wearing any underwear, and with the way Mrs Cutler mistakenly thought she lived as the Romans did.

'Mrs Cutler's behaviour is an insult to every decent Australian,' Mrs MacAdams said loudly, to the room at large. 'Who does she think we are? Abos? And I must get that car of mine back from her.'

'What about Mr Kelly's behaviour?' I asked her boldly. 'He's got murder on his mind and treats Dad like dirt. What about the Colonel? Even the Bishop's talking to him.'

Mrs MacAdams didn't seem to be listening to me. Her eyes were going round the room, looking for someone.

'Why isn't everyone turning their back on them?' I persisted.

Mr Kelly had recovered from his setback with Auntie Annabel and was rubbing his potbelly up against the fat lady from the store at Mudoogla. The Colonel was being as jolly as Santa Claus.

'Ah, Mr Sullivan, there you are,' cried Mrs MacAdams. 'Have

you met the Bishop yet? Let me introduce you. We must get you some interesting tidbits for the *Star*.'

Gloomily I watched Mrs MacAdams take Mr Sullivan over to the Bishop, who now had his arm around the Colonel's shoulder.

Jennifer put her sticky hands over my eyes and said guess who, so I went back with her to the buffet and ate the last of the sardine patties. I looked at her awful tow-coloured hair and was amazed at how thoroughly love had died. Jennifer and I were once more two people who did not really get on, but I knew I would miss her carefree ways. I stood close by her, hoping something of the past would miraculously burn bright once more. Auntie Annabel began upbraiding the twins for their manners. I took a mutton sandwich in one hand and two profiteroles in the other, just to see if Auntie Annabel would upbraid me also. Jennifer's eyes flashed and we smirked wickedly at each other. She put out her tongue at Auntie Annabel and then began to tell me about the koala bears and palm trees down at Woy Woy.

It was then that I saw Mr Sullivan leave the Bishop and go over to the table near the grand piano and grab a whole plate of sausage rolls. It was my chance. I ran over, grabbed a sausage roll too, and began talking. Mr Sullivan obviously didn't believe me.

'No, sir. I am not exaggerating. Mr Kelly is leading Mr Williams astray, just like he is Dad.'

'Mr Ernie Williams is a fine upstanding citizen. I play bowls with him.' Mr Sullivan talked with his mouth full, and flakes of pastry were falling all down his front. 'Bruce Kelly is just a lot of talk. This isn't Russia. We don't arrest people for what they think. We'd have to take in everyone in the Prince William, son.'

'It's a plot. That has to be a crime.'

Mr Sullivan shook his head. 'The thing about stories like this is that we have to confirm them. Do you know what that means?'

'Yes sir, and we should confirm it at once. Mr Kelly will confirm it.'

'Oh, for heaven's sake!' said Mr Sullivan testily. He moved off with the sausage rolls, back towards the Bishop.

I raised my voice. 'We can ask him right now in front of the Colonel and he will be stopped from shooting into the camp. The lives of many prisoners will be saved.'

'Do you think it matters whether their lives are saved? What's a few Japs? We're at war. Thousands of them are being killed in the Pacific every week. Do you think the people around here care about the Japs? I don't. Every Jap eating his head off inside that camp costs me money. The fewer the better, I say.'

'Richard, that's enough,' came Mr Buchanan's voice from the piano.

Mr Sullivan gave a funny snuffling laugh.

'I care about them.' I paused and then said, 'I know one of them quite well. I told you before. He was at our farm.'

Mr Sullivan stopped eating for a moment and looked down at me over his glasses.

'Mum and I are worried about Dad. Brown says that Dad would not even be mixed up in all this if it wasn't for the drought. Drought makes for strange bedfellows.'

'It does indeed.' Mr Sullivan put down the plate and gave my ear lobe a little jiggle. 'Don't you worry. Maybe I can do something with all this very interesting information. I'll get Mr Tappley on to it immediately.'

'I know all about Mr Tappley. You.'

Mr Sullivan gave my ear a sharp parting twist. 'Don't let your mind run away with you, boy. Bruce Kelly's got a powerful hate, and an equally powerful imagination, but there's a difference between what people want to do and what they actually do.'

'It's not only Mr Kelly. It's the Colonel. The Colonel is at the heart of the problem. It's a conspiracy.'

'Get away from me,' hissed Mr Sullivan, shooing at me with both hands.

'You're in it too!' I shouted, and even then I somehow knew that I was shouting in frustration at the whole world of adults, a world I was not privy to, and feared, suddenly, I never would be.

'Richard, come here,' Mr Buchanan called urgently.

I ran away and threw myself at Brown's legs.

'Brown, you've got to take me into the police station in Wudgie.'

'Look out, here comes your dad,' said Brown.

I turned to see.

'Oh, dear God,' Auntie Annabel cried.

Dad was lurching. One of his studs had come undone, and his collar was around his ear. His hat was missing and his hair was up in spikes. Mum went to him quickly and fixed his tie. She tried to get him to leave, and Brown and Mrs Cutler moved over to help, but he brushed them all aside and pushed his way farther into the room. He had something definite on his mind.

He went straight to the long windows facing the portico at the front, where the Bishop was in conversation with Mr MacAdams and the Colonel. They were all smoking expensive cigars, even though there was a war and a drought. The Bishop had doffed his mitre and was no longer anywhere near six feet tall. I found I agreed with Mrs Cutler. What a fraud.

I left the buffet and wove my way through the crowd until I reached the windows. The Bishop looked down as I arrived. He beamed and touched my hair with his hand.

Close up the Bishop smelled of cologne and a strong mustiness. His face had liver spots and his jowls hung over his collar. Dad was standing in front of him, breathing hard, but looking quite respectable. Mum had managed a quick repair job. She stood behind him a little, nervously twisting at her gloves. The Colonel took a step forward as if to deal with Dad and then thought better of it.

'Thank you for your prayers, Your Grace,' Dad began. 'I believe they will be answered.'

'Bishop,' corrected Mr MacAdams.

'If God so chooses,' replied the Bishop sombrely, 'this stricken land will be blessed with soaking rains.'

'You gave Him no choice. His goodness and mercy have become manifest. The clouds have gathered. The drought is over. Water is flowing again in every river, every stream.'

The Bishop closed his eyes, puffed on his cigar, and coughed discreetly. He gave a slight bow in Dad's direction.

Mr MacAdams drank from his glass. The Colonel did the same and muttered something to an officer standing behind him. Dad's eyes were a little off-beam. Somewhere he had found quite a bit of whiskey. It was hard for me to look at him, and I waited in trepidation for what might come next. I found myself staring at the Bishop's hand. His fingers were short and beefy, and he wore a heavy gold ring in which was set a large red stone. His gracefully cocked wrist was no more than a foot away from my face.

'There was a massacre last night,' Dad suddenly shouted, and pointed an accusing finger at the Colonel. 'This man is to blame. War has come. No one was spared. There is blood upon the land.' He spread his arms out wide towards the Bishop, palms upward, and then looked from his left hand to his right and back again.

'There is blood upon my hands. Blood – ' He stopped.

'Bishop, this man is a well-known local ratbag, if you'll pardon the expression. Pay no attention to him,' said the Colonel as Mum moved forward and gently took Dad's arm.

'Jack dear, come away.' She gave a tug. 'Please excuse him. He has not been well.'

The Bishop nodded. Then he looked at the Colonel, and then at Mr MacAdams.

Mr MacAdams drew in his breath and glanced at the faces all around. The room had fallen silent. A circle had formed. Mr Buchanan finished up on the piano with a little trill.

'Mr Armstrong. Jack. You've had a rough day. Enough is enough. Lillian, do you need any help there?'

Mrs MacAdams pushed her way through. 'Let me handle this, Bill.' She stood beside Dad with her hands on her hips. 'Mr Armstrong, you are making a complete idiot of yourself. Get out of my house.'

Dad took no notice of her.

'I did my best,' he shouted at the Bishop. Dad's features were twisted, his mouth opening and closing in such a way as to show all his teeth and gums. 'I have been found wanting. Everything is gone. My last hope. This man is the instrument – ' Dad pointed at the Colonel, and began to cough, almost choking on all the saliva in his mouth. 'This man,' he repeated. 'Your Grace, you are God's vicar, and a great man. You must pray for me. And my babies. We are being struck down. This is the beginning of the slaughter. My father . . .' Dad's voice suddenly trailed off.

No one moved. Then Dad was down on his knees, and all eyes followed. I have never forgotten that unexpected fall to the carpet. Our carpet, I couldn't help reminding myself, even in that dreadful moment. The Bishop's ash dropped in a heap. I looked at Mum. Into the silence thundered Dad's voice.

'Let us pray. All together. On your knees, Your Grace,' he shouted. His arms, sweeping round wildly, indicated that he wanted everyone to join in. Then he leaned forward, pulled hard at the Bishop's robe, and shouted, 'Down!' – and that did it. The Bishop yanked his robe away. Mrs MacAdams got a hammer lock on Dad and dragged him backwards. Mum screamed at her to leave him alone. Heather came running up with Dad's hat.

'Major Oakander,' barked the Colonel.

'Bob,' called Mr MacAdams. Major Oakander and Bob both moved forward and grabbed Dad under the arms. Dad struggled briefly and then let himself be taken.

'More orangeade, Bishop?' I heard Mrs MacAdams ask as I ran off after Dad.

'Bloody drought,' said a voice.

'You're hurting him,' Mum cried. Dad was half walking, half scrabbling as the two men hauled him through the front door and out on to the portico. From there they threw him down the two steps on to the gravel.

Dad remained on his knees where he had fallen. He lifted his hands and stared at them. The gravel had scraped the skin away.

'Jack, let me look.' Mum rushed to him, followed by Nurse McCaddie. Dr Abercrombie appeared at the front door.

'I'll do it, Jean,' Mum said, taking a handkerchief and wiping away the saliva dribbling from Dad's mouth.

'I will go and get my bag,' said Dr Abercrombie. 'I think a sedative . . .'

'They had no right to do this to him,' Nurse McCaddie began.

In that moment Dad jumped to his feet and ran for the front gate. Only then did I see that Belinda and the sulky were out there. Dad disappeared for a moment or two behind the pencil pines, and then he ran back towards us with his shotgun in one hand and a sack in the other. In the time he had been missing, Dad had been home. Mum screamed and screamed again. 'No, Jack, no!'

'Stop him!' cried Dr Abercrombie, holding out his arms. Dad dodged us all easily. He was up the steps. Brown was on the portico and grabbed for the gun, but Dad moved too quickly for him. He was through the door and into the drawing room. I heard screams. Mum tried to hold me, but I followed him inside.

The crowd parted; some people flung themselves on the floor.

Mrs MacAdams was yelling and threw the contents of her glass, Major Oakander cracked him hard with his stick, but Dad reached the Colonel and the Bishop without much opposition and emptied the sack of decapitated rabbits all over them.

FIVE
Nightmares

24

BROWN DROVE MUM into town every day to see Dad at the hospital. It was a week or so before Dad stopped talking about how the Japs had got the lettuces.

After he had thrown the rabbits, Dad had begun running round and round the MacAdamses' drawing room. He knocked over all three trestle tables, and it took six men to wrestle him to the floor. The shotgun wasn't loaded, but Dad kept swinging it around wildly and did considerable damage to one of Mrs MacAdams' chandeliers. Dr Abercrombie gave him a needle and took him that same afternoon to Wudgewunda Base Hospital, where he was kept heavily sedated and under close observation.

Mrs Cutler said there was no longer any question about what the Armstrong family had to do. The first step in the cure for someone who had gone cuckoo, she said, was to get the victim out of the place that had caused it. Mum agreed that our life in Billarooby was over, and accepted Mrs Cutler's kind offer for us to stay in her big house at Woy Woy until we found something of our own.

The last thing Mrs Cutler did before leaving was to push the Vauxhall Cabriolet over the cliff behind her house. Mum was aghast at the waste. 'A blow against the empire,' said Mrs Cutler. 'Needed a new engine anyway.'

Mum became concerned about our throwing ourselves on the mercies of someone capable of such abandon, but she overcame her fears and told Dad firmly what we were going to do. I was there in the ward when she told him. It was for his sake, for the sake of the coming baby, and for the sake of Heather and me. Dad sat in his hospital bed with his hands folded on the Bible and sort of nodded while he stared at the wall.

'I wish it hadn't taken something like this to make him see reason,' said Mum.

Mum had made all the preliminary arrangements for our departure, and I found that I was even looking forward to seeing Jennifer again, when Dad dropped a bombshell. He appeared unexpectedly one afternoon at the farmhouse with Mr Kelly, who had picked him up at the hospital, days before he was due to be discharged. Mum and Heather and I were all on the floor, packing up Mum's china.

'We're not going anywhere,' Dad said. He threw his hat for the peg and landed it.

'That's my boy!' crowed Mr Kelly, and, moving forward, gave Dad a friendly massage with his paunch.

I stood with Brown towards sunset that day, watching a flock of beautiful birds in the orchard.

'What are they?'

'Ibis. Means there's rain about.' He handed me his binoculars.

They were large black and white birds with long red legs and curved beaks.

'They're looking for insects.'

'Break their beaks on that soil.'

'Maybe they've found a soft spot.'

'Ibis are a good omen. If they stay.'

Brown went back to the dairy, but I sat on the hillside watching the ibis. After a while they decided that Billarooby was not the place for them. They rose together in stately fashion and flew off in a V formation across the dry bed of the Lachlan.

Cold winter settled on Billarooby. Dad went back to his rounds and to his rabbiting with Mr Kelly. Weeks would go by without his ever washing or shaving. He had the smell of the dump and the dead rabbits about him and Mum wouldn't have him in the big double bed.

Up in the sulky, with his whip and shotgun, with his dirty, bearded face beneath the old slouch hat rammed down tight, the army greatcoat flapping open, his flies unbuttoned, Dad was a rather scary figure, brooding and dark, like some vengeful appar-ition. Doors were closed against him as much as against the

Japanese. He did not seem to care about the lack of welcome. At first, everyone from Mrs MacAdams to Auntie Annabel tried to persuade him to leave the district, but Dad listened to no one except Mr Kelly, and he was telling Dad something completely different.

Billarooby began a wait and see. Along with the nemesis of the camp, Dad became just another of the trials and sorrows of the drought.

'You must keep him away from the booze,' I heard Dr Abercrombie saying pointlessly to Mum one afternoon when he was out to check her. Dad was passed out on his mattress on the side verandah, breathing heavily, drunk and unsavoury. 'The pills. He has to keep taking those pills. Grind them up in his food if you have to.'

Mrs Cutler kept sending breezy letters from Woy Woy saying how wonderful it was and to hurry on down. Heather kept her new navy blue tunic and blazer perfectly pressed and carried a brush with her on the train for the dust. She said she was making up for Dad's being so unkempt. Heather remained an unrepentant apologist for Dad. She even got him into the tub one night for a good wash. I made a smart remark and got a talking to. 'It's not his fault if he still stinks. It's all the quicklime.'

There was a rumour of the killing of many Japanese prisoners who had attempted to break out of another, smaller camp near Cowra, and confirmation of another rumour that the Colonel had shot to death an older Korean prisoner who had not even been trying to escape. Sergeant Duffy said that there had been a military enquiry but that the Colonel had been completely exonerated. The exoneration had gone to his head, and since then he had been going around as if he had permanent sunstroke. Dad wasn't the only one cracking up.

Sergeant Duffy added that the Japs didn't like the way the Colonel and his crew were slapping them around, and that we should keep our ears glued to the wireless.

The Bush Brigade no longer even tried to conceal that they were a vigilante group. Mr Kelly and Blue Chapman were accused of harassing two Italian POWs working on a farm near Glen Hogan, and the following week there was an editorial by Mr Sullivan in the *Wudgewunda Star* expressing concern that certain sections of the population were taking the law into their own hands against the prisoners of war.

Mr Sullivan went on to say that there were also rumours of a plot to shoot into the camp, which was not only a breach of international law but a crime against humanity, and if the Japanese authorities in Tokyo found out about it, there would certainly be reprisals against Australian prisoners of war in Malaya. The *Star* called for security measures at the camp to be tightened all round and guards to be posted in all the outcrops overlooking the camp.

'Sullivan finally came round,' Mr Buchanan said to me one day after class. 'You can pat yourself on the back, Lindsay.'

'Why doesn't he write something about the Colonel?' I wanted to know. 'About him being so trigger-happy.'

'Censorship. Everything about the camp has to be cleared through the army machine. You'll never read anything about the mess inside that camp. Anyway, you know Sullivan and the Colonel are drinking mates.'

I cut out Mr Sullivan's editorial and pasted it in my scrapbook, along with a paragraph about the police coming out and giving Mr Kelly a warning. Mr Sullivan's reporter took a photograph to go with his story, and I pasted that in too, of course. I still have the scrapbook. The yellowed picture shows Mr Kelly genial as can be, holding up a dead rabbit, and Dad in the dump behind, all eyebrows and stubble, looking grim, like Fagin in his final days.

I checked my outcrop one day. There was no guard posted, and the whole place stank of piss. Beer bottles everywhere. It had to be Mr Kelly and his gang.

There was an outbreak of impetigo at school, and I got it on both knees.

When the end came, it came with a rush.

I sat in the back row, slack-eyed and unable to pay attention to my lessons. When Mr Buchanan made the announcement that the Billarooby school would be closing for lack of pupils and that next term all of us would be going to Wudgewunda on the train, I could not raise a cheer as the Morrisons did. That same morning had come the news that some of Slow George's cows had died during the night. 'Six of them, sir, all swolled up,' said Eric Kiddy, who came by the dairy every morning on his way to school.

'Swollen,' corrected Mr Buchanan.

'They ate something poisonous, down by the river. They stink real bad, sir.'

I closed my eyes and put my head in my arms on the desk in front of me. Mr Buchanan led me to the school couch and took my temperature. I had a high fever and he sent me home.

It was a still winter day. The frost had long since been dispersed by the heat of the sun, and the air had a hot, dry crackle to it. I dragged my feet through the dirt, trailing my satchel. There was an aching behind my knees and a fire in my forehead. Dust coated my swollen throat. Halfway home I had to rest in the shade of the box tree. The bark crunched and broke under me as I lay down and closed my eyes.

When I opened them again, I felt a little better. Time had gone by. A frilled-neck lizard was poised on a nearby stump. And there was Gus, the magpie, pecking at the ground a short way off. I noticed he had developed a bald patch. He looked round suddenly and gave me the evil yellow eye. I stood up in alarm and moved away, my head swimming. The lizard's frill spread wide as I passed, and it spat a soft, warning *pah*.

I was not sure where I was, and momentarily I panicked. Then I recognized the flats and held out my hand to touch the dairy roof. Perspective had changed. A truck pulled up and a voice asked me if I wanted a lift. I was on the road. It was Mr Morrison going down to have a look at the cows.

'You OK?' he asked as I leaned back on the seat. The cabin was full of feathers.

'I'm sick. I should be in bed.'

'I'll drive you home.'

'I want to see the cows.'

The cows lay on their sides in the far paddock, swollen to twice their usual size. Slow George and Brown, working on them with skinning knives, had already taken off two of the hides. The carcasses glistened purplish red. Shiny green winter flies buzzed in the still air. There was a fetid smell I had not encountered before, and the smell of fresh cow shit.

I clung to the fence, my face burning. Brown came over, wiping his bloody hands on his trousers.

'Cows decided to take a good rest,' I heard him say. I wanted to climb through the fence to help but couldn't get my hands off the barbed wire, and although my eyes were open I found I could no longer see clearly. Waves of heat and livid colour took the place of the cows, and then, without warning, no more than a few inches in front of me appeared the Japanese. They were clinging to the barbed wire, like me, their uniforms bright red tongues of fire, their hands and mouths flowing blood. They cried out for help, but their voices were drowned by the cawing of a thousand crows. Louder and louder grew the cacophony until I wanted to do nothing more than put my hands over my ears and shut it off. It was then I realized that I could not find my hands. I cried out. An arm went round my shoulders and I closed my eyes. The Japanese disappeared.

'Come on, boy.' Brown was loosening my hands from the barbed wire. I looked at them. They were scarlet, with little blue punctures in the skin. Brown put his hand to my forehead. I looked at the cows again and noticed they were lying in a black slime.

'Dad, I'm taking the little bloke home,' Brown yelled. 'He's real crook.'

Brown drove fast. The corrugations in the road bounced every bone in my body.

'I'm dying alive,' I informed Brown in a whisper.

Through the dusty windshield I saw the farmhouse. I reached out to touch it; my fingers hit the glass. Brown carried me into the living room, and Mum came forward to feel my brow. Dad was standing in his pyjamas with the Bible in his hand. The whiskey bottle was on the table. He had not left the house for two days. He had made me empty his chamber pot that morning.

'He had better go straight to bed,' said Mum, leading Brown down the corridor to my room. The covers went over me. The fur from the rabbitskin blanket was horrible on my face, and I pushed it off.

Voices came from far away.

'Jean McCaddie . . .'

'Jack can't go, in his state . . .'

'Be back in half an hour . . .'

A cool cloth wiped my face and body. 'Drink this.' It was Mum's voice. She lifted me into a sitting position, and I drank. It was something bitter. I sank back on to the bed.

I don't know how long I lay there, but I was brought back to consciousness by a steady shouting. Sometimes it came closer, other times it went farther away. Slowly I realized that it was Dad reading from the Bible as he paced up and down the living room. His voice became more and more insistent, and I pulled the blankets over my head to shut it out. I knew he had thrown away all his pills. Suddenly I heard Mum cry out, and such a charge ran through my body that I thought for a moment I was cured. I sat up.

'Give me that!'

A chair overturned, and there was the noise of paper tearing.

'There! That's what I think. I'll bring you to your senses, if it's the last thing I do. It can burn for all I care.' There was a crash. 'Oh my God,' she screamed, and then there was silence.

I got out of bed. I clung to the bedpost and then staggered into the corridor. My head hit the wall. By the time I reached the living room door, Mum was backed up between the dining table and the range. Her hair had fallen down, and there was a wet stain on her long green gown. The crystal water jug lay broken on the floor. Dad was advancing towards her, his fists clenched.

'No, Jack, no! Think of the baby.'

Tears streamed down her cheeks. One arm was raised to protect her face, the other held out to stop him.

The room was littered with pages ripped from the Bible. In the middle of the rug I saw a ten-pound note. The Bible itself lay in the coals in the fireplace, and smoke was already beginning to rise. I crawled over and pulled it out. I tried to get to my feet and help Mum, but my head was like a kite in a tailspin. My voice came out in a whisper. 'No, Dad, no.'

He slapped Mum twice across the face with two sweeping blows. She turned and ran outside, with Dad moving slowly in pursuit. I clung to the couch and then launched myself in the direction of the front door. By the time I was on the verandah, Dad was halfway across the front yard, picking up rocks. Mum's gown caught on the barbed wire as she went through the fence.

She gave a wrench. The gown tore down the front, but she was free. She ran to the truck and began to crank it. I knew she could not do it. As Dad lurched slowly past the barbed wire towards her he threw a rock, which missed Mum and crashed against the bonnet of the truck.

'It's his, you whore,' Dad shouted, and threw another rock.

I saw the shotgun resting against a verandah pole and managed to pick it up. I didn't know what I could do, but I suddenly found my voice. 'Leave Mum alone,' I shouted over and over again, the blood pounding in the side of my head. 'I've got the gun.'

Mum flung the crank handle away and went running down towards the dunney. A stone got her in the back, and she fell to her knees. She didn't try to get up or protect herself from Dad. Instead she began to shake her fist at the sun and to shout. She was cursing everything. I heard Mrs Cutler's name. I heard Australia and Billarooby.

'Rain, damn you, why don't you rain!'

She threw dust at the sky and then began rubbing handfuls of it into her hair.

'I curse you, Jack Armstrong, and I curse your father and your whole family,' she screamed at him as he went down the slope towards her. 'You can kill me for all I care.'

I could not get any farther than the barbed wire. I leaned against an iron stake and saw Brown's lorry coming up the driveway, and behind it, just turning into the gate from the main road, Nurse McCaddie's Baby Austin.

Mum was still on the ground and Dad was standing over her when Brown reached the top of the slope. Brown got out of the lorry and ran stiffly towards them. Dad had another rock. He raised his arm.

'Go away, you're not wanted here,' Dad shouted.

'It's all right, Brown,' Mum cried. 'Don't come any closer.'

'Put that down, Jack.' Brown limped slowly forward with his hand outstretched.

'It's all right, Brown,' Mum cried out once more. She got to her feet.

Nurse McCaddie's car was a bug on the slope. Dad threw the rock at Brown, who ducked and then began to grapple with him. I raised the shotgun and then stumbled. The gun hit the ground and went off with a great explosion. I fell sideways against the barbed wire and felt it tear my skin. I lifted my hand up to have a look and found myself in another time and another place. Rain was falling. My hand was wrapped in Granddad's handkerchief and there was blood pouring down my wrist. I began to scream. To scream and scream again.

25

THROUGH MY OPEN WINDOW the sky was a harsh blue. On my bedside chair was a hand bell. The sheet was soaked in sweat. Throwing it off, I climbed out of bed. The compress on my forehead fell to the floor and I walked into the corridor.

Once outside, I climbed through the back fence and then through the barbed wire barricade.

The sun burned me and my legs shook, but I was impelled onward, along one of my pathways. I was walking slowly over a meat ants' nest, and the ants swarmed up my legs. A bite, and then another, and another, and nothing to do about it.

I began to swell up like one of Slow George's cows. My skin grew tighter and tighter, and I floated off into a cold and utterly lonely blackness.

A Japanese knight in ceremonial armour, with the rabbit grin and slit eyes of Mr Buchanan's poster, appeared like a distant pinpoint in the void. He rushed towards me, threw a spear. I raised my hand and deflected it. The knight disappeared, but to my horror he was the first of hundreds. They thought I was the Colonel. I saw I was wearing his uniform. Frantically I waved my arms, warding them off. 'You're making a mistake,' I shouted, 'a terrible mistake.' I tore off the Colonel's uniform, threw it on the ground. 'Look, I'm Lindsay.' It was no use. Tighter and tighter I grew until I was the thinnest of membranes. The least touch would cause me to explode. A thistledown drifted towards me. I screamed.

I was at my circle. In the distance the barbed wire barricade around the farmhouse arose on its stakes and marched towards me. It swarmed with Japanese hurling knives and screaming like monkeys. I looked for Tadao, but he was not there to help. I was lost and all alone. 'Tadao, tell them it's me.' I turned away in despair and closed my eyes.

I began to cry. I waited to die and the wait was unendurable. Then came the feeling that if I was to live, I had to look death in the face.

'Turn and look,' I commanded myself, but I could not. Barbs like needles, teeth razor-sharp, right upon me.

'It's the truth that matters, not the wax,' said Mr Buchanan.

'Be brave,' said Mrs Cutler.

'Jump,' said Brown.

I turned and looked, only to find myself in the middle of my nightmare.

I am running along behind Dad and Granddad on a rainy winter's afternoon. Granddad is dressed in his rust-coloured hunting jacket, black trousers, and high red boots with straps all down the side. He wears a green hat with a partridge feather. His hair is silver-white. His moustache and beard are stained orange around the mouth. He is smoking a cigar and shambling through the stubble. Granddad drinks from a flask. Dad reaches for it and Granddad pushes him away. Dad goes sideways and then recovers. I hear his boots squelch in the mud. Dad is dressed in a long grey overcoat and wears a tweed cap.

'Jesus Christ Almighty! Always in the dark,' Granddad yells at Dad.

We come to a stile. Granddad falls against it, then steadies himself. He takes the cigar out of his mouth.

'Chop chop,' he shouts.

I run forward to hold his gun so Granddad can climb.

Granddad pushes the gun so roughly towards me that he catches me in the chest with the stock. The safety catch scrapes along my hand and I feel the pain as I fall backward into the mud. There is a tremendous explosion that makes the gun jump out of my hands. Granddad is falling. I see the rust-coloured coat hit the ground, I see his legs go in the air.

'Lindsay!' I hear Dad's voice and he takes my hand. There is blood pouring down from my cut, and a fine rain is beginning to fall.

'You stupid old goat!' Dad shouts.

Granddad lies on his back. I hear him begin to laugh, and then to cough.

He sits up against the stile, takes out his flask, and has a swallow. There is mud on his jacket. He reaches for his hat and shoves it back on his head.

'Kill an old man, would you, kill an old man.' Granddad continues to laugh and cough. He looks around for his cigar, but it is gone in the grass. He pulls a handkerchief from his pocket. 'Stop your blubbering, man, come here.' Granddad wraps my hand in the handkerchief. 'Your pretty mother will wash it for you when we get back. We'll go in at the next stile.'

Granddad is on his feet, swaying to right and left. He looks at me, leans down close. His eyes have a network of red lines over the whites, and purple pouches under them.

'Warned you about that catch. Killed your granddad, you did.' Granddad begins to laugh again. 'Ah ha ha ha! Ah ha ha ha!' Granddad laughs like the devil. He pulls me to him, squeezes me up against his legs. 'I dwarf you, little man, I dwarf you,' he cries with glee, and grows to ten feet tall.

A cold wind blows spatters of rain in our faces, and it is a long way across the next cornfield to the cover. Dad and Granddad start yelling again.

'You bastard,' shouts Dad.

'You're the bastard,' Granddad shouts back. 'Would I do such a thing to her?'

And then there is a silence, a pool of eerie silence, but for Granddad's wheezes, which grow louder and louder as we walk forever in the field. Two cock pheasants suddenly crash upward in a whirr of wings. *Cuk! Cuk! CUK! CUK!* They are in full flight and head towards the river. Granddad and Dad both shoulder and fire. One of the birds falls down by the bank. Granddad reloads.

'Go pick it up.' As I run by him, Granddad growls, 'Stop that feeble noise, my man. We're going in.' I wipe away my tears.

I push on down the slope of the bank and out of sight. I know exactly where the pheasant has fallen. I go through the marshy grass and find it, in the reeds. I reach forward and grab it by the tail, admiring the red wattles and the bright shine of the plumage. The river ripples by. It is nice and calm down there by the water, away from Dad and Granddad. I look at my hand. Blood is trickling down my wrist.

I close my eyes for a moment and feel myself rising, rising, rising, until suddenly I am flying high above the river and the field. I am a bird of prey, a kite with long white wings. Below me, Granddad and Dad are approaching the second stile. I pause, fluttering my wings. The sun breaks through the clouds and illuminates me and the stubbly field. Everything is very beautiful. Granddad reaches the stile with Dad close behind him, and they are arguing as usual. Granddad hands the shotgun to Dad and begins to climb. As he reaches the top, Dad steps forward and pushes him. He falls down the other side, and Dad leaps over and begins to kick him. Granddad struggles to rise, but Dad continues to kick and keeps him down. They are shouting, but I cannot hear. Then Dad places the gun at his head and pulls both triggers. Blood explodes outward and turns the sky red. Dad spits on Granddad, a terror seizes me, and my wings turn to stone. I hang motionless in the sky and Dad points his finger at me. 'No, Dad, no,' I scream, but a flash of fire comes from his finger, and there is a terrible pain that shoots up my back and explodes inside my brain.

I am tumbling, tumbling, through the bloody sky and open my eyes to find myself lying on my back beside the river with the pheasant in my hand. 'Lindsay, Lindsay,' I hear Dad calling. I see the blood seeping through the handkerchief and hesitate. I am frightened. His voice calls again, like an echo, and I rise and scramble to the top of the bank.

I see Dad running towards the stile from the centre of the field to where Granddad is lying, and I begin to run also. Dad shouts, 'Stay back, stay back,' but I continue to run, and we reach Granddad at the same time. We look down together. The side of his head is blown away. 'What did you see, what did you see?' Dad asks.

'I didn't see anything,' I reply. 'I was down by the water.'

Dad stares at me and shouts, 'I did nothing, do you hear me, nothing! It was an accident.'

For a few moments we stare at each other, then Dad steps forward and begins to squeeze me in his arms. I feel myself being squeezed smaller and smaller until I disappear into the shattered side of Granddad's head. Then I reappear, squeezed out through the blood that is oozing between Granddad's back teeth, and find that I am standing on my centre stone. I am screaming. I am naked. Heather is running towards me, followed by Nurse McCaddie. Farther behind comes Mum. I cover myself with my hands, and feel the sun hot on my face.

'You little fool, you'll die,' said Heather as she ran up. Nurse McCaddie wrapped a wet towel round me and felt my forehead.

'I'm better,' I said. The weakness in my legs was gone and I felt euphoric, exhilarated. Heather picked up my pyjamas.

Nurse McCaddie helped me down from the stone.

'I really am better.'

'We almost lost him,' said Nurse McCaddie as Mum came up and put her arms around me.

I was put back to bed. Nurse McCaddie took my temperature and found that it was back to normal.

'The boy is right, the fever is broken.'

When Dad came in to see how I was, I had no fear of him. I sensed instead the fear that had come to fill his life, and the fear he had of me.

'I have been with Granddad, and I know what you did to him,' I said.

Mum, Heather, and Nurse McCaddie were all there. It just came out. It was my moment of truth, my one short-lived moment of absolute clarity. It was my same old nightmare, but now, with every shred of loyalty and love for Dad gone, I accepted it as truth, instead of dutifully rejecting it as the most appalling of fantasies.

'Now, Lindsay, you've been at death's door,' said Nurse McCaddie. 'You must stay quiet and not talk a lot of nonsense.'

It might have been nonsense to her, but I knew it wasn't to Dad. Or to me. Dad had done the most terrible thing in the world and never admitted it, so he was doomed to a life of suffering. Somehow he had always wanted me to know because I was his son, just as he was his father's son, but now that I knew, he would kill me before I told everybody else.

26

I ATE MY WAY rapidly through a helping of rabbit pie and a huge mound of fried potatoes. I could not stop. Mum poured me more milk.

'How long was I sick?'

'Four days.'

An alarm went off in my head. 'Are they all right?'

'Who?'

'Did the machine guns fire into the camp?'

'No, of course not, Lindsay dear,' Mum reassured me, casting a look at Dad, who was slumped in his chair near the range and staring ferociously at me as I ate. 'But we must be very careful. Sergeant Duffy says that something is going on there.'

'What?'

'It doesn't matter, just keep inside.'

My head filled with speculations about what might be happening at the camp. I began looking around for food, and Mum gave me more pie. I cut myself another slice of bread and spread it with dripping.

As my hunger went, I became even more aware of Dad's stare. The fear of him came rushing like a torrent. Worse than before.

I looked over at Mum in her chair, but she seemed not to notice Dad's ferocity. I could scarcely believe how big she had become in the days I had been sick. She was wearing her creamy flannel gown that tied under her breasts and fell all the way to the floor. Her hair was tied back with one of her green ribbons, and her face was rosy and calm.

'When does the baby come?'

'Soon.'

'Any day,' said Heather. 'It nearly came when you were sick.

You wouldn't have known anything about it. Dr Abercrombie was all the way out from Wudgie. He hardly even looked at you.'

Heather was both sorry I hadn't been even sicker and glad that I was now well.

There was no sugar or honey. I stirred my tea anyway.

At that moment Dad rose and went to the hat stand. He dusted off his slouch hat, put it on, and then picked up the shotgun from behind the door.

'Jack, please don't go off again. Stay here with your family.'

He hesitated, and I muttered under my breath, 'Go, go, go!'

'Everybody is already warned, over and over. There is no need to do any rounds today.'

'Bruce.' The screen door banged and he was gone.

'What happened to his arm?'

'He fell over,' said Heather, and she began to cry. Mum reached out and stroked her hair.

'He stumbled getting out of the sulky behind the shed and fell on the disc plough,' said Mum. 'It made a nasty cut.'

'How many stitches?'

'Lindsay, what does it matter? Only ten. I want you to go back to bed for the rest of the afternoon. Heather will read something. She's been staying home especially to look after you. And stop worrying about your father. There's not a drop in the house and he has been taking his pills. He has been much better these past few days.'

Mum and I looked at each other for a long second before we dropped our eyes.

'Go on with you,' she snapped.

Heather read to me from *A Tale of Two Cities*. After a while she got up and closed the door.

'Dad didn't do anything to Granddad,' she said. Her voice was intimidating, but I could feel that she was doubtful for once.

I waited a moment and then let her have it.

'He killed him. That's what he did. I saw.'

I shocked her to the extent that she had to restrain herself from hitting a recently sick person. 'That's a really terrible thing to say. You're still sick in bed.'

'No, I'm not. I'm better.'

'You're delirious and I'm looking after you.'

'He did it in the most horrible, cruel way.'

'It was an accident, and you told everyone you didn't see. It was in the papers.'

'If it was an accident, why did we leave England?'

'If Dad had done it, he would have gone to prison.'

'Nobody saw.'

'Because there was nothing to see.'

'I saw.'

'You just said nobody did.'

'Nobody except me.'

'You were down by the riverbank and didn't see anything.'

'I forgot. I was on my stone and I saw.' I almost screamed at her in frustration.

'Your stone! I knew you were lying. You had another one of your silly nightmares.' Heather stood up angrily, her eyes practically boiling with dislike. 'You can lie there and rot until you die as far as I'm concerned. You made me miss three whole days of school. You've always hated Dad.'

'He hates me.'

'That's because you're a sook and a sissy.'

'He knows I saw what he did.'

'Shut up.' Heather threw her book at me and ran out. The door to her room slammed.

I was restless all afternoon. I tossed and turned in bed and wondered. Perhaps it was what it always was. A nightmare. Nothing but a nightmare. Heather came in to reclaim her book. I dozed off, and was wakened by voices from the living room. It was nearly sunset.

'Here he is,' cried Auntie Annabel from the stove. She was stirring the big pot with a wooden spoon. 'He could smell it. Nothing gets a boy well quicker than a good split pea soup.'

'I came in to catch up on what's happening.'

'Nothing ever happens around here.'

I was immediately suspicious of Auntie Annabel.

'Lindsay, come here.' Mum checked my tongue and my eyes. 'You should still be in bed.'

Mum was lying propped up on the couch. Brown sat in Dad's

chair. He had brought up a small churn of milk, which was resting on the table. Beside it was a pair of blue booties with ribbons, and a blue bonnet that Auntie Annabel had knitted.

Mrs MacAdams had been round with a baby blanket. And there was a freshly painted cradle on the other side of the room. Everything blue.

We ate the soup around the big fireplace while we listened to the local news. When it was over, Brown turned the dial to country music and then sat down again in Dad's chair. He stuck his leg out on the stool and made himself comfortable. He was wearing a thick green sweater with leather piping around the neck and wrists. Heather lit the lamps.

'The soup is delicious, Annabel,' said Mum.

Neither Brown nor Auntie Annabel seemed in any hurry to go, and Mum was giving them every encouragement to stay. I was glad. No one mentioned Dad or expressed any wonder about what he was doing. The room was warm, and there were friendly dragons in the burning logs. Mum brought out the sweet sherry, and a discussion began about naming the baby.

Heather thought Sidney would be a good name. Auntie Annabel favoured the Scottish tradition and suggested Angus or Andrew. Mum didn't like the idea of alliteration and preferred something more English, like Geoffrey or Hugh. Nobody asked me. They all knew my attitude. Brown had no opinion about names and he bet it was going to be a girl anyway.

Mum suggested that Brown's hair needed cutting. She got her clippers and the long pointed scissors from the sewing drawer, tucked a sheet around his neck, and began to give him a short back and sides.

We heard a vehicle pull up outside. 'It's Dad,' I cried in sudden alarm. 'Brown!' The last time I had seen Brown, he and Dad were fighting.

'Buchanan.'

Brown was right. Mr Buchanan came in wearing a balaclava and blowing on his fingers. He went straight to the fire and spread his hands.

'You're better. I'm glad,' he said to me as he turned and warmed the seat of his trousers. 'I was hoping Jack would be here. I have terrific news.'

He looked around at us all. His yellow grin split his face.

'The Japs are leaving Monday. The whole bang lot.'

'Oh, Fred, can this really be true?' cried Mum.

'Straight from the horse's mouth.' Mr Buchanan's grin didn't stop, and he did a twirl in front of the fireplace.

'Well, thank God for that. Finally, after all this time.'

'Amen,' said Auntie Annabel.

'All of them?' asked Brown. 'That's a lot of prisoners.'

'They're splitting them up. The officers and the NCOs are going to Myrtleford in Victoria, and those below the rank of lance corporal are going to Hay. The official reason is the drought. The real reason is the Colonel. It was move the Japs or move the Colonel. The scandal is finally breaking. That shooting. Other things. They're going to leave him with just the Itis and hope it will all blow over.' Mr Buchanan looked over at me. 'See, Lindsay. Every little bit helps. You should feel proud.'

'Let's have some more of that sherry, Lillian. I feel like getting a little tiddley,' said Auntie Annabel.

'Take your hat off, Fred, and relax.'

But I was panic-stricken. 'That means there will be a war. They will take over the camp.' I tried to shout, but it came out in a squeak.

Auntie Annabel looked askance at me. Mum gave a sigh and refilled the sherry glasses.

'Come now, Lindsay, what's got into you?' queried Mr Buchanan kindly.

'The samurai are blood brothers,' I explained. The words came tumbling out. 'If you split them up they will fight. It says so in my book. We must tell the Colonel.'

Mr Buchanan coughed and took a sip of his sherry. 'It's not much use telling the Colonel anything.'

'We'll tell Major Brent,' I cried, looking at Brown. 'He runs the camp, really.'

'Lindsay, I wouldn't take your book too seriously. The Japs in the camp are not samurai.'

'Yes, sir, they are. I saw. This morning. Out in the field.'

'He had his nightmare again,' said Heather.

'They will do it the night of the full moon, sir. Tomorrow night.'

'Saturday night out.' Mr Buchanan laughed. 'It almost sounds as though you are looking forward to it.'

'I'm not. I want everyone to live. It's Mr Kelly that wants them to escape,' I shouted. 'So he can shoot them. And Dad wants them to escape so he can save Billarooby and prove he's brave for Granddad. And he'll kill too. He's used to killing.'

There was a chorus of protest.

'That's enough, Lindsay,' said Mum angrily. 'How dare you. You can get straight back to bed. Your father is doing his best in his own way to protect us all.'

'Tadao will get him.'

'I wouldn't mind if they got rid of those Italians too,' said Auntie Annabel. She tossed her head. 'Then what would Elsie Cutler have done?' They all laughed. Even Mum.

'We have to face it,' I cried.

'Give me another look at your book,' said Brown. 'Maybe you read it wrong.'

'I don't have it. It's in my cave.' I was so disappointed, I began to cry.

'Stop it,' Heather yelled.

Mum carefully gathered in the sheet from around Brown's neck and shook the cut hair into the fire. There was the smell of singeing. Brown stood up, brushing at his trousers, and Heather swept the floor.

'The Japanese and the soldiers will fight, Brown, and I don't know what to do,' I cried in desperate confusion.

'Hey, come on. The big shot in the family doesn't know what to do?' Brown reached out and grabbed me. He swung me high and knocked my head twice on the ceiling. 'Wood on wood. We'll get that book tomorrow and work it all out.'

'Let me down. I'm going to get the book now.'

Brown grinned up at me. I could see the firelight reflected in his eyes. 'Japs been here once. Lightning never strikes the same place twice.'

'That's not the point – '

Bonk. He gave my head another bump on the ceiling. For a split second he let me go, then caught me by an arm and a leg and began to spin me around. Mr Buchanan jumped out of the way. Brown had me, and I wound up upside-down on the rug in front of the fire. I looked up. Everybody was smiling down at me. I felt a stab of doubt. Mr Buchanan was watching me closely. Perhaps I was mistaken. 'Young kooka,' said Brown.

I got to my knees and gazed for a moment into the fire. Yes, I could check the book with Brown in the morning. I would be proved right and I would go with Brown and Mr Buchanan to the camp to see Major Brent. We would go to the *Star* and talk to Mr Sullivan again. We had a whole day to do it. I felt my head clear and looked up at everyone. I gave a smile.

'There you go,' said Auntie Annabel.

'Relief of Mafeking,' said Mr Buchanan. Everyone laughed and began talking at once. Heather turned up the wireless, and a few minutes later Auntie Annabel began to put on her coat.

'Nice coat, Annabel,' said Mum, of Auntie Annabel's ugly checked coat.

Auntie Annabel preened for a moment or two in front of the mirror. 'You're just being kind, but it's the sort of thing I go for. George chose it for me.'

'I would like to be here when Jack comes home,' she continued, 'but George will be wondering what has happened to us.'

I began to panic again. I realized it would be safer if they stayed. 'Brown – ' I began.

'Trust in the Lord, Lindsay, and He will guide you along a safe path. With Him, there is nothing to fear,' said Auntie Annabel, covering her head with a scarf.

'Children, wait in here with Mr Buchanan. It's cold outside,' said Mum, going on to the verandah with Brown and Auntie Annabel.

As she closed the door behind her, I heard Brown say, 'Auntie, you go sit in the lorry. I want a short word with Lillian.'

Something was going on. I walked quietly out the back way and was round the house in a flash. My body was light as a feather. Mum and Brown were talking on the other side of the pepper tree. I crept up behind the trunk.

'He was very strange with Lindsay this afternoon,' Mum was saying, 'but on the whole . . . Fred has been coming round every day. He's a stabilizing influence. Got him to take a good wash the other day.'

'I don't like the way he can suddenly snap.'

'That was the only time he's ever hit me. He's been apologizing ever since. And he's been taking the pills. I think he realizes he needs them.'

Mum put an awful lot of faith in those pills. I sneaked a look. Brown was holding Mum's hand in his.

'It's Bruce Kelly who has been scaring me these last few days.' Mum paused. 'He's been firing shots around the camp. Jack says he had to stop him from firing right in.'

'I know. He's itching to do it,' said Brown. There was a silence. 'We'd better be going, Lillian. All we have to do is sit tight until Monday. Don't forget to tell Jack.'

'Oh, Brown, of course not.'

I peered out once more. The moon was sailing up into the sky, so high and bright that I could see almost as clearly as day.

'I'll be up in the morning with fresh milk and cream. Dad's good management.'

'Thank you, Brown. Jack and Lindsay both love cream on their porridge.'

'Check on the little bloke.'

'Oh, he's almost better.'

Brown leaned forward and gave Mum a quick kiss. 'Look after yourself, love.'

'Oh, Brown, what will happen when it comes?' whispered Mum in sudden alarm. 'It could be tomorrow.'

'Don't even think about it,' I heard him say.

Auntie Annabel called to Brown from the lorry to hurry up, and I turned and went back inside. My suspicions were unfounded. There was nothing going on I wasn't already aware of. For some reason Mum mightn't know what to do when the baby came, but I did. Move to the dairy, and if that wasn't safe, Brown would help me get down to the coast, to Mrs Cutler's. From the way things were going with Dad, I might have to move to the dairy even sooner.

Mr Buchanan had poured himself another sherry.

'Well, Lillian, looks like I am going to miss Jack,' he said, when Mum came in. 'But I'm glad to hear he's doing better. He must have got delayed at the McCaddies'.'

'He may be staying the night at Mr Kelly's.'

'What's Mr Kelly got that I haven't got?' asked Mr Buchanan, and laughed.

'Please stay as long as you like, Fred.'

'I'd better be getting back. The Sarge is cooking dinner tonight. We're celebrating the end of the Jap era.' Mr Buchanan ran his fingers across his hair and gave a nervous grin. 'Just came by with the good news.'

He pulled his balaclava back on. As he went out the door he said, 'Hear there's a big duststorm on the way. Might hit us tomorrow sometime. Keep the hatches battened down.'

We were alone once more. Mum settled down in the big chair with some sewing. Heather, who was reading by the light of the flames, had not moved from her place by the fire. Her legs were all mottled from the heat. I prowled about the room restlessly. I turned the wireless down slightly, then turned it up again.

'Go to bed, Lindsay. You're going to bring your fever on again.' Mum bit off a thread and looked at me. 'I hope for your sake your father has decided not to come home tonight. You're a bad influence on each other.'

Mum could not get me to go to bed, and I was out in the moonlight when, half an hour later, Mr Kelly's truck pulled up outside. I could see the hurricane lamps on the sulky coming up behind on the hill. I dashed back into the house and slipped the bolt across the door.

Dad made such a noise when he found the door bolted that I thought he was going to break it down.

'Lindsay must have done it,' said Heather when she opened it. Dad lurched in, followed by Mr Kelly. Heather was startled and ran back to her place by the fire. She took up her book.

Dad and Mr Kelly rested their shotguns by the front door and headed across the room. Dad threw his hat for the peg and missed. Mr Kelly let his black and red lumber jacket fall to the floor, removed his earmuffs, and then banged a bottle of rum down on the table.

'Ho, Mrs Armstrong. What a condition, what a fine condition. You look like you're ready to drop it. I am going to indulge in a premature celebration of the auspicious event.'

After drinking from the bottle, Mr Kelly held it out to Mum, who declined. Dad snatched it and took a swallow. He stuck the bottle in the pocket of his greatcoat, and Mr Kelly pulled it out.

'Up from the bed of pain.' Mr Kelly came over and tried to put a hand on my head. I twisted away. 'What a snowy little sweet pea he is.'

He reached out for Heather also, and Heather rose at once. 'I'm going to my room, Mum.'

'Ach!' said Mr Kelly, squinting down the corridor after her. We heard the door of her room slam.

'Plates,' said Dad thickly.

'I'm not feeding either of you.'

'Plates. Plate for Bruce,' Dad shouted.

Mum ladled out two bowls, and Dad and Mr Kelly sat down.

Mr Kelly burned himself on the first mouthful and then, in an attempt to cool it, blew soup across the tablecloth. 'Pea soup makes me fart like a beaut.'

Dad ate with his head down almost to the level of the table. 'What are you staring at?' he suddenly bawled over at me. 'Those eyes!'

'Jack, I won't have you talking to your son like that.'

'My son, my son! No son of mine.' He stood up at the table and yelled, 'Get out of my sight.'

I hesitated and he was on me. I squirmed from his grasp and ran into my room. I got a chair against the doorknob a second before Dad's hand reached it. He began kicking and I crawled under the bed. Mr Kelly's voice, and then Mum's, came from the living room, and Dad desisted. I listened to his strangled breathing close by the door, and then he moved away, back down the corridor.

I waited under the bed. After a minute or two there was a tentative knock and then Heather's voice. 'Lindsay, open the door.'

I let her in quickly and replaced the chair.

'Lindsay, I'm sorry he's mean to you. I really am. He's been mean to me lately too. It's Mr Kelly.'

In the light of the moon coming through my window, we looked at each other and experienced some long and unprecedented moments of complete sympathy.

Heather gave my hand a squeeze. 'What will you do?'

'He usually passes out. But Mr Kelly is here.'

'About the rabbits, I suppose.'

'No. The camp.'

There was a crash from the living room. Heather gasped.

'Dad's broken his plate again,' I said.

The sound of angry voices rose.

'Shall we look?'

We sneaked back along the corridor. Heather went first. 'Mr Kelly has soup all over his face. Mum threw it at him.'

Mum was shouting '. . . yes, they're leaving, Mr Kelly. I only wish they could take you with them. You and your disgusting fantasies.'

Mr Kelly began wiping himself off with the tablecloth. 'You saintly bitch. You've scalded my face.'

'Get out of my house. And take my husband with you. You got him drunk.'

'Your cowhand's going to slip you one?'

'Oh, get out,' said Mum contemptuously, and turned away. Mr Kelly put on his jacket and earmuffs and headed for the door.

Dad followed him out.

'Shut up, you useless pile of shit,' I heard him snarl at Dad as the door slammed.

'Lindsay, is that you there?'

Heather and I ran into the living room.

Mum waved her shawl about at the smell that Dad and Mr Kelly had left. Dipper was licking up soup from the floor. 'Oh, Mum,' said Heather.

Mum lined us up in front of the fire. 'You must have noticed your father is in a dreadful state. I don't know what he and Mr Kelly are up to, but – '

'The Bush Brigade is going to attack the Japs before they leave.'

'Oh, Lindsay, Blue Chapman and Ernie Williams are not even around. They took those cattle to Armidale. I do know that Mr Kelly is setting up camp down the hill in his truck, and that means your father is going to be in and out all night. I don't want either of you staying in your rooms. You're to sleep in the Landgirls' old room. It's the only one with a bolt. They won't find you there.' Mum held her hands against her belly. 'If by any chance they do, under no circumstances are you to open the door to either of them. Heather, do you understand?'

'Yes, Mum.'

'I can go and get Brown.'

'There's no need for that,' said Mum firmly. She paused and added, 'Lindsay, you said the one thing this afternoon to your father that you shouldn't have.'

I stared at her. Mum knew. Mum had known about Dad and Granddad all along.

There was a heavy footfall on the verandah. 'Here he comes again. Go on quickly, the both of you.'

Heather and I raced for the Landgirls' room.

27

I WAS WAITING for him and he came. First it was cursing, then the drag of his boots on the verandah, a rattling of the doorknob, a loud knocking, and finally, 'Open up, I know you're in there.'

Heather sat up in bed. I put a finger to my lips.

Dad began pounding on the door with his fists. Heather jumped from her bed, dashed over to mine, slid down, and pulled the blankets over her head. Through the noise he was making came his voice again: 'Lindsay, let me in.'

There was a pause, followed by a thud. The door shook, the bolt gave a creak. Dad had put his shoulder to it. I shrank down beside Heather.

'Heather, I want Lindsay.' The door was kicked and then pounded by fists once more. 'Open up!'

Heather screamed from under the blankets, 'Mum, make him stop!'

I was out of the bed at the back window, pushing hard. It was stuck. 'Christ!' I swore for just about the first time in my life. The window hadn't been opened since I painted the frame after the departure of the Landgirls. I struggled with it and at the same time looked around for something to break the glass with.

'Wait until morning. Please, Jack.' At last, Mum's voice.

Dad shouted my name once more. 'Lindsay!'

'I beg you, leave him alone. Come on in out of the cold.'

There was another crash. The door shuddered, the bolt was almost wrenched away. One more time and it would go.

'Jack!' Mum's voice rose in a desperate scream.

The window shot up a few inches. I pushed it higher, vaulted up on to the sill, and was through and running before I realized that Mum was leading Dad away along the verandah. She was remonstrating with him, her voice cajoling.

The ground was cold on my bare feet. I hoisted myself back into the room, ran to my bed, and pulled the rabbitskin blanket off Heather, who screamed.

'It's only me. I need this,' I said, rolling it up. 'I'm going to my cave. If I stay here, he'll come back and get me.'

Heather stared at me, terrified.

'He killed Granddad, and now he's trying to kill me.'

Heather ran across the room and jumped back into her bed. 'Dad would never hurt me.'

She was right, but I said darkly, 'I wouldn't be so sure about that.'

It took only a few moments to get ready. I sneaked back to my room for an extra pair of pants and a sweater. I pushed them into my satchel and then, back with Heather, sat immobilized on the bed. Enormous doubts began to assail me.

'You can come if you want to.'

'No,' said Heather.

'You must promise not to tell Dad or anyone. A terrible thing might happen if you do.'

Mr Buchanan always said she had eyes like gimlets. Now I could see he was right. But maybe it was because she wasn't wearing her glasses. I didn't trust her. She was still in Dad's pocket. At that moment she reached out to the dresser and put her glasses on.

'I promise,' she said.

Mum was at the door. I let her in and bolted it behind her. She had her head in a scarf against the cold, and had a shawl wrapped over her dress.

She took me gently by the shoulders and said, 'Lindsay, I want you to stay the night down at the dairy. Go in the back way and wake Brown up. There is no need to disturb Auntie Annabel. Brown will understand. Tell him you want to sleep there and that Heather and I are all right. Just to come up in the morning as usual.'

'Where's Dad?'

'He's in the bedroom. You have unleashed a demon, Lindsay. You cannot stay here tonight.'

'He murdered Granddad,' I cried. 'You know he did. It would be safer if we all went down to the dairy.'

Mum glanced at Heather and then leaned down towards me. 'A terrible killing, but there was no murder in the heart.' Her voice was a whisper. She did not want Heather to hear. 'No murder in the heart,' she repeated, fiercely this time. 'Except by your granddad.'

'What do you mean?'

'Never mind. Get going.'

'I can harness up Belinda and take us all in the sulky.'

Mum hesitated for a moment. She almost said yes before saying no. 'That's enough. Heather and I can deal with your father. Off you go, quickly. Before he gets up again. Brown will find you blankets and a place on the sofa. Or with him. He's got a big bed.'

'I'll stay here and protect you.'

'He was going to his cave,' said Heather.

'Oh, Lindsay, you would have frozen to death.'

'I've got blankets there.'

'Forget your cave.' Mum began pushing me towards the door. 'Hurry. Go straight to the dairy and get warm as soon as you can. Take some soup with you. It's still hot on the stove. I haven't locked the front door yet.'

She held me close against her belly. I reached up and gave her a kiss.

'Now, run!'

The Aladdin lamp still burned in the deserted living room and the mantelpiece clock said twelve. A log flared in the fireplace. I opened the door carefully and made a dash for the kitchen dresser. I filled a large pewter mug with soup and then shoved a big hunk of bread in my pocket.

A sound came from their bedroom. Dad's voice, and angry. I began to panic. I took my overcoat down and had it on in a second. At the door, I noticed Dad's hat still on the floor. For some reason I picked it up and put it on the peg. My eyes flared as I caught sight of the tomahawk in the kindling box. I stuck it in my satchel, gave a final look around – I was never coming back – and was out the door.

Mr Kelly's truck was gone, as I had suspected it would be. There was frost on the ground, but the cold meant nothing on that midnight flight. I sped down the hill, through the orchard and the blackened ash of the thistles, along the paths by the old irrigation ditches. The moon was palest cream and lent a sepulchral glow to the flats.

At the junction near the pump I stopped dead. To the left was the dairy; to the right, my cave. Everything that had happened in Billarooby flashed through my mind. I stood there so long my teeth began to chatter, my head to ache with the indecision.

Suddenly I was off, running towards the river. I carried the soup all the way to the cave without spilling a drop.

I gathered sticks and lit a fire, then crouched over it, warming my hands. I stuck a piece of bread on the end of a stick and toasted it. Then I dipped it in the soup and ate it hungrily.

The firelight flickered and threw shadows. Smoke curled up through the overhanging roots and away into the moonlight. A wind began to stir the gum leaves high above.

The minutes passed, and an immense loneliness grew. I leaned forward and put more twigs and a piece of bark on the fire. As it began to crackle and blaze I thought of Dad. That memory of Mum, on the day I first saw Tadao, calling out Dad's name again and again in a kind of despair, as though she had some premonition of what the future had in store for us in Billarooby, came to my mind. And what had she meant when she said that about Granddad? A thousand years had passed since my fever had broken that morning.

'I have to cheer myself up,' I said aloud to the night. From my satchel I drew my tin whistle and played 'The Rose's Age,' a rather lugubrious tune that failed to lift my spirits. My eyes fell on the tomahawk, and I gave a shudder. Dad would never find the cave again, or would he?

It was no use. I would be safer at the dairy. Mum was right. As the fire died, I picked up my satchel and then remembered my book. Perhaps that was all I had come here for in the first place. I took it down from the ledge. I would wake Brown up and make him see that I was right about the Japanese, and about what the Colonel must do.

As I held the book, my sacred text, I closed my eyes, and as I pictured it, page by page, my blood began to race, my temperature to rise. The next night was the night of the full moon, and they would be honour-bound to take on the mantle of the samurai warriors. They could not permit the Colonel to humiliate them further. They would have to try to rejoin their Emperor, and the machine guns would kill them. But I would save them. I would save Tadao. I had no doubts. I would stop the Colonel. Major Brent would understand, and so would Mr Sullivan.

'Tonight,' I said tenderly, 'the warriors are asleep.' Suddenly there was no question in my mind. I had to see the camp again, see that the warriors were in fact safely sleeping. I felt responsible. I was the shepherd watching over his flock by night.

As I crossed the dry riverbed at a run, I felt that I was approaching the end of a great adventure. The Japanese would not be split up, they would go, samurai brothers all together, to Myrtleford, free of the Colonel. Him they could send to Hay. As I sped through the trees on the other side, I began singing, 'Silent night, holy night, all is calm, all is bright . . .' I sang it loudly into the night. At the top of the slope I paused to look up. It seemed the moon above was tinged with red, or rust. The air smelled of dust. There were great clouds of it drifting in from the western sky.

My boots crunched as I raced over the barren, frosty slopes, and soon the outcrop rose ahead of me. Its battlements were silver-grey against a bright incandescence – the floodlights at the camp. The kurrajong trees dropped in graceful silhouette.

I was still weak from my fever and was breathing harshly by the time I climbed over the last rocks. Before I reached the flat area beneath the trees, I crouched down and scouted it out. There was the sound of snoring.

I knew at once who it was. Beyond the bulky sleeping figure was a rum bottle. A shotgun rested against a boulder by his head. Mr Kelly was waiting for the morning, and in the morning he would fire his shots into the camp. If he didn't do it then, he wouldn't be able to do it at all.

I moved a step nearer. He was making so much noise, it was a wonder he did not wake himself up. Or that the guards did not hear. Drool came from a corner of his mouth and glistened like an icicle in the moonlight. I thought of how he had frightened Mum that evening, and what he had done to Brown. Of what he had done to Dad, and what he was about to do to the Japanese. I wanted nothing more than to stop Mr Kelly in his tracks.

I stole forward and took his shotgun. Then I picked up his cartridge belt, thrust his bottle of rum into my overcoat pocket, and crept away to the other end of the little amphitheatre, as far away from him as I could get. Then I clambered down a few yards towards the cold dazzle of the lights from the camp. I settled myself in a cranny in the rocks, well hidden from above, and thought no more, for a while, of Mr Kelly.

My eyes roamed over the camp below. The circle and the cross were even clearer under the glare of floodlights than they had been on the afternoon I had first seen them, but having come with expectations of a ghostly, gleaming sight, a crystal pale city under the moon and the Milky Way, a city that held captive the knights of Bushido, I was immediately conscious of a deep disappointment. Without sunlight or shadows the patterns held no magic. I found myself staring at the huge red cross painted on the Fibro roof of the hospital block, and listening to the sound of Mr Kelly's snores.

My feet were frozen and I decided it was time to go. I forced down a little rum to warm me up, then stood and waved my hand in ceremonial farewell to the sleeping samurai. I wished Tadao a restful night, and smiled at the thought that the next day I would be saving the samurai not only from the Colonel but from themselves.

I slung on the cartridge belt, picked up the shotgun, and took one last look.

Was that a figure running? A scream, long and wavering, rose up into the cold night air. The hair on my neck stood on end and I almost dropped the gun. Yes, a man, arms waving wildly, was racing towards the main gate of the camp. He screamed again and pointed back towards the huts. Two guards appeared from nowhere and blocked his way. While one of them had a shouting match with the man, who had fallen to his knees, the other raised his rifle in the air and fired three shots. At the same time flames erupted from one of the huts. Smoke billowed into the air. A second hut began to burn, then a third and a fourth. The air was rent by the sound of a bugle. Hundreds of figures suddenly emerged like a red wave into the light, and from their throats rose the sound that has haunted me ever since, no matter where I go — like the high-pitched shrieking of a flock of cockatoos, the harsh cawing of a thousand crows, the sound in my head as I lay ill with fever, the sound that Brown had heard one morning in the jungle at Isurava, it was the sound of the samurai screaming and cheering for their honour and their Emperor as they charged for the wires. *Banzai, banzai, banzai!* And in answer to that cry, there began the crackle of rifle shots.

I stood transfixed at the sight. The Japanese had stolen a march on me. And on the Colonel. A quarter of the camp was on fire, and the wind caught the thick black smoke rising skyward and sent it in the direction of the outcrop. I coughed and sat down in panic.

Many things were happening at the same time. Guards caught out in the open were running for cover. I saw the garrison coming out of its quarters into the electric glare, men putting on uniforms over their pyjamas as they went. The camp was like a kicked-over meat ants' nest, with Japanese and soldiers scurrying frantically this way and that. One group of prisoners was headed for the very centre of the camp. Two other groups were covering the barbed wire fences below me with blankets and makeshift ladders and climbing over.

The Japanese were rushing for the Colonel's new machine guns, cold and stark, mounted on their flat-bed trailers outside the camp perimeter. And then, as I saw soldiers running in the same direction from their barracks, I realized that a race for those guns was in progress. Tadao was surely one of those in the race.

In that moment the camp floodlights went out, and it was as though someone had turned the clock back to ancient days. There was the moon above, and there at last, below on the plain, was my pale, ghostly city, no longer merely silently gleaming in cold, crystal light, but a city aflame. Taking place right in front of me was yet another of the battles to end all battles, the escape from the Great Captivity. All I wanted to do was join it.

'Where the fuck, where the fuck, where the fuck . . .' Mr Kelly was looking for his twelve-bore. I had forgotten him. My heart stopped and then began again. His voice came closer and closer. I

shrank myself small and pulled my overcoat up over my hair like
a dark cowl. Crouched down tight, I imagined myself to be just
another rock. I prayed that the moonlight would not give me
away. Out of the corner of my eye, I saw the top of Mr Kelly's
head come into view.

'God Almighty, where the fuck!'

He took one step down and bent towards me. I held my breath.
He was so close I could smell him. The enemy wasn't the Japanese,
it was Mr Kelly. I thought I would burst, so hard and still did I
keep myself. 'Fuck you, Jack, where's my gun?' His voice receded
and then came back crashing in my ears like a wave on the
seashore. Receding, crashing, receding, crashing, the voice went
echoing far, echoing near. I wondered if I was drunk from the
rum. Then I decided, drunk or not, that I had to find a safer place.
The battle below, lit by the fires and the moon, drew me
irresistibly, and as Mr Kelly's voice receded one more time, I
broke cover and headed down.

I really find it difficult now to describe what happened to me as I
made that steep descent into what of course was absolute hell for
everyone involved in it. I think I went completely mad. Perhaps
the state I got into was similar to the one that occurred that
fateful day on the riverbank back in England, the day that
Granddad died. Although I had some understanding of the turmoil
and carnage below, at first there was no fear, only fascination and
euphoria.

By the time I was halfway down the outcrop, the Japanese had
reached the big guns and were swarming over them. I saw the
guns swing round and the garrison soldiers scatter for cover.
Triumphant shouts went up from the Japanese. The guns went
into action, and the last real thing I remembered for a while was
standing on a prominent rock thirty yards or so above the closest
gun, waving my arms, orchestrating the battle. I disappeared into
some vainglorious, escapist trance of victory and exultation.
Somehow, I became surrounded by beautiful cicadas – red princes,
black princes, yellow mondays, green grocers, double drummers
– all as large as I was, who crawled out from every rock and
boronia bush to exult with me. There was no harsh machine gun
fire in this world, only the cicadas, all singing away louder and

louder until the air rang with thunderous joy. The cicadas were Tadao and his friends, and we were in the presence of the Emperor of the Sun, who sat above us at the top of a perfect, pink volcano. The Emperor smiled down serenely, bathing everything in a warm, heavenly glow. In his lap was a glass bowl, filled with water in which swam iridescent goldfish. The volcano was erupting fireworks of every possible colour . . .

I felt a sharp pain in my shoulder and, for a moment, thought I had fallen from a dream in my bed to the floor. Below me the camp still burned, the smoke still billowed skyward. The machine guns were silent. And around them, locked in a seething hand-to-hand struggle, were hundreds of prisoners and soldiers. The fight for the camp was continuing. Rifle fire filled the night. A shot sang through the air and hit the outcrop just above my head somewhere. A piece of rock flew by me. Another shot splattered to my right, then another, and finally I knew that this was no sensible place to be. I had to get away from there.

As I rose to go, I saw below me, no more than ten yards away, a group of Japanese ascending the outcrop, under fire from the camp.

They wore white headbands, each with a large red circle in the middle, and they carried knives, barbed wire switches, and sticks. Steam came from their mouths and noses. One had blood pouring from his ear, and another was hitting the rocks, as he climbed, with a baseball bat studded with nails.

The closest Japanese looked up, straight into my eyes. He bared his teeth in a snarl and raised his knife high. My bowels melted; I jerked back, and knew I had shat my pants. Whether I screamed I had no idea, but I turned and ran for my life.

The next thing I knew, I was flying down the open hillside towards the river. Pale green lights exploded in the sky, Very lights, which slowly spread a spectral glow over the landscape. Behind me the machine guns started firing again. Only then did I realize that I was carrying the shotgun, clutched in both hands horizontally in front of me. I shouldered it on the run and became conscious of the shit running down my legs. Without missing a stride, I hoisted my overcoat up around my waist to keep it clean.

Near the river I heard an engine coming towards me from the direction of the camp. Headlights appeared and I dashed for a tree, panting hard. As the truck went by, I saw that it was Mr Kelly, and I could not be sure whether he was alone or with someone, but I knew that he must be going home for his other gun.

It took me no more than a few minutes to reach the little pool of muddy water below my cave. I leaned the gun against the trunk of the granddaddy tree and took off my overcoat, then my pants. In a frenzy of fear and cold. I scooped out handfuls of the icy water and washed myself clean.

My knees were knocking, my teeth were chattering. I could not remember ever having been so cold. I will get pneumonia, I thought, or frostbite. I clambered up the final yards of the bank, trembling so violently that I did not trust myself to make a jump into the cave. Gingerly I lowered myself down the sides and then reached up for the gun.

I dried myself on my overcoat, changed into the other pair of pants. I unloaded the gun, put the cartridges in my pocket, and lay down under the blankets. I dared not light a fire. I would get warm and then go straight to the dairy. I curled myself up into a ball and gradually my shivering stopped.

The sound of the machine guns was faint in the distance. I put my head deeper under the blankets and closed my eyes, straining hard to shut everything out.

In a minute, I kept saying to myself, I will get up, run to the dairy, and warn Brown about the camp. That was the proper thing to do. Brown had been right all along – samurai or not, the Japanese were the enemy. And I would tell him what had happened with Dad, and he would know exactly what steps to take. Even as I felt my drowsiness, I was convincing myself that I was still alert.

It may have been that in the deepest part of me I did not want to do the proper thing, but I recited over and over again my determination to go to the dairy and warn Brown, until I fell into a deep sleep.

28

IT WAS DAWN. I smelled tobacco smoke. From below my cave came the sound of voices. Japanese voices. A terror exploded in my head. I immediately pulled the blankets over me and screwed myself up tightly. My heart hammered and banged. The voices continued, the minutes went by, nothing happened.

I uncurled a little and poked my head out of the covers. Curiosity getting the better of me, I found the courage to stand up and then, cautiously, to take a look.

I counted four of them, and there were at least two others out of sight. They were a few yards down the bank, gathered in a group by the trunk of the fallen tree. My eyes went farther down to where I had thrown my dirty pants, but clearly they were paying no attention to them. They seemed, in fact, to be in the middle of an argument about which way to go. One gestured in the direction of Billarooby and another pointed, with a club wound about with barbed wire, upstream towards Mr Kelly's. The man closest to me was stabbing savagely at the ground with a long knife while he talked. They all looked rough, dirty, and grim-faced.

I slid back down in horror, praying that they would not see the cave. It is well concealed, I said to myself. There is no danger. Soon they will move on.

I was shivering in the morning cold, but my palms were wet with perspiration. I put on my overcoat and then took it off. I thought of breakfast and picked up the pewter mug. The soup had set solid and acquired a coating of dust.

At that same moment, the sun broke through the trees and lit the tangle of roots above me. I looked up and was aghast. The flag! It was beyond carelessness, almost an advertisement of my presence. Even as I looked, a wind caught the flag and sent it flapping. I jumped up and ran this way and that in despair and confusion. Somehow, I thought, I'd get it down. Or the gun. I could load the gun.

But it was too late. The jabbering from below suddenly became more animated, and I could hear one of them come scrabbling up the bank. I dived for the blankets and covered myself. I pulled Mr Kelly's gun in beside me, along with the cartridge belt. I held my breath and lay perfectly still.

'Ha!' The cave was discovered. A voice above me began to call excitedly. I heard the others begin to climb the slope, and then there was a loud thud of someone landing right by my ear. My eyes were wide in the dark.

He was moving around, and a voice called to him from above. There was the jiggle of marbles and another 'Ha!' My ledge and all its treasures had been found. Something heavy fell on me, and my body gave an involuntary spasm. I closed my eyes tight. A second passed, and then the top of the blanket was pulled back. I opened my eyes and found myself face to face with a Japanese. It was the angry one, and impaled on his knife was the embroidered cap, my talisman.

I pulled the covers back around my neck and drew up my knees protectively. 'No, no, please!' I said. My hand closed on the tomahawk.

We stared at each other. Without taking his eyes from mine, he called up something to his companions. Their heads were appearing one by one and formed a half ring around the top. He held up the cap for them to see.

'Ha!' said the first Japanese again. 'Good morning. I am sorry. Friends. Speak English very good.' He inclined his head politely and gave a sad smile.

I could not speak. My hand still clutched the tomahawk.

'It OK, little girl. Friend.'

I found my voice. 'I'm a boy.'

'Ah.' His eyes continued to roam around the cave and fell on the pewter mug. He stuck his knife in his belt, bent down, and picked up the mug. He gave a sniff, then stirred the contents with the spoon. 'Soup?'

'You can have some if you like.'

'Thank you.'

He tasted it and I sat up. I brushed the hair out of my eyes and saw that it was my book that had fallen on me. I realized that I was no longer afraid of them. Looking hard at him while he ate the soup, I took a deep breath and asked, 'Did you capture the camp?'

There was a silence. He handed up the soup, which started going from hand to hand. Each man took a mouthful. One man took two, and there was a reprimand. They hadn't had breakfast, of course. 'Auntie Annabel made the soup,' I said. I scrutinized every face, trying to turn each one into Tadao.

I waited a few moments and then asked about the camp again.

'Shikishima die. Many die. We like chicken with no head.' He laughed and then added, 'We go now to join Emperor.'

I took another deep breath. 'Are you samurai?' I asked, very shyly, terrified I would not get the answer I wanted.

'Samurai?' He turned up to the others, and every one of them broke into a smile of some sort. There was rapid discussion.

'Yes, samurai.'

'Do you follow the Code of Bushido?'

Another head appeared at the top of the cave. My heart jumped with an intense delight. It was Tadao. He was handed the mug, and they all started talking to him. I heard the word 'Bushido' several times. Tadao had a bandage around his left hand.

'Yes, Bushido.'

Tadao said something and there was laughter.

'Me, yes,' said the first man. 'Him, no.'

'I know you. Your name is Tadao. I met you here. And on the bus in Wudgie.'

'Ah. Wudgie.'

I could tell he did not recognize me. His scar still travelled up his face, but it had gone white, like Dad's welt.

'That's your cap. I found it in the river.'

Tadao took it from the man next to him and exclaimed something.

'My name is Lindsay. Lindsay.'

He took a good look at me. 'Ah, Lindsay. Small boy.'

He remembered. Tadao spoke rapidly to the first man and they all began to talk. There was great interest, I think, in the fact that I had met one of them before.

He indicated the cap and put it on. 'Thank you, Lindsay.'

We smiled at each other.

'Did you get my letter?'

'Letter?'

There was more talk, and it was clear that the letter had not been received. I changed the subject by picking up my book.

'Your name's in here, Tadao,' I said as I thumbed through it. I wanted to show them one of my favourite pages. 'Here's Yoshit-sune Minamoto.' I stumbled over the pronunciation. 'He turned into a great white bird and escaped.'

The first man took the book from my hands and stared at the picture. His eyes did not seem to be very good and he held the book first at a distance, then very close to his face. Turning the pages, he began calling out to the others.

I looked from face to face. They were all very young, about the age of the recruits from the Training Center whom I saw each time I went into Wudgie. One of them was cleaning his nails with a screwdriver and looking at them, like Joan.

The first man handed up the book for the others to look at, then leaned back against the wall of the cave.

'Your house?' I saw that his eyelids drooped with exhaustion.

'My cave. I could light the fire and make some tea, if you have time.' I doubted that they did, but I indicated the billy.

'Ha! Plenty of time.'

'And while you wait, you might like some of this.' I pulled out Mr Kelly's bottle of Bundaberg rum.

'Aha!' Such a shout went up, such laughter and excitement, that I began to get nervous. The threat of Mr Kelly flashed over me, but I decided not to alarm them. They all tried to grab the bottle at once.

'Aren't you worried about the soldiers coming?'

'Soldiers come, we fight. We die. No problem.'

'Well, you're probably safe as long as you are with me.'

I set to work getting the fire going. The rum went round and round. One of the men up top, who was lying on his back smoking a cigarette, pointed to the flag up in the sunshine and asked something. The first man translated.

'Why you got?'

'It's the Red Ensign,' I explained. 'It's the only one I had. I should have taken it down, really.'

The twigs caught fire and smoke began to curl upward.

'I'll run and get some water,' I said. 'We'll have to boil it and boil it again.'

'No hurry,' said the first man. He closed his eyes. 'Emperor wait.'

I looked from him to the ones flipping through my book, and realized that they were men who had nowhere to go, at least for the moment. I began to wonder what could be done. They couldn't possibly go back to their Captivity. They had burned down the camp anyway.

As I picked up the billy and prepared to climb out of the cave, the man who had asked about the flag stood up, stuck his cigarette in his mouth, and reached up for it with both hands. In that instant a shot rang out. I saw him clutch his chest and fall sideways out of sight. There were grunts and exclamations, the heads all disappeared immediately, and I could hear the prisoners sliding back down the slope. There was a second shot. The man with me in the cave drew his knife and went into a crouch.

I pressed myself against the rock wall. His eyes blazed at me for a second, and then he pounced on Mr Kelly's gun, which was poking out from beneath the blanket. He began looking around for cartridges. He held out his hand. 'Where?' he hissed. I shook my head.

'Lindsay?' Dad's voice came in an angry shout from somewhere out in the big trees, and if I'd had shit to shit, I'd have shat my pants again. There was a flash of the night before, of Dad at the door, and the crash of his fists hammered in my head. My eyes fixed on the fire. The flames were bursting upward brightly now, the smoke curling thickly, blue and white. The Japanese man's hand was there in front of my face, insistent.

'Lindsay?' The shout came again, closer this time.

I do not excuse what I did next. Throughout my life, I have avoided thinking too much about it, although I have always had the grace to admit the deed. At least to myself. The Japanese prisoner of war would probably have found the cartridge belt anyway, but I reached under the blankets and not unwillingly handed it over.

Swiftly he loaded the gun, moved to the bottom step, leaned the barrels on the platform, and poked his head out. His eyes scanned the riverbank. He barked out a stream of urgent questions. Answering shouts came from below. Then there was a silence. I stared at his back. He had a big tear down the middle of his red flannel shirt, and there was dried blood on the woollen singlet underneath.

I was suddenly shaken by paroxysms of regret. 'No! You mustn't!' I shouted, darting forward and pulling him by the trousers.

He shook me aside roughly, took another quick survey, and then leapt upward with a bloodcurdling shout. On the platform he stood, legs apart. He adjusted the gun and took aim.

'No!' I cried desperately.

He fired. At almost the same instant I heard another shot. The Japanese man threw up his hands and tumbled backwards.

There was no time for me to get out of the way. He came down shoulders first on top of me, knocking me to the ground. At the same time there was a deafening explosion, and a sulphurous smell filled the cave. Mr Kelly's gun had gone off as it hit the floor beside me. The Japanese jerked two or three times and then lay still. From outside came another shot.

'Get off,' I gasped. He had taken the wind out of me, and there was a painful constriction in my chest. My ears were ringing from the blast.

I saw that he had been shot in the neck. He made a gurgling sound and moved slightly. Blood bubbled out on to his shirt and then to the floor. I shrank away from it as I pushed, but it got on to my hands, warm and sticky.

From outside there were more shots, and then I heard the remaining Japanese begin to shout their battle cries. They were fighting. Dad was still alive. It is hard to say that I wished for the Japanese to kill Dad, but I knew that my fear of him was greater than my fear of them.

'You're hurting me,' I shouted, continuing to wriggle. I extricated one leg. The man stirred, rolled over on to his side, and began to pull himself up on his elbows.

All over my sweater there was blood, and the cave was full of the smell of it. I scrambled to my feet, determined to run, anywhere. I had to get out of there, away from Dad, away from the Japanese, back to Brown. I made my first step up and found my ankle grabbed.

'Let me go!' I screamed in a panic. 'Let me go!' I kicked, but the Japanese's grip was strong. I looked down. His eyes stared back blankly as though they did not see.

'No, little boy.' I watched in horror as blood poured from his mouth and flowed down his chin. 'Safe here.'

Suddenly his head fell to one side. The grip on my ankle slowly slackened, and I shook him off. I was up the steps and on to the platform, my mind already charting a course for the dairy.

I stopped dead. Down along the slope, beneath the tree with the growths on the trunk, was Dad, and he had his gun aimed at Tadao, who was ten yards away and shouting at him, making no effort to run.

'Dad!' I cried desperately. 'Don't shoot. It's my friend. It's Tadao.'

Dad heard my voice and turned towards me. I gasped. One side of his face was nothing but blood. The second that Dad turned, Tadao dashed forward and grabbed for Dad's shotgun. Dad hung on. Tadao began to kick him.

I jumped down into the cave, seized Mr Kelly's gun, and loaded it from the cartridge belt. In seconds I was out and running towards them.

'Stop!' I shouted, levelling the gun. I was no more than a few yards away. 'Both of you.'

At that moment Tadao twisted the gun out of Dad's hands. Dad fell forward on to his stomach and then lay still. Tadao took a quick look at me and then aimed the gun at Dad's head.

'Tadao,' I yelled sternly, admonishing him, moving forward with the gun, 'it's Dad. My dad. Leave him alone. I'll shoot you.'

If Tadao had not taken a step back, I would have shot him even though up to that time I had never fired a gun, except accidentally that once, and I had not really thought of firing this one. I had thought only in terms of bluff.

'Ah, Dad. I sorry.'

Tadao kept his gun pointed at Dad but gave me a look that was both a smile and a scowl. He did not seem to care whether I was going to shoot him. Suddenly he bent over Dad, removed his cartridge belt, and began to run off. Then he stopped and turned. He looked at me for a moment and gave a deep bow. I lowered Mr Kelly's gun and bowed in turn.

But I didn't like his stealing the gun, and had a thought.

'Take this one, and give me Dad's. It's his special gun.'

I stepped towards Tadao, indicating the swap, and that both guns used the same ammunition. Tadao was taken by surprise and hesitated.

'Very good gun. Mr Kelly's.'

'Good gun?'

I held out my gun and reached for Dad's, and there was a moment when we each held both.

He suddenly wrenched Mr Kelly's gun away and still hung on to Dad's. 'I take two.'

'No.' I stamped my foot. 'That's not honourable. You samurai. Samurai!'

He smiled, the white scar travelled up to his embroidered cap, and I felt my fear beginning to return.

'Dad's gun, Tadao,' I shouted quickly. 'Dad's!'

'OK, Lindsay.'

He let me take the gun, and then, with one final, mocking glance at me, he ran off across the river and disappeared into the trees on the other side.

He wasn't very honourable, but he had taken pity on me. And Dad. 'Tadao . . .' I called one last time.

Dad was conscious and began to move. I watched, transfixed, as he rolled on to his back and levered himself into a sitting position against the tree. He looked at me through a single dully gleaming eye, and it was only then I realized how desperately he was hurt. I gave a little cry.

It seemed that all of one side of his face had been bashed in. An artery in his right temple spurted blood. I could not even see his right eye, which was covered with earth and bloodied leaves.

'Oh, Dad.' I knelt down beside him. Gingerly I place my hand against his temple. Bright, warm blood sprayed through my fingers. I took my hand away quickly. I picked dead leaves away from his eye. I snatched at rabbit dirt.

As I tried to clean him up a bit, I noticed that he had taken a bath that morning. His hair was washed and freshly brilliantined, he had shaved, and Mum must have run an iron over his khakis. He had prepared himself for battle. Just like a samurai. 'Oh, Dad,' I said again.

I thought of my flag and ran to get it. There was a Japanese lying half in the waterhole below, his red uniform covered in dust. He had rolled all the way down. Beyond him were two more bodies. I saw the empty rum bottle. On the other side of the waterhole, a few scrawny rabbits were out.

I tore the flag into strips, wound them tightly around Dad's head, and then turned my attention to his chest. He had been stabbed several times. No arteries had been cut, but blood flowed down freely from just below his neck. I pushed my handkerchief into his neck, but it was no good. Blood was everywhere and I began to panic. The big slug from Mr Kelly's gun had gone into his right shoulder. I squeezed my eyes tight, not wanting to admit the fact of it.

'Dad, I'm going to get help,' I shouted in his ear. 'Can you hear me?'

'Lillian. Go help . . .'

'It's all right, Dad. They're not going to hurt Mum. I told you.'

'I'm sorry. My fault. Japs . . .'

'I'll be back real soon, Dad.' I turned and ran. I knew that Belinda and the sulky would be at the ford.

'Lindsay . . .' came his voice.

I stopped and looked back. He lifted his arm.

'Gun.' His mouth hung open, and it oozed blood.

I stared at him. His eye held mine. Something told me not to give Dad his gun, and I looked away, intending to refuse it. I saw in the tree on the other side of the dry riverbed the red of a shirt and the glint of metal. He was still there.

'Tadao,' I shouted. 'I need help.' Dust suddenly obscured the sun, dead leaves swirled in the wind . . . I waited. I was mistaken.

I felt that Dad was safe from the Japs, but with his eye upon me, like the eye of God, I obediently put the gun in his hands, handed over the cartridge belt. Laboriously he began to load it.

He coughed. Blood gushed from his mouth, and terror seized me.
I had been here before, and so had Dad. Granddad's face sprang
into view. Dad raised the gun and I ran for my life, as well as for
his.

'I'll be back,' I shouted, and dodged behind the very first tree.
Into the murk across the river I yelled, 'Tadao, if you are there,
stay away. That's my Dad and he'll shoot you.'

The eucalyptus groaned and cracked in the wind blowing up from
the direction of the ford, and the treetops roared like a freight
train. Strips of bark, leaves, and twigs were flying. The sunlight
still shone down in dusty shafts, but the storm that Mr Buchanan
had warned us of was engulfing Billarooby. I held my arms up to
my eyes against the dust as I ran.

'I'm not getting anywhere,' I cried.

I was pushing my way through the thick belt of silky oaks on
the steepest part of the bank when I received one of the biggest
surprises of my life.

'Brown!' I shouted in relief and joy.

'Thank Christ,' he said. I clung to him, suddenly trembling
violently.

'Dad's bleeding to death. We have to take him to hospital.'

'Japs get him?'

'Yes. Near my cave.'

'They still around?'

The face of Tadao came into my mind. But he was not really
like a Jap. I again had the thought that we could ask him to help.
But then again, I was not sure I could trust him.

'Well . . .' I began.

'Kelly's down by the ford. Get him up here.'

I hesitated. Now that I was no longer alone I was too frightened
to leave. At that moment the sound of shots came on the wind
from the direction of the ford.

'Fucking Kelly. You better come with me. We can carry your
dad together.'

With the wind behind us, the return journey to the big trees
was much easier. I felt we were flying.

'Is Mum all right?' I shouted.

Brown grinned. 'Having her baby. Few days early. Japs helped it along a bit. Jean McCaddie's there. And the doc.'

'Be careful,' I shouted as we got closer. 'He's got his gun.'

'Who?'

'Dad.'

It was hard to see anything for the dust. Above the noise of the storm, and being carried away from us by the wind, came the sound of shooting.

'It might be Tadao,' I cried, hoping so much that it wasn't.

There must have been nine or ten shots, and they all seemed to be coming from the same location. We proceeded warily from tree to tree. High above us the sound of the leaves was like rushing water.

Fifteen yards from the bloody spot where I left Dad, I stopped.

'He's gone,' I exclaimed.

'Can't be hurt that bad.'

There was the sound of another shot, very close this time, and a new fear seized me.

'A trail,' said Brown. There was blood leading across the clearing and up the bank towards my cave.

'Stay here,' he said, taking a step into the open.

A shot whistled right between the two of us.

'Down!' A second shot went over our heads almost immediately.

'Jack!' shouted Brown.

We waited. There was nothing but the roar of the storm, the terrible swaying, snapping, groaning dance of the trees all around us.

'Bugger thinks we're the Japs.'

'It's us he wants to kill.'

'Jack, mate,' shouted Brown once more. 'It's Brown. Lindsay.'

Again the ominous silence amid the storm.

'We should crawl down to the river and up along the big trunk,' I said. 'That way he won't see us.'

We found Dad on his back by the platform outside my cave. He was lying in a pool of blood. The end of the barrels of the shotgun rested in his mouth. His finger was on the trigger. He was breathing but unconscious. His face was wet. I realized he had been crying. Expended cartridges were scattered around him.

Brown bent over and quickly knocked the barrels out and off to the side.

'Just a shot away,' he said. 'What's that all about?' Then he looked down into my cave. 'Christ!'

Brown took off his blue shirt, ripped it up to make better bindings for Dad's wounds, and then slung him over his shoulders in a fireman's carry. Before we had gone far, Brown's bare back was glistening with Dad's blood, and it seemed to take us so long to reach the ford that I thought Dad would surely die. Brown had to rest his legs several times, and at one point he tripped in a rabbit hole and fell. He began swearing. Dad recovered consciousness and started to groan. I looked down at the two of them lying there. Brown rubbed his leg and his ankle.

'I can't do it, mate,' gasped Brown. 'Not without a rest.'

'Oh, Brown, he's going to die.'

'Run ahead, get Kelly up here. It's our only chance.'

Again I hesitated, and in that moment a figure loomed out of the storm. Brown made a grab for his gun.

'Brown, don't shoot, it's a friend.'

It was Tadao. He inclined his head. 'Dad.' Tadao hoisted Dad on to his shoulders and headed for the ford at a run.

I helped Brown to his feet and we followed.

By the time that Brown and I stumbled out through the salt bushes, Tadao had placed Dad in the back of Brown's lorry and was untying Belinda. As Brown went to have a look at Dad, Tadao jumped up into the sulky, took the reins, and brought the whip down on Belinda's back. Belinda took off slowly up the track to the flats.

Tadao smiled grimly and waved.

'Strange bloody friend,' said Brown, wiping sweat and dust from his face. 'Bugger's running off with Belinda.'

Mr Kelly's truck came bouncing through the ford from across the river. He pulled up beside us and saw Dad lying in the back.

'Gone to a better fucking place?'

'We get him home, he's got a chance.'

The sulky was at the top of the rise, almost hidden in the dust.

'Who's in the sulky?'

'Jap,' said Brown, starting up his lorry.

'Bunnies, that's what the cunts are, mob of fucking bunnies,' shouted Mr Kelly. The dust had turned his sweating face into a muddy mask. He was a roiling, wild-eyed, fearsome sight. 'Get that cunt,' he yelled, taking a quick swallow from his bottle. 'Yes indeed.'

'Leave him alone. He's got a gun,' I shouted, but I don't know whether Mr Kelly, in his murderous mood, heard or was concerned. He roared off in pursuit.

'Bad storm,' said Brown as we set off up the track after Mr Kelly. A flock of crows beat against the wind, seeking better shelter along the riverbank. *Quark, quark*, came their desolate cries. The air was filled with debris, and up on the level our farmhouse and the dairy were blotted from view.

Only dimly could we see the chase going on ahead of us. Tadao was not having much luck with Belinda, and Mr Kelly was closing the gap rapidly.

'Bruce is having a fucking field day. Let's keep out of it.'

When Mr Kelly reached the sulky, he veered to the right, forcing Tadao to haul on the reins. The sulky slowed, and I could see sparks fly from the wheel as it scraped up against the barbed wire fence. The wind brought us Belinda's neigh of terror as she beat at the air with her forelegs and tried to rise up between the shafts. Mr Kelly pulled up his truck in front of the sulky, where two big posts marked a narrowing of the track, and forced it to stop. Tadao jumped out and hid behind the sulky wheels.

Mr Kelly was slow. By the time he climbed out of the truck with his gun and turned to fire, he was too late. Tadao had shot him and shot him again. Mr Kelly slumped to the ground. Brown pulled up fifty yards from the scene and fired a couple of quick shots, but Tadao did not even look our way. He ran for Mr Kelly's truck, climbed in, and drove it off into the storm.

Brown checked, but there was nothing we could do for Mr Kelly. 'He had his day,' said Brown. 'He certainly had his bloody day.'

'More rattles than a boneyard,' shouted Brown of the corrugations as he drove the lorry furiously along the road towards our farmhouse. 'Gonna be the death of the poor bastard.'

I looked back at Dad, laid out on the truck bed. Brown had

covered him with a tarpaulin, but it had half blown off. Farther behind, at full gallop, came Belinda, trailing the empty sulky. An immense orange cloud was banking above the line of trees along the Lachlan.

'When did Dad find out about the breakout?'

'Didn't know a bloody thing until yer mum woke him up this morning. She heard it on the wireless.'

'Did Dad come to rescue me?'

'Might have been one of the things on his mind.' Brown glanced back at Dad. 'And I came to rescue the bloody both of you.'

As we turned into our gate a Lincoln bomber came roaring out of the dusty sky. It was camouflaged green and brown and flew almost directly overhead, louder even than the storm. I had never seen a plane so close or so large. I thought it would surely crash into our farmhouse, but it cleared the roof ('Good twenty feet,' said Brown) and then headed north along the river, away from the billowing orange cloud.

Outside the house was Mr Buchanan's Morris, Nurse McCaddie's Baby Austin, and Dr Abercrombie's big Chevrolet from Wudgie.

'Not a word to anyone about how we found your dad,' said Brown.

By the time I had dealt with Belinda and got her into the stable shed, the big dust cloud had enveloped the farmhouse completely. Blinded and choking, I found my way in through the front door, and pushed the bolt across behind me.

I wiped the dust from my eyes and saw that Dad had been laid on the couch and stripped of his clothes. Nurse McCaddie was washing him and binding up his wounds swiftly. Heather took a steaming pan of water from the stove and headed down the corridor.

'Don't,' said Nurse McCaddie as I started to follow. 'Your mum's doing fine. If you want to make yourself useful, help keep some of this dust out. Stuff up those cracks around the door. Use newspaper.'

Mr Buchanan was sitting with Brown at the dining table. There was a bottle of brandy between them.

'Oh my God, Lindsay, oh my God,' said Mr Buchanan as he watched Nurse McCaddie.

'It's a big storm,' I yelled at him. 'Help with the newspapers.'

Mr Buchanan paid no attention to me. Brown poured himself a drink and stared at the table.

It grew even darker. I heard the wooden tub crash into the charcoal safe and then roll off the verandah by the water tank. The whole verandah was creaking, and a corner of the roof flapped with every gust. Fronds from the pepper tree splattered up against the windows. We sat and waited in such a haze of dust that soon it was difficult to breathe. I found myself thinking of Mr Kelly, of him slowly being covered up by the dirt and leaves, being buried by the hand of God. And I pictured Tadao heading through the storm, hunched over the wheel of Mr Kelly's truck, driving away across the plains to join the Emperor. I filled my head with thoughts – anything to avoid thinking about Dad.

Heather came out of the bedroom to sit by Dad, who was deathly white. A bandage covered his right eye and most of his head. Heather wiped what she could of his face with a wet flannel. Blood still seeped through the dressings about his neck and chest, and the water in the enamel bowl was bright red.

'Ah, Jack, mate,' said Mr Buchanan, coming over from the table and sitting beside Heather. He took Dad's hand and gave it a squeeze. 'Don't leave us now. Now that you've done your bit.'

Dr Abercrombie appeared from the bedroom and took his blood pressure again.

'He needs blood. If we could get him into Wudgie, he might make it.'

'Oh dear, what can we do,' said Nurse McCaddie.

Mr Buchanan put his head in his hands.

'If the will to live is strong,' said Dr Abercrombie, 'there is always a chance. Even if we can't get him to hospital.'

Brown had been listening from the table. 'I'll take him in,' he said. 'I've seen worse storms.'

'You seriously think you can drive through this?'

'I'll make it.'

'Good man,' said Dr Abercrombie. 'We'll get him into the Chevrolet. It's more comfortable.'

Brown stood up. 'I'd like a quick word with Lillian.'

'I'm sorry, that's impossible at this point,' said Dr Abercrombie.

'I've got to see her. Wish the missus good luck.'

'Please, Mr Douglass. It's not done. On your way. Every second is precious.'

'Get Fred to help you put him in the car.' Brown pushed Dr Abercrombie aside and almost ran down the corridor. I heard him close the door to the bedroom.

Brown wasn't very long. Dr Abercrombie, Nurse McCaddie, and Mr Buchanan had got Dad only as far as the verandah when he came bursting out again. I clung to a verandah post as the Chevrolet disappeared into the storm. With my eyes closed, I pictured Brown struggling through the dust. I wondered why he had so urgently wanted to see Mum, and thought of how he had the power of life and death over Dad.

The wind blew steadily for hours, not getting any worse or any better. We became hoarse from shouting at each other and eventually were silent.

At two in the afternoon, as the wind was beginning to abate, Dr Abercrombie came into the living room and announced that Mum had given birth to a baby boy.

Mr Buchanan got out the glasses and had us all – Nurse McCaddie, Dr Abercrombie, Heather and me – toast the new baby in brandy. Shortly thereafter I was let in to see him, along with Mr Buchanan.

The bedroom was very dark, with drawn curtains, and better protected against the dust than the rest of the house. Light came from two hurricane lamps and Mum's little bedside oil lamp with the pink shade. Mum was lying back, exhausted, her hair spread out on the high pillows behind her head and shoulders. Her face shone waxily in the dim light. I couldn't even see my baby brother at first. He was well wrapped up against the dust and hidden in the folds of Mum's nightgown.

'Dear Lindsay, what a fright you gave us this morning. Your father was sure the Japs would get you. He was in no state to rescue anyone, but off he went.'

To rescue me or kill me? I was still not quite ready for the truth.

'How did he know I was in my cave?'

'When Brown came up without you, we knew you must have gone there.'

'If you had stayed at the dairy like you were told, this would not have happened,' said Heather.

'That's enough, Heather.'

Heather dropped her eyes. For once.

'Didn't you try to stop him?'

'You know what your father's like.' Mum reached out and brushed dust out of my hair. A twig fell to the floor. 'I always knew we'd have to send a search party out for you one day.' She managed a smile.

I listened closely to her voice, both for explanation and for blame, but neither was there. She was happy to have me back, and glad that things were not any worse than they were.

'Brown will have got him there,' she said, and then began to cry.

'Storm's clearing,' said Mr Buchanan at the window.

He pulled back the curtain, and we could see the orange cloud moving across the plateau. It was as if a great invisible hand were rolling it away.

'The school's still there,' said Mr Buchanan.

'Now we can have a good squint at the little one,' said Nurse McCaddie. Sunlight was suddenly and miraculously illuminating the room.

Mum pulled back the blue covering and we all looked. The baby was bright red and wrinkled.

'It's Jack's,' said Mum, in a voice so low and so shocked that Mr Buchanan, who was standing as close as anyone, could not hear.

'What?' he queried.

'Well of course, Lillian,' said Nurse McCaddie.

Mum burst into tears.

'There, there, dear,' said Nurse McCaddie. 'If he made it through the storm, there's every chance.'

'Probably lose that eye,' said Dr Abercrombie.

Back in the living room we opened up all the windows to clear the air. Heather got out the brooms, and I turned on the wireless. There would be news of the breakout.

'You won't hear anything,' said Heather. 'They made one announcement this morning and said there won't be any others. We have to stay inside, but there is no cause for alarm.'

'It didn't happen,' shouted Mr Buchanan, drunk at the table. 'That's what they'll say. You'll see. Let's just thank God the roof held. Here's to the Armstrongs' roof.'

I made tea in the big silver pot and took a tray in to Mum. The tea was just what she needed, she said, but she was in no state to make conversation.

'I know what you must be going through, Mrs Armstrong,' said Dr Abercrombie. 'Please let me give you something to steady your nerves while you wait.'

Mum refused. I think she was very grateful for Dr Abercrombie's skill with her delivery, but she did not think much of his powers of diagnosis.

Dr Abercrombie was still making offers of sedatives when Brown came back with the Chevrolet and his news.

29

THE ROOF DID HOLD that day, but there was another, much more devastating duststorm three days later that ripped it right off, except for the addition, which was the Landgirls' room. The kitchen tank and the shed tank both fell from their stands and wound up in the barbed wire. The chook shed collapsed, and our various fowl were scattered across the district. A large amount of Dad's topsoil went east somewhere. New Zealand, Mr MacAdams said, pity about that.

The wattle and daub held, however, and none of us was seriously hurt. We spent a week up in the shearers' quarters adjoining the woolshed while Brown organized a work party to replace the roof of our farmhouse.

Mum appreciated everything that was done for us in our hour of need, but this time it really was the end of our days in Billarooby. Long before Dad got out of Wudgewunda Base Hospital, she had written to Mrs Cutler and received a reply. Mrs Cutler's invitation to the whole family, including Dad and whatever we had left of our belongings, she said, still stood. We were welcome to stay at Woy Woy for as long as we wanted to.

'How can we leave Brown, just like that?' I demanded. 'He's part of the family. I'm going to stay with him at the dairy.'

Mum was very patient with me in those dazed days.

'It's decided, and that's all there is to it. Mr MacAdams is buying the farm and there is nothing left for us here. You're coming with us and Brown can visit you down at the coast.'

I found I was not only crying for Brown, but angry, for some reason, about Mr MacAdams buying the farm.

'MacAdams has wanted the flats ever since your dad showed

him what could be done,' said Mr Buchanan. 'Now he's getting them for a song.'

'But there's no water.'

'It'll rain one day. Then MacAdams will put in a manager and make a packet.'

Mr Buchanan was leaving Billarooby too. The Department of Education had confirmed its decision, he said, and the school would be closing at the end of the Christmas term. Now he could go and live it up in Sydney.

After the breakout Billarooby lived in a state of siege for over a week. There were search parties going up and down the Lachlan, planes flying overhead, and jeeps and military vehicles rattling by on our back road to nowhere all day long. We had a three-man guard at school and played rounders with them at lunchtime. Mr Sullivan from the *Star* and dozens of reporters from papers such as the *Daily Telegraph*, the *Sydney Morning Herald*, and the *Melbourne Argus* came to Billarooby and talked to the residents. Mrs Packman told everyone how her booby trap had captured two very nice prisoners, and how she gave them breakfast and drove them back to the camp herself. Heather told them how she had to travel on the milk truck to school in Wudgie because there were Japs hiding in the hills. Gordon Morrison reported that four of them lay down on the tracks near the Glen Hogan siding and were decapitated by the train he and Heather usually travelled on. When the army closed in on two prisoners hiding out near Mudoogla, they killed themselves. 'By ritual stabbing,' said Eric Kiddy with relish. 'My dad found a whole mob of them hanged dead in the trees.' None of these extraordinary stories appeared in any of the papers we read. Mr Sullivan filled a whole page about Wudgewunda's being the focus of Australia-wide press attention but only hinted at why. Mr Buchanan said that censorship by the federal government prevented the publication of the real facts. The government was concerned that information about the breakout and its aftermath might get into the wrong hands, particularly in Singapore and Batavia.

'The Colonel would probably be worth a headline or two in Tokyo,' said Mr Buchanan.

Well, even if the rest of the world had to be kept in ignorance, everyone knew that the Japs had finally mutinied, as had long been expected, and that hundreds of them had been massacred that night. Hundreds more fled into the bush or wandered off along the back roads in places far from Billarooby, and it was weeks before the last of them were recaptured. When their plan to die as Bushido warriors failed, most of them lost their spirit force and did not know what to do with themselves. Sergeant Duffy said that they were very happy to be back in the camp with their three square meals a day, ice cream, and Ping-Pong.

Auntie Annabel and her church crowd sent ripples of good Christian shock and distaste through the district for the hangings and ritual stabbings and other examples of suicidal behaviour, but sitting alone at school in the back row, with *The Knights of Bushido* a fixture in my satchel, I felt I knew too much about it to be shocked. After all, I had been there, even though I had to keep reminding myself of the fact, so unreal did it all seem sometimes. When I wasn't crying about it, I was very detached. 'It's better to die with honour than to live with shame. The Japanese have gone to join their ancestors and live in glory,' I wrote in my exercise book, proud that they had accomplished their mission. Then I would recall my handing over Mr Kelly's gun to the Japanese in my cave, and I would hide my face in my arms on the desk, overcome with horror and guilt. I felt it was all my fault. If Dad had not got shot, he would have beaten the Japanese and then he would not have tried to kill himself. If I . . .

'It's the truth that matters, not the wax.' Mr Buchanan's words came back to me again, but I found that I wasn't telling the truth to the reporters or to anyone about what happened down on the riverbank. My mind kept going back to Granddad and another riverbank, and other problems with the truth, a long time ago.

'Snap out of it.' Mr Buchanan was worried about my moody silences, day after day, there in the back row. 'Your dad's recovering well. Everything's turning out for the best.'

Mr Buchanan said that the authorities had decided that people like Dad and Mr Kelly, who had been responsible for the death of several Japanese, had acted in self-defence. It was an incendiary situation, and it was not necessary to go into the details of what happened, or confront the fact that many Australians took advantage of the breakout and used the Japanese for sport more

exciting than hunting rabbits. Dad and Mr Kelly were not the
only ones, by any means, who had had a field day.

Sergeant Duffy found out that the breakout was masterminded
by two very nobly intentioned officers, Sergeant Major Shikishima
and Sergeant Pilot Okamura. Shikishima had been killed, as I
knew, but Okamura gave evidence at a preliminary inquiry that
the Japanese, under their code of honour, known as the Code of
Bushido, regarded themselves as being at war with the military
and not with the general population, to whom they wished no
harm.

'That's a lot of bullshit,' said Blue Chapman. 'Bruce wasn't
wearing no uniform.'

We learned that an army patrol ran down Mr Kelly's truck on
a back road beyond Goondiwindi and surrounded it. Tadao was
not alone. He and his companions fired on the advancing soldiers,
seriously wounding two of them. When the soldiers eventually
closed in, they found that the two Japanese had shot themselves
with the last two cartridges rather than be recaptured.

Mr Buchanan wondered about Goondiwindi. It was three
hundred miles to the north, across the Queensland border.

'They were on their way to rejoin their Emperor,' I explained.

I carved Tadao's name on a piece of willow and placed it in a
place of honour in the centre of my circle of stones. I had had an
enemy for a friend, but he was no enemy of mine.

Up in the woolshed there were prayers for Dad's full recovery,
and when he came home, a special service. The Reverend Pitts
commended Dad for his supreme valour. I was a lost, misguided
lamb, and Dad had rescued me from certain death at the hands of
the Japanese.

Dad had been right about the Japanese from the start, everyone
decided. All was forgiven, and at church that day the entire
congregation was invited by the MacAdamses to an impromptu
morning tea up at Moorellen.

'Looks like Al might be relieved of his command,' said Mr
MacAdams. 'Japs are one thing, but to lose ten good men . . .'

'He's lucky the army looks after its own,' said Mr Buchanan.
'Allowed those poor bastards to accumulate weapons. Didn't even
have those guns manned at night. Tempted them.'

'That's boredom for you. Al always hated that camp. So humiliating for him. They should have given him combat duties overseas. That's what got him drinking.'

'His conduct was appalling, Bill. Admit it. Duffy says it was getting like he wanted them to go for the wires. So he could have a go at them, like Bruce.'

'Come off it, Fred. If there was proof of that, he would have been court-martialled.'

'I'm sure he's glad it's all over, more than anything else,' said Mrs MacAdams. 'He and Edwina have that nice beachfront place down near Bulli.'

There was regret that we had decided to leave Billarooby, although of course no raised eyebrows. Mr MacAdams offered Dad the job as stockman that Mum had always wanted Dad to take, and to rent us the Bridges' former house. 'See you through the drought.'

Mum thanked him very much but stuck to her decision.

'The Bridges' old house is very nice. If you stay, Brown and George will help you fix it up,' said Auntie Annabel. 'It's right by the woolshed.'

Mum shook her head.

'Had enough of Billarooby, have you, missus?' asked Brown.

'It's not the best place to deal with a newborn baby.' Mum was busy wiping a few bubbles away from the baby's mouth. 'The drought. All this dust and desolation.'

'Billarooby's best place in the world after it rains.'

Brown gave Mum a grin, but she would not look up at him. She turned to Auntie Annabel and said, 'The sky is the same, day after day. It's time for us to move on, to start again.'

I could tell from Brown's forehead that he was feeling left out. One day when we were out ferreting, he had said that Mum hadn't spoken to him since the baby was born. 'I'd do anything for your mum.'

Mr Buchanan and I watched Dad walking slowly about the MacAdamses' drawing room smiling at everyone. Since coming home from hospital Dad had said scarcely a word and hadn't taken a drop. He seemed to have no objections to any of the decisions Mum was making. He made no complaints, ventured no opinions.

'Auntie Annabel says he's a man at peace with God,' I said.

'Maybe. Something in his life did come to an end that day,' said Mr Buchanan. 'Pity about the eye.'

Dad still had a large bandage covering one side of his face.

'The one he has left is his good one. Dad says he is going to call himself Old Hawk Eye.'

'If you ask me, he's rather proud of it.' Mr Buchanan gave an affectionate laugh. 'The war wound.' Then he became very serious. 'Tell me, Lindsay – was your handsome dad really ready for *anything*, down there on the riverbank that day?'

I swirled my lemonade around in my glass as befitted the importance of the question.

'He's a brave man. Almost as brave as Brown. They both came to rescue me at whatever cost. I was very foolish because of my inexperience. I let my imagination run away with me.'

'You mustn't start blaming yourself.'

'Dad was prepared to die for his sins.'

'I don't know if he managed to take it that far. Let's just say he struggled all the time to face the music – apparently the music had to be faced. Whatever happened to your granddad, your dad tortured himself over it far too long.'

'He was in prison,' I said, 'suffering. Just like the samurai.'

Mr Buchanan and I looked at each other, and I could see that I had surprised him. And then he surprised me. 'We all suffer, Lindsay. You too, or have you forgotten your nightmare already?'

I didn't know what to say. I hadn't thought in those terms before about myself, suffering. Mr Buchanan was talking to me, man to man.

'I'm sorry,' he went on. 'Forget I said that. There may be something in what you say about your dad. It did become a question of just how far the guilt would take him. Do you think he sought death at the hands of the Japanese? As some kind of final atonement?'

'What's atonement?'

'Salvation.' He took a sip of tea and added a little more sugar. 'The Japs play it even rougher than we Christians.'

I was getting lost, although I sort of knew what atonement

meant. When Dad felt he had failed Granddad one more time and the Japs were going to overrun Billarooby, rape Mum and Heather, and do all the terrible things that he believed the Japs did, he decided to kill himself rather than face Granddad's wrath any longer. Mr Buchanan had almost got it right but not quite. But then, he wasn't in full possession of the facts. Nobody was, except me. And what Brown knew about how we found Dad was a secret between Brown and me forever.

'Personal salvation at whatever cost can be very expensive,' Mr Buchanan went on. 'Well, it's over now. Jack settled for an eye.'

I drank the rest of my lemonade. Mr Buchanan understood in his own way about Granddad and Dad, just as Mum did.

Dad took the baby from Mum over by the tall windows. He held him whenever she would let him. Heather said he was the best baby in the world. As if she would know. Oh well, he certainly didn't cry very much, and he got more interesting and less wrinkled by the day. He had hazel eyes, and he looked right back at me when I stared. I liked to watch Mum feeding him. He had been named James Gunning William, which was Dad's choice, the only thing he had insisted upon since he came home.

'Sometimes Jack looks as though he can't believe it's his,' said Mr Buchanan.

'It's just that eye,' I said.

I finally told Mum everything I could remember about my Granddad nightmare and, to ease my guilt, dropped a hint or two about what had happened down on the Lachlan, but she did not express much interest in what was true and what was not in either case.

'Your father did something. Whether it was like you say we will never know,' she said. 'Granddad died his own death. He fired that shot the day your father was born. If only your father had been able to grasp that, we wouldn't be in the mess we are in now.'

A flash of soft, green fields, and friendly clouds full of moisture filling the English sky, went past my eyes. Rainy days.

'You are your father's son, of course, but you must stop yourself from dwelling on all this. Sometimes the truth matters, sometimes it doesn't. Learn a nice honest discretion, and if you get caught, put a brave face on it. Above all don't torture yourself. When we go down to the coast, there will be a big school for you to go to and lots of other children to play with. Next year you will be going to high school. You can learn French and Latin and things like that. We will put Billarooby behind us.'

Our last week at Billarooby went by very quickly. Mr Buchanan had a Parents' Day at school and took a photograph of everyone assembled out by the dead wattle trees in the back playground. Dad put his hand on my shoulder for the photograph and gave me a friendly squeeze. I was almost convinced.

Mr Morrison repaired our truck, and Dad made a deal with him about taking Belinda and the sulky when we left.

'Why don't you read the Bible anymore?' Heather asked one evening at the dinner table.

'Read it for me,' said Dad.

Heather did, but she felt awkward and did not do it again. The Bible sat on its stand day after day untouched. All the ripped pages had been collected and the damage from the fireplace was very slight, but Dad made no effort to repair it.

'Shall I fix it for you?' I asked.

'What's a few torn pages?' Dad replied.

One morning Mum quietly took the Bible from the stand and packed it away with the other books.

30

THE THING I remember most about our last morning at the farmhouse was the episode of the dinner plates.

Heather and I had dropped a box of china when we were loading it on to the truck. We watched guiltily as Mum stood with one of the broken plates in her hands. It was from her very best set. The plate had broken into two halves. She waved at the flies with the halves and then ceremoniously let them fall into the dust.

'Billarooby can have the plate. It took everything else.'

I picked up the pieces and found that they fitted perfectly.

'I'll mend it right now. Then you would have a full set again. At least of the plates.'

'The glue is packed away.' Mum sighed. She took baby James from Heather and walked towards the empty house. 'Come on, Heather, one last look.'

Brown followed Mum with his eyes and blinked when the screen door slammed, as though it hurt him. Brown had been at the farmhouse all morning, helping us load up our things. Mrs MacAdams had taken a few more pieces, and everything we had left was going on to the truck.

When she returned, Brown said, 'I keep wishing you weren't leaving, missus. It's gonna rain. Billarooby – '

'Are you asking me to wait for it?' she demanded.

The sky was overcast. It was another of those hot, grey days we had become so used to in Billarooby.

Brown was disconcerted by the knife in her voice.

'Here, Brown. I want you to have the plate.' I held out the pieces and felt it was the perfect symbol.

Mum hit the roof.

'What do you think you're doing?' she shouted. She thrust the baby into Heather's arms, seized the pieces from me, and threw them down the hill. 'I don't care, I don't. I just want to get out of here.'

She then went to the box of china, selected an unbroken plate, unwrapped it, and handed it to Brown.

Brown turned it over slowly a couple of times. 'Thank you, Lillian. I'll treasure it. It's a beautiful bit of china.'

'I'd give you anything you want, Brown.' Mum began to cry. 'You deserve it all.'

Dad appeared from the direction of the shed, carrying a rope.

'I'm sorry if I have been dreadful,' said Mum quickly, in a low voice. 'Forgive me.'

'Ain't nothing to forgive, missus.' Brown walked away. 'I'll get the tarp. Looks like this is about it,' he called over his shoulder.

Brown's bare back gleamed in the morning light. Mum followed him with her eyes for a second, then turned away and dried her tears.

Fifteen minutes later we were ready to go. We all shook hands with Brown. Dad thanked him for everything he had done, and then Brown said, 'Jack, mind if I give yer missus a farewell kiss?'

Dad paused for a fraction of a second and then replied, 'Go ahead,' and walked away to the truck. Heather followed him, and I walked away also, but I couldn't resist sneaking a look.

Brown smoothed his moustache with his thumb and forefinger, put his arms around Mum, and gave her a hearty, lingering kiss, full on her lips. Then he buried his face in her neck and it looked as though he whispered something. Finally he picked her up and whirled her around. Mum began to smile in spite of herself.

'The one-legged woolshed waltz,' said Brown, laughing.

'Brown, dear, put me down,' said Mum, and the sadness seemed almost to have gone from her voice.

'A kiss to build a dream on, mate,' Brown called to me.

'Oh, Brown, we'll see you again,' said Mum. 'Lindsay will make sure of that.'

It was the end of October 1944 when we left Billarooby, a little more than two years after our arrival. We left in the old shark-nosed, round-fendered 1930 Ford truck we had come in, except that this time Mum did the driving.

The day before there had come some bad news, but Mum had refused to let it interfere with our plans for the coast. Mrs Cutler had written again. She hated Woy Woy and was on her way to New Zealand. Awfully sorry if we were inconvenienced, and we were absolutely not to think of her as a fair-weather friend. She would write from New Zealand when she had an address, and we were perfectly welcome to stay, of course, for as long as we liked. She had heard that army surplus tents were going very cheap in Sydney and that lots of families dispossessed by the drought were buying them up.

'It does look like rain,' I could not help saying as we drove through the gate at the bottom of our hill. 'I can even smell it.'

No touch of colour enlivened the desolation of the flats. The Douglasses had sowed alfalfa, but it had not taken. Nothing but the dust and the crows. Even the Patterson's Curse and paddy melons had failed to materialize. There was no sign of any thistles.

'The ant nests are up, and those birds are flying for cover,' I exclaimed. Two galahs flapped ahead of the truck and then went off towards the river. The air was thick and humid; the birds almost had to carve their way through it.

The truck hit a bad section of corrugations. Looking slyly over at Mum, I remarked, 'More rattles than a boneyard.' She did not respond, and I realized she didn't want to be reminded of Brown for a while.

James slept through it all. Heather kept him well sheltered from the hot wind rushing by the windows.

'I'm so glad we're leaving, Dad. I'm never, never, never going back,' said Heather.

I suppose we had been travelling for some twenty minutes when the first drop of rain hit the windshield. It was followed by another, and then another. Soon it was raining so hard that Mum had to stop the truck. We could see no more than a few yards in front of us. No one said a word. The rain came in through the gap at the top of the window; it trickled down inside the windshield and seeped through the breaks in the pane at the back. I thought of Dipper trying to keep dry in her cubbyhole in the furniture. Torrents of muddy water rushed along the side of the road.

'I always said it would rain,' said Dad.

'Shut up!' Mum's voice lashed at him in a terrible fury. 'It's not raining. It didn't rain the whole time we were in that bloody place, and it's not raining now.'

She dug her elbow hard into Dad's side, and he winced with pain. She revved up the engine, put the truck in gear, and sent it charging forward. Dad sat impassively in the centre. I clung to the door. Heather sat squeezed between us with James in her arms. The windshield wiper worked, but it made no difference. Mum was taking us blindly into a world of nothing but watery grey.

'Mum, stop, we'll all be killed,' screamed Heather.

The baby woke up and began to cry. His cries grew louder and louder.

'Lillian . . .' began Dad. Mum put on the brakes, and the truck skidded sideways in the mud and came to a halt at an angle, one of the back wheels in some sort of hole, or it might have been a ditch at the roadside. The rain was so heavy it was impossible to see. Mum burst into tears. She rested her head on the steering wheel and cried and cried.

The tears, like the rain, did not stop. Dad tentatively put his arm around her back, then rested his head on her shoulder.

From Mum's tears, Dad's silence, the crying of the baby and Heather's attempts to hush it, the solemn thunder of the cloud-burst, there came upon me a hypnotic state of contentment. The wiper swept steadily back and forth across the glass. The windshield with its wash of water and the rain dancing on the blue bonnet of the truck dissolved into the picture of a river. The river flowed into a brilliant, sunlit sea, and there I was on a boat, gliding towards the shore. With me was Brown, and on the shore was Mum, waving to us and waiting. She held the baby in her arms, and Heather was standing beside her, smiling at the baby. They stood with their feet in golden sand, palm trees swaying above them. I looked up at Brown, he grinned down at me, and the air was filled with radiance. It was a vision of paradise that began to fade as soon as it was fully formed. I tried to cling to it and whispered words that Brown had uttered in a different

context outside my cave on the riverbank – 'Just a shot away.'
My whole body gave a little spasm, and I found myself back in
the truck, with the paradise lost to a new pitch in the wail of the
baby. Heather handed him over to Mum to deal with, Mum
opened her dress, and I opened the cabin door.

'I'm getting out,' I announced. I hated myself for the words I
had whispered, for they were an expression of deepest regret that
things had turned out the way they had.

I stood on the running board and then jumped down into the
road. I was immediately soaked to the skin. I closed my eyes,
exposed my throat, and held out my arms as wide as I could. I
wanted the rain to wash away forever my cruel, sad longing, wash
away all the terrible things that had happened in Billarooby.

Dipper jumped down from the back and joined me. She grinned
and snorted, loving the rain.

'Come and get wet,' I shouted to the others, suddenly happy,
and happy for Brown and everyone in Billarooby that the rain
had finally come. From the earth came a smell I will never forget
– like ripe peaches. Mrs MacAdams' roses, and mud all rolled
into one. I went to the side of the road and took a leak into the
gushing flow. I could have peed my pants and it would not have
mattered. It was a permitting, purifying rain. Everything was
possible in this rain, and it would all be good. 'Let it rain forever,'
I cried to the rain gods, up there with the buckets.

I saw approaching from the direction of Billarooby two head-
lights in the grey. Ever so slowly they came closer. A red lorry
loomed like a ghost out of the rain.

A lightning bolt charged through my body. 'It's Brown!' I
exclaimed.

The lorry pulled up beside me, and the driver leaned out with
his elbow on the open window. He had his shirt off and he was
soaking wet, like me. His battered hat dripped water. It was a
stranger.

'Everything OK?' he asked.

I stared at him. As I accepted him as a stranger, my disappoint-
ment evaporated.

'Yes, everything's OK. Terrific, in fact,' I said with a grin.

The stranger glanced at Mum and Dad and Heather and James

inside the cabin of the old truck, all trying to keep dry, and gave a chuckle. He revved up the engine.

'Not bad for a shower, eh?' he said, and touched his hat. He drove off into the pelting rain and out of sight.

Heather called from the truck. 'Come on, Lindsay, we're off. And Dad's going to drive, so there.'